The Foreign Relations
of China

Comparative Foreign Relations Series
Edited by
David O. Wilkinson, University of California, Los Angeles
Lawrence Scheinman, Cornell University

Comparative Foreign Relations: Framework and Methods
David O. Wilkinson, University of California, Los Angeles

The Foreign Relations of the United States, Second Edition
Michael H. Armacost, U.S. Department of State
Michael Stoddard, Pomona College

The Foreign Relations of China, Third Edition
Robert C. North, Stanford University

The Foreign Relations of Russia
Morton Schwartz, Univeristy of California, Riverside

The Foreign Relations of India
Sudershan Chawla, California State University, Long Beach

Volumes available from Dickenson Publishing Company, Inc.,
Belmont, California.

The Foreign Relations of China

Third Edition

Robert C. North

Stanford University

Duxbury Press
North Scituate, Massachusetts

Library of Congress Cataloging in Publication Data

North, Robert Carver.
  The foreign relations of china.
  Includes bibliographical references and index.
  1.   China—Foreign relations—1949—1976.   I.   Title.
DS777.55.N598   1978   327.51   77-20819
ISBN 0-87872-157-6

Duxbury Press
A Division of Wadsworth Publishing Company, Inc.

The Foreign Relations of China, 3d edition, was edited and prepared for
composition by Martha Gleason. Interior design was provided by
Martha Woodbridge and the cover was designed by Elizabeth
Rotchford.

L.C. Cat. Card No.: 77-20819
ISBN 0-87872-157-6

Printed in the United States of America
1 2 3 4 5 6 7 8 9 - 82 81 80 79 78

Contents

v

Contents

7

Asia, Africa, Latin America, and the World Revolution   179

8

Current Chinese Foreign Policies, the Death of Mao and Future Possibilities 201

Foreword

The Comparative Foreign Relations Series is designed for foreign policy courses that employ a comparative approach, as well as for courses in comparative politics and international relations that survey the foreign relations of key states. Because the basic literature is lacking, few courses today are able to make a genuinely comparative examination of national actors in the international system, in the manner increasingly adopted for the study of domestic politics. This series has been prepared to fill the need for such a basic literature.

The series presents an analytical model and case materials for beginning a comparative study of foreign relations. As a method of studying foreign relations phenomena, comparison allows us to investigate the differences and similarities among states in relation to the international system, and thereby generate or test propositions about the external relations of states.

In order to compare cases, as analytical model or framework should be used—that is, the same set of subjects and questions should be used to arrange and present information about each case. The analytical model of the series is presented in the core volume, *Comparative Foreign Relations: Framework and Methods,* which outlines a framework for describing the international situation and foreign policy of a state, explaining its current policy, analyzing its current problems, and projecting its future problems and policy alternatives. The case materials are presented in the various country volumes, which, following the analytical model, describe and explain the foreign relations of specific important states since 1945 and sketch their main current and anticipated problems.

The books in the series make comparison possible by presenting material of the same nature about each case; however, the actual comparisons must be made by the reader. Some ways in which the series might be used to further the comparative study of foreign relations are presented in the preface to the core volume.

David O. Wilkinson
Lawrence Scheinman

Preface

As soon as the People's Republic of China was established in October 1949 foreign observers began to speculate what would happen to the Chinese Communist movement and to the country at large when Mao Tse-tung died. Would the new regime collapse? Would it become more conservative? More radical? Would the Peking government move closer to the Soviet Union? Closer to the United States? There were almost as many hypotheses as there were observers, but one consideration was shared universally: everyone had to wait a long time to find the answer. For Mao—unlike Lenin, who died only a few years after the establishment of the Bolshevik regime in Russia—continued to live on and on. Of course, from time to time there were rumors that he had died, or grown wholly senile, or been placed under house arrest. But sooner or later he always reappeared—to be photographed, perhaps, swimming the Yangtse.

In this third updated and revised edition, *The Foreign Relations of China* includes a report, however sketchy and tentative, of the first months of Chinese foreign affairs without Mao. It is much too early to draw firm conclusions, but to date, at least, events do not suggest the likelihood of any abrupt or radical changes. On the contrary, the Maoist years appear to have provided a sound basis for post-Maoist stability well into the immediate future. The main problem is how to interpret the vast amounts of material that are currently available.

During the 1950s and early 1960s there was a feeling among many observers of events in the People's Republic of China that they had at their disposal, even then, greater amounts of data about that country than the citizen at large suspected. If anything, the difficulty was that more material came out of China than the very small numbers of qualified scholars could absorb and interpret. However, with the Great Proletarian Cultural Revolution this situation changed. Many of the more dependable sources of information became increasingly difficult to tap or perhaps disappeared altogether. Stories coming out of Communist China about events there often differed substantially, and one was at a loss how to evaluate many of them. Was Mao Tse-tung in power or out of power? Had he suffered one or two or three strokes? Was he senile? Was he perhaps dead? Were all those who labeled themselves Maoist really Maoists, or were they anti-Maoists posing as Maoists? Had the government of the People's Republic come almost wholly under control of the military? Was it true that Kiangsi Province had broken away to become almost autonomous?

Given such wild rumors and genuine uncertainties, conscientious writing about the People's Republic has become a hazardous occupation at best. The ink was scarcely dry before a manuscript needed rethinking and revising. Who would have thought, in the 1950s or early 1960s, that a few years later sober observers, would be reporting a Russian anxiety that the United States might ally itself with China in a world power struggle against the USSR; that numbers of Chinese Communist were afraid that the United States would side with the Soviet Union against China in that same developing power struggle; or that a new American administration might soon find itself with wholly new possibilities for dealing with both of these Communist giants? Who would have predicted, moreover, that the United States president who first opened serious negotiations with the People's Republic and paid the first formal state visit to Peking would be a political figure who had built his political career in large part upon a reputation of bitter anticommunism?

However unlikely such eventualities might have appeared to many observers in the 1950s and early 1960s, events have moved along since then, and this third edition records the direction of Chinese foreign policy developments through the first months of 1977. The Great Proletarian Cultural Revolution has receded into the past. Westerners are visiting China in considerable numbers, more people are studying about the country, and far more data are again becoming available than could be properly analyzed or interpreted. The People's Republic of China seems to have established for itself a strong and widely recognized position in the community of nations. But the possibility still exists that observers of the middle and late 1970s might be as much surprised by Chinese events of the future as they have been from time to time in the past.

Since the death of Mao, the Sino-Soviet conflict has thus far continued, however, in many respects its future course is even more difficult to predict than it was in earlier years. The United States and the

People's Republic of China have achieved and maintained a partial détente, but not an alliance, and relations between each of these countries and the Soviet Union are still characterized by ambiguities. Yet, whatever the new uncertainties and whatever the outcomes, evidence has been accumulating to suggest that China, with its extensive territory, large and still rising population, developing technology, expanding commerce, and increasing nuclear capability will exert a profound and growing influence on world affairs and the future of mankind.

This book is intended for undergraduate students of foreign affairs, international politics, and comparative foreign policy, as well as for people in many walks of life who are interested in China and concerned about the future of human life on this seemingly shrinking planet. In many respects, the materials and analysis presented here are spin-offs from a longer range, quantitative and qualitative analysis of China's attributes, predispositions, role in world affaris, and interactions with the USSR the United States, Japan, Taiwan, India, and various other countries in Asia, Europe, Africa, and Latin America. In some respects, then, the book might be viewed less as a definitive analysis and more as an updated monitoring of policies and events as they unfold.

In carrying on this work I am deeply indebted to more of my students and colleagues at Stanford University and elsewhere than can be enumerated here. Without their contributions over a number of years, the book would not have been written. I am also indebted to the coeditors of this series, Professors David O. Wilkinson and Lawrence Scheinman, for their early advice and hard work, to those who have read and criticized the draft of each edition before it went to press, and to Judy Adams, Gaye Passell, and Helen Grace, who did the typing and a great deal more. Finally, I owe special debts to Alice Kung, Kelly Bufton, and Matthew Willard for their generous research assistance. For all errors of omission and commission, however, and for whatever flaws may appear in the analysis, I am solely responsible.

Robert C. North

Chapter One

Introduction

In studying the foreign policy of any state, one looks first of all for a general description of that policy. What is it? What are the leaders of the state after? What are the national goals and by what means are they being pursued? How orderly and coherent is the policy, or how confused and inconsistent? Is it stable or erratic, adaptable or rigid, efficient or inefficient, successful or unsuccessful? Is it realistic? How farsighted is it?

Unfortunately for ready analysis, the goals, motivations, and patterns of the People's Republic of China have been matters of considerable controversy and not easily ascertained except partially and tentatively. Few issues of the post-World War II world have generated more heated debates in the United States than the nature, intents, and implications for mankind of Maoist China. During the 1950s and much of the 1960s, it was widely believed that the People's Republic of China aimed to conquer much of Asia and even to control the world through revolution on five continents. Others were equally convinced that Mao Tse-tung and his colleagues sought no more for their country than recognized membership in the international community and a fair opportunity for modernizing Chinese society and providing more adequately for their people's needs.

Difficulties in Studying Chinese Foreign Relations

For the first two decades or more of the Maoist regime's existence, many people felt that the foreign policy of the People's Republic of China had been consistently deceitful, hostile, and aggressive and that only containment by the Nationalist Chinese and by the United States had prevented the overrunning of much of Asia by Chinese Red Army hordes. There was also a conviction in some quarters that United States policies toward the People's Republic had been far more lenient than they should have been — sometimes dangerously lenient — as a consequence of irresolution or an underestimation of the communist threat by the leaders in Washington. Many people holding these views believed that the Sino-Soviet controversy was of minor importance, that it might even be something of a deceit to mislead the West, and that Chinese and Russian programs and activities were all part of a single, highly integrated plot for gaining control of the world and making it communist.

Other people believed that the People's Republic, although admittedly communist, was also strongly nationalistic and concerned with many of the same problems that any strong Chinese regime would be. There was a tendency among these people to feel that the Chinese Communists had not been particularly aggressive, except when they had perceived themselves as seriously threatened or when they had tried to reacquire territory they considered rightfully theirs. Often associated with these views was a tendency to perceive the Sino-Soviet controversy as real, stemming from a variety of historical considerations and from sharp differences in national interest.

There were also disagreements about the primary sources of Chinese Communist motivation. According to one representative viewpoint, Communist China's foreign policy derived primarily from ideology. "Specifically," according to one scholar writing in 1968, "it is what Peking terms 'the thought of Mao Tse-tung' which directs Red China's methodological approach to the long-range goal it shares with Moscow. This 'thought' is Marxism-Leninism, mixed with elements of Stalinism, and 'adjusted' to the conditions and requirements in Communist China. It is derivative rather than inventive. Mao has been overestimated as an original thinker."[1] The principles directing Chinese Communist foreign policies were thus "akin to those of the USSR except that they embody an even more aggressive and revolutionary intent."[2]

Other views suggest that Chinese Communist foreign policy derives in part from Maoist ideology but also from a variety of other factors — some historical, some demographic, some economic, some nationalistic, and so forth. Many observers perceive powerful elements of Chinese traditionalism in Maoism itself — sufficient, along with other factors, to set Chinese communism quite apart from Russian communism on a number of critical issues. Against this background, it was all the more dramatic, ironic, and confusing when the first concerted efforts toward improved relations with the People's

Republic of China were undertaken by President Richard M. Nixon, who owed much of his political career to the rigor with which he had opposed communism and its apologists in both Russia and China, as well as elsewhere in the world. One of the problems in the study of international politics and foreign policy is how to explain such major and seemingly sudden shifts in the relations of states as dramatized by the eruption of the Sino-Soviet conflict and the Nixon visit to Peking.

The effort in this book is to proceed from assumptions of multi-causality, that is, from the belief that the foreign policy of any nation is likely to be the outcome of numerous considerations, that unicausal explanations are likely to be inadequate and perhaps dangerously misleading, but that, of many influential factors, some are substantially more significant than others. It is our intention to identify some of these critical factors and show, insofar as possible, how they relate to each other and how they combine to account for extensive aspects of China's international activities and relations with other countries.

One of the difficulties in understanding Chinese foreign policy and behavior has stemmed from the uneven and often uncertain quality of available information. This is a recurring problem that will be discussed at greater length in other parts of this book. A second, perhaps even more formidable, difficulty emerges from seemingly abrupt changes that have taken place over the last quarter of a century with respect to China's role in the international system and the ways in which the country has been viewed and evaluated by outsiders, especially in the USSR and the United States.

The Main Determinants of Foreign Policy

The role of any country in the world is probably first and best accounted for in terms of its capabilities — economic, military, and other — that determine its position and stature in the systemic hierarchy of powers at the moment. How do a country's capabilities compare with those of other countries in the world — with the capabilities of its trading partners, allies, and rivals, for example? And, are the country's capabilities — its technology, economy, production facilities, trade capacities, military capabilities, and so forth — growing or declining relative to the capabilities of other countries?

Next in explanatory importance is the presence or absence (in degrees) of dissatisfaction with things as they are, combined with a conscious, centralized (organized) will expressed by a vigorous, powerfully motivated leadership. The greater the extent of such political leadership in a country, and the greater its dissatisfactions with the status quo, the more that leadership's characteristics and peculiarities will tend to replace more stable historical, traditional, bureaucratic elements in the formulation and explanation of foreign policy. In these terms, the ideological factor is best understood, on the one hand, as the ideas — the belief system — of a conscious leadership and, on the other hand, as the traditions of a routinized leadership. But a society's will cannot be made effective unless appropriate capabilities are available. Often a strong-willed country must build an array of specialized, facilitating capabilities before its larger purposes can be pursued more directly.

When will and dissatisfaction are high, one may expect to find strong tendencies toward innovation, the establishment and pursuit of new values, new goals, and new ways of doing things as compared with persisting, longterm, traditional habits, routines, customs, and institutions, and the conscious development of basic capabilities that were previously lacking. Often a change from old routines to new patterns involves a social, political, economic, and intellectual revolution — the uprooting of an old world view and an old belief system and the substitution of something almost entirely unprecedented — at least within that particular society. Many of these considerations are peculiarly characteristic of China over the years since World War II.

Third in explanatory usefulness are certain residuals — by no means unrelated to the factors already mentioned — such as the political culture and institutions, the competitions and struggles among domestic political factions, and other influential processes. After the capability factor has been analyzed, these residuals tend to explain individual policies and resemblances of policies among states. When goals are strongly influenced by tradition and history, these factors may be more necessary and adequate to explaining policy than when goals are set by decisionmakers, who are freer from restraints of their own past.

Despite the extraordinary influence of capabilities and dissatisfactions in explaining a country's role, policies, and behavior, there are, however, good reasons for reviewing some of its history, tradition, and other background conditions first. It is these considerations that chapter two will focus on.

Notes

1. Kurt London, *The Permanent Crisis* (Waltham, Mass.: Blaisdell, 1968), p. 151.
2. Ibid., pp. 149-50.

PART 1

Explaining Chinese
Communist Foreign
Policy

Chapter Two

Tradition and Consciousness: Historic and novel objectives and principles

Any society, even a revolutionary one, is the product of its historical development. Therefore, in order to comprehend China's basic economic and military capabilities more fully, it is important to consider the tradition and consciousness of Chinese society, or what might be called its *world view*. By world view, we mean specifically a people's image of the universe and their role in it, their recorded history and recollections of past experience, their long-range goals or sense of purpose, and whatever values and beliefs they hold about human relations. Included in a people's world view would be significant aspects of their history, culture, ideology, and special principles and objectives. As early as the 1950's it seemed evident to many foreign observers that the People's Republic of China was not at all a carbon copy of the USSR. Since then, developments not only in China, but also in North Korea, Vietnam, Cuba, and elsewhere have suggested that Marxist-Leninist principles tend to be influenced in powerful ways by the individual cultures in which they take root. The organization and doctrine is likely to remain distinctly Marxist-Leninist, but the applications and manifestations may be expected to incorporate elements, styles, and tendencies from deep within the local culture and history.

In each case a distinction should be drawn between the world views of elite groups, including the political leadership, and the world views of the rank and file of people. The two may be quite different. The more dissatisfied and active a political leadership is, the more likely it is that its special world view, rather than the world view of the mass, will dominate foreign policy. China's leaders are highly dissatisfied and have worked out an elaborate set of ideas about the world as it is and as it ought to be; ideas that go well beyond those of the mass of the Chinese population. Furthermore, China's modern social and political structure has made the political culture and thought of the bulk of the population largely irrelevant to explaining foreign policy, just as did the traditional social and political structure. In the early 1950s, established continuities, based on the widespread illiteracy, lack of education, and primacy of local and familial concerns that characterized the Chinese Empire, were combined with a high degree of political centralization and leadership dissatisfaction to make the world view of Mao Tse-tung and a relatively small number of other Party leaders. That view is most relevant to understanding Chinese foreign policy at that time. Therefore, our major references in this book are to the images and ideas of Chinese Communist leaders rather than to those of the Chinese people at large.

The more or less traditional perspectives of the Chinese rank and file, including their views of themselves, their environment, and their leaders, are powerful political realities nevertheless. Deeply ingrained world views do not change easily. But increasingly, during the twentieth century, the world views of Chinese political leaders have been deeply influenced by the West and have tended for this reason (and for others) to diverge rather sharply from the more traditional notions of the Chinese rank and file. These views have profoundly influenced — but have also been tempered by — the time-honored views of the people.

When we examine the world picture of China's Communist leaders, we find both extreme novelty and, perhaps surprisingly, some ancient and some modern precommunist themes. Marxism-Leninism-Maoism is itself a Chinese interpretation of an essentially Western-derived world view. A distinguishing characteristic of Chinese Communist political power has been the effort by Mao Tse-tung and his colleagues to transform the historical Chinese world view into an overall Marxist-Leninist world view — through the close blending of theory and practice, through thought reform and other methods — while moving many traditional concepts into the new context where their meanings and implications have been transformed.

Prior to the twentieth century, its leaders had traditionally considered China, on account of its advanced civilization, paramount in the world. The proper role of other states was to pay homage, to imitate, to absorb Chinese culture. But in the late nineteenth and early twentieth centuries, the superior technology of the West brought about the subjugation and exploitation of China. Chinese leaders responded to this fall with a demand for revitalization, modernization, and material equality (at least) within the international system. Maoism, the current leadership's system of ideas, hopes and claims to achieve such modernization. And the revolutionary Marxist-Leninist element of Maoism has merged with traditional ideas to engender a foreign policy of competition in economic and military capabilities, isolation from and hostility to stronger states, and an attempt to present the People's Republic as a model of modernization techniques. Some of the dynamics of Chinese Communist behavior undoubtedly arise from a strong desire on the part of the leaders to reestablish China's historical position as a powerful state; but this tendency is combined with a Marxist-Leninist-Maoist belief in certain laws of history that are operating to transform the country into a major element in a new world order.

The Traditional View of China's Primacy

For the better part of two millennia, at least, China perceived itself as the only great empire on earth, the only civilization, the only culture that really mattered. The Emperor — or Son of Heaven — represented all mankind, whether Chinese or barbarian, in his ritual sacrifices before the forces of nature. He was the crucial link — the mediator — between heaven and earth, and he enjoyed the mandate to rule all men. Envoys bearing gifts from other sovereigns were viewed by the Chinese as paying tribute, and, in approaching the Emperor in later centuries, even the representatives of Western powers were expected to perform the kowtow, the three kneelings and nine prostrations. Thus, as pointed out by John Fairbank and by S. Y. Teng, "The tributary system, as the sum total of these formalities, was the mechanism by which non-Chinese regions were given their place in the all-embracing Chinese political, and therefore ethical, scheme of things."[1] There was a 2000-year-old predisposition to view China as the single major power in a world of less important states.

Until the beginning of the nineteenth century, China remained geographically isolated from direct confrontations with other advanced societies. In general, up to this time neither Chinese emperors nor their bureaucrats, literati, and military leaders had possessed any means of comparing Chinese culture, society, and empire with anything but the cultures, societies, and political structures of seemingly lesser peoples, who were normally viewed by the Chinese as barbarians or semibarbarians. Chinese merchants had traded with India and Roman outposts, and Chinese pilgrims had made overland journeys to the Indus and Gangean valleys, often by way of the Oxus and what is now Afghanistan. Marco Polo brought China vaguely in touch with Venice and the Mediterranean, and during later centuries early Jesuit missionaries resided in China. But distances were vast, and interchanges were intermittent at best. For China, the consequences of this geographical and cultural isolation have been unusually significant.

As the West was developing its nation-state and international treaty system, the Chinese emperors, scholars, and bureaucrats, insulated from much of the world because of their geographical position, were practicing a diplomacy that emerged from the monolithic prestige of their empire. In consequence, the concept of a community of legally equal sovereign states and of international transactions on the basis of such legal equality failed to evolve in China. Historical circumstance provided no milieu comparable to that of Western Europe for the training of diplomats in the give and take of foreign affairs, characteristic of a multistate system of roughly equal state actors.

There were ebbs and flows in Chinese fortunes. At times the country was integrated into a powerful and effective empire. At other times it broke down into petty kingdoms or warlord preserves on a regional basis. Many times it was overrun by outside forces. In the long run, however, China was always able to reintegrate itself, to absorb the invader, and to preserve its integrity as one of the oldest cultures of human history.

Whatever their other differences, Mao Tse-tung and his colleagues, and Chiang Kai-shek and Sun Yat-sen, shared many of these traditional views of Chinese superiority and of the central role and vast sweep of the ancient Chinese Empire. As pointed out by Harold Hinton, "Communist China, like traditional China, believes that it is the repository of unique values that ought to be accepted by all mankind and that this acceptance should create a willingness to acknowledge Chinese political leadership even in remote areas where China's power cannot reach, and still more where it can."[2] It would not be surprising if this Chinese predisposition were to increase the dissatisfactions of any Chinese leadership that perceived the country as occupying a secondary position and being exploited, threatened, constrained, or dominated by other states.

Fundamental to imperial Chinese diplomacy was the tributary system based upon the age-old tradition of Chinese superiority over foreign barbarians. By barbarians, the Chinese meant whatever people had not yet been Sinicized.[3] The Chinese viewpoint was that

> *Those barbarians who wished to "come and be transformed" [lai-hua] and so participate in the benefits of [Chinese] civilization, must recognize the supreme position of the Emperor; for the Son of Heaven represented all mankind, both Chinese and barbarian ... This supremacy of the Emperor as mediator between Heaven and Earth was most obviously acknowledged in the performance of the kowtow, the three kneelings and nine prostrations to which European envoys later objected. It was also acknowledged by the bringing of tribute ... , by the formal bestowal of a seal, comparable to the investure of a vassal in medieval Europe, and in other ways.*[4]

The status and prestige of other peoples thus varied according to their acceptance of Chinese ethics and culture. Non-Sinicized barbarian peoples had their place in the world scheme somewhere below that of partially Sinicized people. "I have heard of men using the doctrines of our great land to change barbarians," asserted the Chinese classics, "but I have never yet heard of any being changed by barbarians."[5]

When China was penetrated or conquered, the invaders normally stood in awe of Chinese culture and tended to be absorbed or at least profoundly influenced by Chinese culture and technology. At times of greatest power and influence, traditional China was the center of a large but loosely connected system of tributary states. As described by Mary Wright, "The tributary system, which included all the world known to China, had proved through centuries to be an enduring and effective system of international organization, a hierarchy in which the place of each people was determined by the degree to which it was permeated and transformed by the Confucian doctrine."[6] China — the Middle Kingdom — occupied the magnetic center, so to speak, of this Confucian world order.

It is doubtful whether tributary states interpreted their relations with the empire as did the Chinese, who accepted their own suzerainty as part of the natural order of things. Moreover, there was considerable variability in the nature of tributary ties; those between China and Burma being looser and more intermittent, for example, than those between China and Korea. Viewed from within its own frontiers, however, China looked like the center of world power and culture. Under these circumstances, it is not surprising that for many generations the

Chinese assumed themselves to be "more intelligent, more cultured and more capable than any other people"[7] and that they tended to view their empire as the world's primary political power.

The Fall to Backwardness and Exploitation

For centuries at least until the end of the Middle Ages in Europe, China more than held its own in technology (in the application of knowledge and skills), and consequently there tended, on the whole, to be a match between Chinese pretensions and Chinese capabilities. "The compass was invented in China very long ago," Mao Tse-tung has reminded his followers. "The art of paper making was discovered as early as 1800 years ago. Block printing was invented 1300 years ago. In addition, movable types were invented 800 years ago. Gunpowder was used in China earlier than in Europe. China, with a recorded history of almost 4000 years, is therefore one of the oldest civilized countries in the world."[8]

But the scientific renaissance that swept the Mediterranean and other parts of Europe in the fifteenth, sixteenth, and seventeenth centuries largely passed China by, as did the industrial revolution some two centuries later.

With the so-called Opium War between China and Great Britain in 1839 and the subsequent acceleration of Western economic, political, cultural, and technological penetration, the traditional pattern was rapidly disrupted. Within the course of a generation or two, the barbaric, but technologically superior, Westerners effected a reversal of the traditional relationship: China, vulnerable to Western commercial exploitation — and also to good works and all manner of new concepts and ways of doing things brought by Western missionaries, merchants, soldiers, and diplomats — became, in effect, a tributary of the West.

Mao, Sun Yat-sen, Chiang Kai-shek, and many other Chinese of varying political persuasions, whatever their disagreements, have tended to identify as still Chinese the extensive territories that were alienated from Chinese sovereignty or suzerainty by foreign "imperialists."[9] (These regions include the North-East Frontier Agency and Assam, lost to Britain after 1820; the left bank of the Amur River, lost to Russia in 1858; the Maritime Territory, lost to Russia in 1860; the Tashkent area as far west as Lake Balkhash, lost to Russia in 1864; Bhutan, lost to Britain in 1865; Sakhalin, lost to Russia and Japan after 1875; Ryukyu Islands lost to Japan in 1879; Indochina, lost to France in 1885; Siam, lost under pressure from Britain and France in 1885;

Burma, lost to Britain in 1886; territory along the Sino-Burmese frontier, lost to Britain after 1886; Sikkim, lost to Britain in 1889; Taiwan and the Pescadores, lost to Japan in 1895; Malaya, lost to Britain in 1895; Korea, lost to Japan in 1895 and 1910; the Ladakh area, lost to Britain in 1896; and Nepal, lost to Britain in 1898. The original Chinese edition of *China's Destiny,* published in Chungking in 1943, included Korea among the territories lost to China.) It is true that each of the regions so considered has been at least tributary to China at one time or another, but a Westerner might argue that the Chinese would not be much more justified in rebuilding the ancient empire on this basis than the Italians would be if they sought to reincorporate all the regions ruled by the Romans at one time or another in their history.

During the nineteenth century, Western powers established settlements or concessions in Shanghai, Tientsin, Canton, Hankow, and other Chinese cities, over which the government of China had no jurisdiction.[10] Other parts of the country were leased outright: Weihaiwei, Deep Bay, and Mirs Bay to Great Britain and Kwangchowan to France for ninety years; Kiaochow to Germany for ninety-nine years; Darien and Port Arthur to tsarist Russia for twenty-five years, and so forth. Similarly, Western powers — and later, Japan — claimed large spheres of special interest in China. It was said that Shantung Province belonged to the German sphere of interest, Manchuria to the Russian sphere of influence and so forth.[11] In the concessions and settlements, and indeed in China generally, resident Westerners enjoyed extraterritorial status that exempted them from Chinese law and authority.[12]

Mao Tse-tung, like other Chinese of quite different political inclinations, has frequently referred to the unequal treaties imposed upon China by more powerful nations of the West and by Japan and to the ways in which they acquired control of China's "customs and foreign trade as well as her sea, land, air and inland water communications." Also, how they ran "many light and heavy industries in China," and, by granting loans to the Chinese government and establishing banks in China, "monopolized China's banking and finance."[13]

The Ideology of Maoism

It was Mao's firm conviction, however, that China — once properly aroused, mobilized, and organized — had the capacity for throwing off these alien constraints and influences. According to him, the country was "not only famous throughout the world for its stamina and industriousness, but also as a freedom-loving people with a rich revolutionary heritage." It was a nation, moreover,

he said, "with a glorious revolutionary tradition and a splendid historical heritage," one that "would never submit to rule by dark forces."
Whenever such a rule was temporarily imposed in the past, stated Mao,
the Chinese people had always succeeded in overthrowing or changing
it by revolutionary means.[14] This view has been an important factor in
providing Maoist China with the will and cohesion required for a policy
of self-sufficiency in world as well as domestic affairs.

After the Chinese revolution of 1911, which brought an end to the
ancient empire, the country broke into regional warlord regimes not
unlike some of the petty kingdoms of earlier eras of imperial disintegration. In many instances, Western powers and Japan supported one
or another of these warlords with funds and military assistance —
partly in order to exploit a particular region economically or to protect
their investments.

During early decades of the twentieth century many Chinese, sensitive to the decline in the power and prestige of the Chinese state, had
a tendency to feel apologetic about their culture. Much of Mao Tse-
tung's personal influence and power stems from his success in alternat-
ing this situation. "Soon after the Chinese Communists came to power,
their soldiers could claim to have won victories over the troops of some
of the world's most powerful nations, and Communist China became a
force to be reckoned with."[15]

National revitalization

An extremely important element in recent
Chinese thought, Nationalist as well as Communist, has been the protest against inequality and demands for greater equality with other
nations. An examination of both Nationalist and Communist statements suggests, however, that the goal is something more than mere
legal equality with great and small nations. According to the Nationalist
leader Sun Yat-sen, "Japan studied from the West for only a few
decades and became one of the world's greatest powers. But China has
ten times the population and thirty times the area of Japan, and her
resources are much larger than Japan's. If China reaches the standard
of Japan, she will be equal to ten great powers . . . and will then be able
to recover her predominant national position."[16]

After China reaches "her predominant national position," what
then? A common phrase in ancient China, according to Sun Yat-sen,
was "Rescue the weak, lift up the fallen." Because of this noble policy,
the Chinese Empire had prospered for thousands of years, and
Annam, Burma, Korea, Siam, and other small states were able to maintain their independence. "Consequently, if we want China to rise to
power," Sun Yat-sen wrote, "we must not only restore our national
standing, but we must also assume a great responsibility toward the
world . . . Only if we 'rescue the weak and lift up the fallen' will we be

14

carrying out the divine obligation of our nation. We must aid the weaker and smaller peoples and oppose the Great Powers of the world ... Then will we be truly governing the state and pacifying the world."

If Sun Yat-sen's sentiments were translated into Marxist-Leninist-Maoist language, they might represent rather closely the predispositions of the current leadership. A major Chinese task, at the very least, was and is to modernize the country and reestablish its status as a great power — possibly, in the longer run, to achieve some primacy.

In committing themselves to this mission, Mao and his colleagues — while relying selectively upon their own Chinese heritage — also, drew heavily from the West, bringing about a blend of the familiar with the alien. Among influential Western concepts after the beginning of the twentieth century were those of V. I. Lenin, which reached China in the period of turmoil following World War I. Influenced by the writings of an English political economist, John Atkinson Hobson, Lenin had developed a theory of imperialism, which sought to explain the prolonged power of capitalism throughout the world and the juxtaposition and conflict of economic and political forces producing what he called imperialist wars.

Mao, following Lenin, saw World War I and the establishment of the USSR as crucial turning points. Previously, the Chinese revolution, like many other revolutions in various parts of the world, had been bourgeois-democratic in nature, but after World War I and the October revolution in Russia, the "world capitalist front" had collapsed in one-sixth of the world, and in other places "its decadence was revealed." In remaining parts of the earth, capitalism could not survive "without relying more and more on the colonies and semicolonies." The working classes of the world were freeing themselves day by day.

World revolution

In China and certain other colonies and semi-colonies, according to Mao, the revolution would now develop in two stages. The first stage would be characterized, not by a capitalist society under "the dictatorship of the bourgeoisie," but by the establishment of a new democratic society "under the joint dictatorship of the revolutionary classes headed by the proletariat." In this stage, important elements of the national bourgeoisie would cooperate with the workers and peasants, but later, as the revolution progressed, they would go over to the reactionary side. The second revolutionary stage would lead to the establishment of socialism.

Under these circumstances, the world would be characterized for some time by a "multifarious state system" including "republics with bourgeois dictatorships," "republics under the dictatorship of the proletariat," and "republics under the joint dictatorships of several revolutionary classes" (for example, China under the new democracy).

Maintaining the revolutionary struggle and preparing for socialism, the new democracy would be characterized by (1) the confiscation of landlord holdings and their distribution among the peasants who had no land or only a little land; (2) state control of certain enterprises, some foreign owned, some Chinese owned, that would be too monopolistic or too large for private management (banks, railways, airlines, and so forth); and (3) the maintenance of various lesser enterprises under private management for the time being, at least. In the course of the revolution there would be revolutionary struggles on two fronts—against the reactionary classes within China and against imperialism throughout the world. Mao's strategy and tactics for the domestic revolutionary struggle involved the establishment, through guerrilla warfare combined with political class warfare, of rural revolutionary base areas on the Chinese countryside and the gradual encirclement, attrition, and absorption of the cities therefrom. This combined procedure was put forward as "of outstanding and universal practical importance for the present revolutionary struggles of all the oppressed nations and peoples in Asia, Africa, and Latin America against imperialism and its lackeys."[17]

The history of such people's wars in China and other countries, according to Chinese Communist authorities, had provided "conclusive evidence that the growth of the people's revolutionary forces from weak and small beginnings into strong and large forces is a universal law of development of class struggle, a universal law of development of people's war. A people's war inevitably meets with many difficulties, with ups and downs and setbacks in the course of its development, but no force can alter its general trend toward inevitable triumph."[18]

The question can be raised why, in view of Mainland China's limited economic, technological, and military capabilities, Mao Tse-tung and his colleagues seem to view the future of their regime and of the world revolutionary movement with such optimism. Experience provides one part of the answer. Without doubt, the long and unique experiences of the Chinese Communist leadership, in the mountains of Kiangsi and Hunan during the epic Long March, in the border regions of the northwest during the Japanese war, and later in the successful struggle for power against the Nationalists, have profoundly influenced both the political culture and the institutions of Communist China.

Over the course of two decades, Mao and his associates operated against formidable forces—the Nationalists, the Japanese, and, especially during the Long March, nature itself. They became extraordinarily successful at harnessing meager resources and concentrating them against the enemy's weakest points, devising ways of turning the enemy against itself, and seizing the moment for vigorous action when the opposing forces were scattered or off balance. This long, essentially guerrilla experience tended to engender among the Chinese Communist leaders a profound reliance upon ingenuity, patience, stamina, persistence, will, self-reliance, and other almost puritanical virtues.

These undertakings endowed the Chinese Communists with a deep-seated confidence in their ability to play the role of David against a variety of seemingly invincible Goliaths. The record reveals, moreover, that up until 1956 or 1957, at least, these somewhat spartan virtues contributed to spectacular victories in spite of momentary defeats. This background has predisposed the leadership to continue its dependence upon these virtues and operational modes in the drive for industrialization and to counsel other revolutionary movements in Asia and elsewhere to practice similar self-discipline and to take primary responsibility for the furthering of their own revolutionary struggles.

Ideology—the Marxist-Leninist-Maoist world view—provides another considerable part of the answer. Chinese Communist leaders may well have a fairly realistic assessment of their limited capabilities at the present time, but they believe firmly that the balance of world forces will change in the future, that revolutionary forces will grow stronger and capitalist, imperialist, and revisionist forces crucially weaker.

In a September 1965 essay, Lin Piao put forward a set of predictions about the ways in which a Chinese Communist style of revolution would eventually triumph over capitalism and imperialism everywhere in the world. Much of what Lin said had been stated before, but some of his assertions were new.[19] Lin, who had risen to high leadership in the Chinese Communist hierarchy, drew a startling analogy between the strategy of people's war within a single country such as China and prospects for the "world-wide struggle against imperialism."

Lin Piao stated that in "committing aggression" against the underdeveloped countries—the colonies and semicolonies—the imperialists usually began by seizing the big cities and the main lines of communication, but that they had always been unable to bring the vast countryside completely under their control. The countryside, and the countryside alone, could provide broad areas in which the revolutionaries could maneuver freely and bases from which the revolutionaries could go forward to final victory. "Precisely for this reason," Lin Piao asserted, "Comrade Mao Tse-tung's theory of establishing revolutionary base areas in the rural districts and encircling the cities from the countryside is attracting more and more attention among the people in these regions."[20]

The analogy with Chinese Communist experience was close. "Taking the entire globe," Lin said, "if North America and Western Europe can be called 'the cities of the world,' then Asia, Africa and Latin America constitute 'the rural areas of the world'." His meaning was clear: the contemporary world revolution also provided for the encirclement of cities—the United States and other capitalist countries—by the rural areas. In the final analysis, the whole cause of world revolution hinged on the revolutionary struggles of the Asian, African, and Latin American peoples, who make up the overwhelming majority of the world's population.[21]

World War I had been followed by the birth of the socialist Soviet Union. World War II was followed by the emergence of a series of socialist countries and many nationally independent countries. "If the U.S. imperialists should insist on launching a third world war," Lin predicted, "it can be stated categorically that many more hundreds of millions of people will turn to socialism; the imperialists will then have little room left on the globe; and it is possible that the whole structure of imperialism will collapse."[22] He expressed optimism about the future: "We are confident that the people will bring to an end the epoch of wars in human history. Comrade Mao Tse-tung pointed out long ago that war, this monster, 'will be finally eliminated by the progress of human society, and in the not too distant future too. But there is only one way to eliminate it and that is to oppose war with war, to oppose counterrevolutionary war with revolutionary war'."[23]

From a Western point of view, these Maoist beliefs, assumptions, and predictions about the future may seem farfetched, even ludicrous, especially in view of Communist China's admittedly limited capabilities. On the other hand, it is clear that many countries in the so-called underdeveloped parts of the world are in a precarious situation and vulnerable to revolution if their basic problems are not solved. The dissatisfaction of many people in these countries is profound. If the People's Republic of China should manage to solve its own problems effectively, the Maoist model would undoubtedly appear attractive wherever other, more conventional attempts at solution had failed. This appeal might persist long after Mao Tse-tung's death and the passing of his colleagues. Moreover, it must also be recognized and reemphasized here, that achievement of advanced nuclear and missile capabilities by the People's Republic of China has already begun to alter the world military balance of power in ways that are difficult to foresee.

To a considerable degree, the successes of the Chinese Communist regime can be attributed to Mao Tse-tung's genius in relating Marxism-Leninism—an essentially Western ideology and organizational system—to important elements of Chinese culture in ways that the peasants and other Chinese rank and file could understand and appreciate. The political culture of the leading circles of the People's Republic consists of a subtle blend of traditional Chinese and Marxist-Leninist-Maoist elements that find expression in foreign policy. Among the more powerful traditional Chinese elements are the predispositions to view Chinese society as unique in the world and China itself as occupying a central position among all nations. Emperors of the past were viewed as Sons of Heaven serving as arbiters between universal forces on the one hand and the Chinese people on the other. In this sense, domestic and external affairs were perceived as interconnected and even interdependent.

Somewhat analogously, the Chinese Communist leadership perceives its domestic revolutionary program not only as industrializing the country but also as providing the capability for a reassertion of Chinese power and status. Domestic organization, development, and worthy (as well as successful) leadership thus emerge as prerequisites to effective foreign policy. It may not be pressing the analogy too far to suggest Mao Tse-tung, his colleagues, and his successors as playing the Son-of-Heaven role as arbiters between a unified Chinese people and the rest of the universe, including other countries.

The Political Culture
of China's Masses

The political culture of China's leaders has already been examined. The political culture of China's masses is also worth studying, even if it is only marginally relevant to policy, because it shows how tradition as well as the current regime's practice has made the world views of a narrow stratum most important to overall Chinese policymaking. The political institutions and political processes of China are no doubt more vital than the political culture of the rank and file in explaining foreign policy; unfortunately, they are also more hidden. Even now, as the Mainland has become more accessible, relatively little can really be said with any degree of assurance about current Chinese political processes. But despite the opacity (and recent disruption) of China's political institutions, there are at least some formal notes we may provide, if only to reveal once again the centralized character of foreign policy decisionmaking and to emphasize once again the critical importance of the views of the leaders of the People's Republic to the comprehension of its policy.

Traditional Chinese political
and social order

Traditional Chinese concepts of political order were based on homogeneity of ideas and culture, not on a forced obedience to a common body of law.[24] Over many centuries the empire maintained considerable stability "through an exceedingly clever use of Confucianism as the basis of the state government, coupled with a system of administration which, though centralized, at the same time left to the locality and the individual a large measure of self-rule." As an outcome, the Chinese Empire achieved "a remarkable evenness of civilization throughout a vast country and a continuity of culture longer than that enjoyed by any other living nation."[25]

Universal good government derived from the people's acquiescence to their roles in society. "Let the ruler be the ruler," Confucius had asserted, "and let the minister be the minister. Let the father be the father, and let the son be the son."[26] When names and actualities were in accord with each other, when men behaved in harmony with their roles, there was good government, according to the Confucian concept. When these were not in accord, there was disorder. If the Emperor did not act as an emperor should, then he was not truly an emperor. He no longer had the mandate of Heaven. Each person, then, ought to perform, without complaint or discontent, and as well as his ability allowed, the functions expected and demanded of him by his role in society and should act toward his fellow men in ways appropriate to his position and theirs.[27]

Confucian China thus depended upon a social, economic, and political ordering that defined the rights, benefactions, and obligations of every person and every group from the top to the bottom of the system. The overriding purposes of the society, as handed down by tradition, were the maintenance of domestic and international peace, the furtherance of the material welfare of all members according to their stations, and the fostering of individual serenity and universal harmony. There was an assumption, moreover, that these various benefactions would be achieved precisely insofar as people throughout the system were mutually aware of their various rights and corollary duties—and to the extent that the state and its officials were competent to serve as arbiters. This view has remained an important factor in Chinese policy despite recent attacks on the Confucian heritage.

There was no place within this arrangement for Western-style concepts of individualism, of the supremacy of law, or of personal freedom safeguarded by law. The individual was subordinated to his family group, and the whole of society was ruled by the bureaucrat. The state was "politically centralized while economically decentralized, and strong in the customary ethical sanctions which preserved the patriarch and the ruler at the top of the social hierarchy, while weak in the institutions of property and enterprise."[28] Essentially, however, it was the system in its broader aspects, Chinese culture and the Chinese way of life, rather than the state and its lesser symbols, that the people absorbed as a part of them. This distinctive system was deeply internalized by the people, being largely accepted psychologically as well as physically, and was depended upon the individual in the ordering of his life and his expectancies.

The Chinese hierarchy thus consisted of mutually interacting roles extending from the Emperor down through metropolitan and provincial officials to local officers, the gentry, and the peasants. Each role operated within one of various institutions, of which the family was the basic unit. Larger institutions encompassed smaller institutions, and within this nesting arrangement an individual might play several roles. Binding all these elements together were a highly developed legal system and the *li,* or principles of social usage, which defined each person's place in the society and determined his proper behavior. The ideal was to resolve conflicts through persuasion, compromise, and concession rather than through exercise of force. A well-developed legal code and a family-based system of collective responsibility sanctioned these milder processes.

In its totality, the Chinese social structure was family centered. The extended kinship group served as a social, economic, and political unit, and many scholars view it as the chief source of Chinese social stability.[29] As with other institutions in Chinese society, however, the stability of the kinship system increased and declined with cyclical changes in the empire itself, although it was always a potent force.

The role of the family within Chinese society was clearly defined, and by the Ch'ing era (1644-1911) the power of the institution was unmistakable. Discipline was so firmly established that those possessing power within a family structure found few obstacles to its enforcement. The would-be rebel had almost no place to go outside the family boundaries; furthermore, he knew that the other members would be held collectively responsible for his actions. Behavior that separated an individual from his family tended to isolate him from the possibility of establishing new relations with other parts of the society.[30]

The new order

The Chinese Communists, however, have not been satisfied with a politically centralized but economically decentralized China. Their effort has been to bring the whole society, economy as well as polity, into a unified system in which centralization and decentralization combine in characteristic Marxist-Leninist-Maoist ways. Moreover, they have made powerful efforts to destroy the ancient, patriarchal extended family (often including an impressive assemblage of relatives and retainers), to uproot the gentry and eliminate them as a class, and to pulverize other time-honored institutions. One would not be surprised, however, to find new players filling some of the old roles and to find both the rank and file and elites carrying over or transforming some of their old habits and predispositions.

In many ways Mao Tse-tung and his colleagues have managed to fill traditional roles with their own substitutes. Cadremen have tended to take the place of gentry in providing crucial links between the rank and file and the government. Instances have been reported from rural areas of party secretaries performing the traditional functions of the marriage go-between. It is entirely possible that Mao became the Son of Heaven in many peasant eyes. Mass indoctrination and thought-reform techniques were used to bring resisting elements—especially among petty shopkeepers, recalcitrant intellectuals, and others—into the framework. In these and other ways, the people have been linked with the government in an overlapping of political cultures.

From time to time the Chinese Communists have gone too far, of course, especially in attacking the family. To dismantle the extended family—often viewed as a petty tyranny—was one thing, but to disrupt the nuclear family of husband, wife, and small children was another. However, with some notable exceptions, Maoist forces were sufficiently in touch with the rank and file, and sufficiently sensitive to fundamental, widespread resistance, to retreat from their more untenable positions. Mao's genius in harnessing discontent is probably best illustrated by the Cultural Revolution, during which he seized upon what seemed to have begun as spontaneous discontent with the regime on the part of the young people and turned it against the party—to a large degree his own creation—to his own personal advantage.

As suggested by Franz Schurmann, in traditional China Confucianism was the ethos, the gentry were the status group or elite, and the paterfamilias was the model personality or wielder of authority. By 1949 the revolution had virtually destroyed all three, and today, after many years of Communist rule, "there is no evidence that China will ever return to this ancient trinity."[31] Ideology has now been substituted for ethos, Schurmann believes. "A belief system that expressed basic social and human values has been replaced by an ideology that expresses values and goals of socio-political action and achievement." Organizational leadership, especially party leadership, has replaced the gentry as the elite or status group. And the cadre—the revolutionary leader in organization—has taken the place of the paterfamilias as the model personality.

It has been pointed out, however, that some of the old views and concepts have survived under the surface and sometimes peep through. Even today, according to John Weakland, "human relationships and especially the family system are often a rather explicit model for thought and expression."[32] This seems particularly true of Chinese politics: "In old discussions of the Chinese Empire and of bandit groups, and in recent discussions of business organization and government reform, there occur overt imagery of family organization, family relationship terms, and statements of principles just like those proclaimed by Confucius and by ordinary Chinese informants in regard to family ordering."[33]

Such expression is very evident in the sphere of Chinese foreign policy and international relations, being found in Imperial, Nationalist, and now in Communist pronouncements by Mao Tse-tung and his successors. Prior to the Sino-Soviet controversy, Chinese Communist sources ranging from elementary school texts to city newspapers used images of the Soviet Union as the "elder brother" and China as the "younger brother" within the "socialist world." The capitalistic world was perceived, on the other hand, as resembling the "feudalistic big family" with the United States playing the role of "elder brother."[34] South Korea has been referred to as the "younger brother" of the United States and North Korea as the "younger brother" of China.

The use of these images indicates that the views of the population as a whole are by no means to be ignored in any serious study, for they are not ignored by the leadership of China. There is a concerted attempt by the leaders to secure consensus or assent to policy. As viewed by Mao and his associates, the task of leadership was, and is, to go to the masses, understand their scattered, unsystematic views with respect to needs and aspirations, sum up these views and translate them into party and government policy, take them back to the masses (explaining and popularizing them until the masses embrace the policies as their own), translate them into action, test the activities and outcomes through close interaction with the populace, sum up the views of the masses again, translate them into revised policy, and so on.

Much of Mao Tse-tung's genius has lain in translating and transforming selected lessons and aphorisms from history, tradition, and the Chinese classics, from Marxist-Leninist theory, and from his own guerrilla experience, into colloquial speeches and traits that the peasants could understand. Over the years, and particularly during the Yenan period, the Chinese Communists also developed a special literature as they had built a party organization and an army—as an instrument of policy in accordance with Marxist-Leninist-Maoist principles. Like the organization and the army, this literature has served the needs of the revolution, whipping up popular support for the new government, providing flesh-and-blood behavior patterns for the new society, and giving instruction in practical communism.

Cyril Birch has pointed out that "just as the resistance and guerrilla warfare against the Japanese, however exaggerated in its scope, had been the means of instilling patriotic loyalty into the peasants and of identifying the Communist party as their leader against the national enemy, so the land reform was the means of instilling political consciousness and enforcing participation in the party's crusade against the class enemy."[35]

The major outcome has been not so much "that the peasant received his patch of land; he was not in any case to enjoy the thrill of possessing it for very long. The real and astonishing achievement was that he was goaded into attending political meetings, into believing that he was being guided, not directed, by the Communist party to a position of control over his own destiny."[36] The same could be said for women, whose lives were also transformed by the revolution.

The continuing revolution

Maoist theory provided for more than a one-shot revolution, however. It presented a context within which the workers and the downtrodden could pursue a continuing revolution, or series of revolutions, even within the Chinese Communist party and state. It is largely because of this consideration that, of the several epic events in Chinese Communist history that Westerners have had difficulty understanding (the 3-Anti campaigns, for example, or the Great Leap Forward), it is the Great Proletarian Cultural Revolution (1966-1969) that seems least comprehensible. At that time, it appeared from the outside that Mao was rebelling against Mao, that the whole vast Chinese dragon was bent on consuming itself. For considerable periods of time, it was difficult to ascertain who the real Maoists were, the revolutionary Red Guards, or their victims.

The Anti-Lin Piao, Anti-Confucius campaign offered further evidence, along with the earlier fall of Liu Shao-ch'i, that even veteran Communist leaders of the Party, the Red Army, and the state—heroes, if you wish—were not safe from destruction by the continuing revolution if evidence were found of reactionary tendencies. Indeed, Maoism holds that inner-party struggle is the reflection within the Party of class struggle in society, and this precept was used as a basis for explaining the fall of Lin Piao.[37] According to Chinese theoreticians, Lin and his followers—despite many years of Party membership and activities—had tried to lead China away from the socialist road and "reduce it to a colony of Soviet revisionism."[38] Early in 1974, as reported in the *Peking Review,* "the workers at the Peking Art Handicrafts Plant raised their political consciousness and developed their plant's excellent situation in revolution and production" by deepening their criticism of Lin Piao by repudiating Confucius. Through his attempt to "liberate politically all the overthrown landlords, rich peasants, counterrevolutionaries, bad elements and reactionaries," Lin Piao had revealed himself as "a truly faithful disciple of Confucius and his reactionary world outlook."

Like Confucius, Lin had tried to "turn back the wheel of history."[39] To analyze Confucius from the historical-materialist viewpoint, according to Chinese theoreticians, "one must put him in the context of the class struggle of his time and see which class standpoint he took and which class interests his ideology served." Confucius did all in his power to uphold the slave system, just as Lin Piao had sought to betray China to Soviet revisionism and social imperialism.[40]

Clearly, the political culture of China still contains many powerful holdovers from the past, perhaps more than are evident to the outside observer today. Many of these persisting elements have been combined with Marxism-Leninism-Maoism into a complex, all-embracing ideology or world view. But to date, the Marxist-Leninist-Maoist revolutionary outlook is relied upon to keep the country and its people on a correct path. Currently this world view remains an important factor in influencing Chinese goals, policy styles, and methods of procedure. However, the extent to which it survives and continues to shape the course of affairs now that Mao Tse-tung and many of his older colleagues have passed from leadership, remains to be seen.

Some Notes on China's Governmental Institutions

The question arises: How are the many impulses, predispositions, habits, and innovations of Chinese political culture translated today into policy and action? What institutions give them expression and implementation? Unfortunately, there are serious difficulties here. As Franz Schurmann has indicated, "One of the most important yet least known areas of organization in China is that of state administration, or government. The Chinese Communists have created the most powerful government in Chinese history, but extreme secrecy about its operation makes it impossible for us to study it in detail."[41] The difficulty is compounded by the fact that we must go behind the government to find the major concentration of power. Thus, "Important as the organization of the government is, it is only the machinery for implementing the program of the Communist party."[42]

The guiding principle of organization in the party and in national life generally is *democratic centralism*. The 1956 Constitution of the Communist Party of China (Article 19) defined democratic centralism as "centralism on the basis of democracy and democracy under centralized guidance." According to the basic conditions of democratic centralism, the leading bodies of the party are elected. All higher bodies must "pay constant heed to the views of their lower organizations and the rank and file party membership, study their experiences, and give prompt help in solving their problems." Party organizations at each level combine collective leadership with individual responsibility. "All important issues are to be decided on collectively, and at the same time, each individual is enabled to play his part to the fullest possible extent."

Party decisions must be carried out unconditionally. Once a decision is reached, individual party members "shall obey the party organization, the minority shall obey the majority, the lower party organizations shall obey the higher party organizations, and all constituent party organizations throughout the country shall obey the National Party Congress and the Central Committee."

Many basic decisions made by the party are implemented by organs of state. To a large extent, indeed, the government may be viewed as executing the will of the Party in many spheres of activity. In 1975 the revised national constitution defined the People's Republic as "a socialist state of the dictatorship of the proletariat led by the working class and based on the alliance of workers and peasants."[43] The Communist party of China was identified as the core of leadership of the whole Chinese people and Marxism-Leninism-Mao Tse-tung thought was declared to be the theoretical basis guiding the nation's thought. "The organs through which the people exercise power," according to the constitution, "are the people's congresses at all levels, with deputies of workers, peasants and soldiers as their main body."

The National People's Congress is designated the "highest organ of state power under the leadership of the Communist Party of China. The Standing Committee of the National People's Congress is its permanent body and is composed of the Chairman, the Vice-Chairman, and other members," all of whom are elected and subject to recall by the National People's Congress. The functions and powers of the Standing Committee are to convene sessions of the Congress, interpret laws, and enact decrees. The Standing Committee is also responsible for the dispatch and recall of plenipotentiary representatives abroad, the receiving of diplomatic envoys, and the ratifying and denunciation of treaties with foreign states.

The State Council is responsible to the Standing Committee and to the Congress. Composing the Council are the premier, the vice-premiers, ministers (including the foreign minister), and ministers heading commissions. The functions of the State Council are to formulate administrative measures, issue decisions and orders, exercise unified leadership over the ministries, commissions, and local organs of state, draft and implement the national economic plan and the state budget, and direct state administrative affairs.

The Supreme People's Court, local people's courts at various levels, and special people's courts exercise judicial authority and are responsible and accountable to the people's congresses and their permanent organs at the corresponding levels.

The Chinese People's Liberation Army and the people's militia "are the workers' and peasants' own armed forces" and are "led by the Communist Party." The chairman of the Central Committee of the Communist Party of China "commands the country's armed forces" (Article 15).

The state sector of the economy is the "leading force in the national economy" (Article 6) and socialist public property is considered inviolable (Article 8). "The state applies the socialist principle: 'He who does not work, neither shall he eat' and 'from each according to his ability, to each according to his work'."

The Ministry of Foreign Affairs functions as the principal operational arm of foreign policy.[44] Subordinate to the foreign minister are vice-ministers and assistant ministers who probably direct the day-to-day implementation of foreign policy.[45] The departmental structure of the ministry is simlar to that of foreign offices in many other countries.

In the past, at least, the People's Republic has been represented in Communist bloc nations and noncommunist nations by quite different diplomatic types. The representative in a Communist bloc nation is likely to be a man of army or cadre background with little or no previous diplomatic experience. His academic training is likely to have been limited to a Red Army academy in Yenan or its equivalent. He is not likely to know the language of the country to which he is accredited. Ambassadors stationed in noncommunist capitals tend to have been better educated and to have had considerably greater diplomatic experience.[46]

In the past, at least, the People's Republic has also maintained an unofficial foreign ministry and has been represented abroad by equally unofficial ambassadors. The unofficial ministry has encompassed several people's organizations, including the Chinese People's Institute of Foreign Affairs, which was established, in part at least, to conduct foreign policy research. In the past, these unofficial bodies and their representatives have been particularly important with respect to nations that did not maintain diplomatic relations with Peking, particularly in Latin America and Africa.[47]

With respect to the details of Chinese Communist institutions and political process, we are dependent upon limited data and insights. In explaining foreign policies and actions, however, we are not entirely blocked by this lack of detailed knowledge of institutions and process. With reasonable assessments of Chinese Communist capabilities—low today, but with future potential—some knowledge of tradition and political culture, and a feeling for the political consciousness and will of the leadership, we can go a considerable way in explaining foreign policy and actions. And at least one important point about institutions, which is not concealed from us, lends credence to this view. Chinese government is highly centralized (or was until the onset of the Great Proletarian Cultural Revolution). Chinese foreign policymaking, at least, is still highly centralized. The ideas of the men at the top, therefore, assume primary importance in explaining policy. And these ideas are available to us, while detailed analyses of institutions and processes are not.

In the Aftermath of the Great
Proletarian Cultural Revolution

Even today, little is known about many aspects of the Cultural Revolution. What does seem clear is that, by undertaking a revolution from within against its own bureaucracy, capitalist remnants, revisionists, and the like, the Chinese Communist movement was merely bringing into larger, nationwide play a whole range of peculiarly Maoist political instruments, such as self-criticism and behavior-change-through-hard-labor-and-revolutionary-action, that had been developed during the thought-reform campaigns of Yenen in the late 1930s.

It is important to note that Mao's wife, Chiang Ching, was viewed by outsiders, at least, as one of the most radical of the militant revolutionaries—although the careless use of terms such as radical, leftist, and rightest can be misleading when one deals with China. It is also important to note that no leader seemed so highly placed as to be safe from Red Guard attack. There were times when even Mao's own position appeared to be threatened. Finally, in retrospect, it turned out that soon after Mao's death—and well after the end of the Cultural Revolution—Chiang Ching herself fell victim to the continuing revolution, having been charged as one of a Gang of Four with creating splits and stirring up struggles through armed force.

Mao Tse-tung saw the Great Proletarian Cultural Revolution as having been "absolutely necessary and most timely for consolidating the dictatorship of the proletariat, preventing capitalist restoration, and building socialism." The socialist revolution was a continuing struggle to bury capitalism. The proletariat had already won great victories in China, but the defeated capitalist remnants would continue to struggle. "These people are still around," Mao warned, "and this class still exists. Therefore, we cannot speak of final victory. Not even for decades. We must not lose our vigilance."[48]

According to Mao, it was essential to wage intra-Party struggle correctly, to make a correct distinction between the two different types of contradiction and struggle—"those between ourselves and the enemy and those among the people themselves."[49] There might be some Communists who were not conquered by enemies with guns, but who could not withstand "sugar-coated bullets."[50]

Despite this seemingly endless revolutionary turmoil, certain aspects of traditional Chinese society have remained influential in the contemporary economy—especially the cellular organization of the countryside whereby the small, farm village (most of whose inhabitants are likely to be related) is linked economically to a larger, market village and thence to several market villages that "pay economic and political homage to a still larger administrative town."[51]

Overall, the foreign relations of the People's Republic have been the outcome of many factors. Maoist ideology has shaped the world view of Chinese Communist leaders in critical ways and has provided the Peking regime with a powerful instrument for mobilizing the national will, organizing the society on local, regional, and national levels, disciplining the economy, and guiding policy formation. "Socialist revolution is the powerful engine for developing the social productive forces," Chou En-lai told the National People's Congress early in 1975, the year of his death. "Only when we do well in revolution is it possible to do well in production." He warned against the dangers to China and the world of "colonialism, imperialism and above all superpower hegemonism." Normal state relations with the USSR should be maintained, but no one should forget that the Soviet leading clique had betrayed Marxism-Leninism. Despite fundamental differences between China and the United States, relations might be expected to improve as long as recently established principles were observed in their interchanges. In order to strengthen its position in the world, China must "bury dogmatism," "break down blind faith," "do away with slavishness," "go in for industry, agriculture and technical and cultural revolutions independently," "rely mainly on its own efforts," and "learn from the good experience of other countries conscientiously," being sure "to study their bad experience, too, so as to draw lessons from it."[52]

Chapter three will discuss some of the fundamental development programs and capabilities achieved by the Chinese Communist leadership and centrally important to an understanding of contemporary China's position in the world today.

Notes

1. J. K. Fairbank and S. Y. Teng, "On the Ch'ing Tributary System," *Harvard Journal of Asiatic Studies* 6, no. 4 (June 1941), pp. 138-39.
2. Harold C. Hinton, *Communist China in World Politics* (Boston: Houghton Mifflin, 1966), p. 5.
3. Mary Clabaugh Wright, *The Last Stand of Chinese Conservatism* (Stanford, Calif.: Stanford University Press, 1957), p. 222.
4. Fairbank and Teng, "*Ch'ing Tributary System*," pp. 138-39.
5. Wright, *Chinese Conservatism*, p. 222.
6. Ibid.
7. H. G. Creel, *Chinese Thought from Confucius to Mao Tse-tung* (Chicago: University of Chicago Press, 1953), p. 1.
8. Mao Tse-tung, *Selected Works*, vol. 3 (New York: International, 1964), p. 73.

9.   Sun Yat-sen, *San Min Chu I* (Chungking: Ministry of Information of the Republic of China, 1943), p. 35; and Chiang Kai-shek, *China's Destiny* (New York: Macmillan, 1947), p. 34.

10.   For Western analyses of foreign syndicates, spheres of influence, and control mechanisms, see P. H. Kent, *Railway Enterprizes in China* (London: E. Arnold Co., 1907) and T. W. Overlach, *Foreign Financial Control in China* (New York: Macmillan, 1919).

11.   For primary Western sources documenting foreign encroachments on China, see W. W. Willoughby and C. G. Fenwick, *Types of Restricted Sovereignty and of Colonial Autonomy* (Washington, D.C.: U.S. Government Printing Office, 1919), and William Woodville Rockhill, *Treaties and Conventions with or Concerning China and Korea, 1894-1904* (Washington, D.C.: U.S. Government Printing Office, 1904).

12.   Rockhill, *Treaties and Conventions,* p. 50.

13.   Mao, *Selected Works,* vol. 3, p. 79.

14.   Ibid.

15.   Creel, *Chinese Thought,* p. 4.

16.   Sun Yat-sen, *San Min Chu I,* trans. Frank W. Price (Shanghai: China Committee, Institute of Pacific Relations, 1927), pp. 146-48.

17.   Lin Piao, "Long Live the Victory of the People's War!" in commemoration of the twentieth anniversary of victory in the Chinese people's war of resistance against Japan, in *Jen-min Jih-pao,* September 2, 1965, in William E. Griffith, *Sino-Soviet Relations, 1964-1965* (Cambridge, Mass.: M.I.T. Press, 1967), p. 432.

18.   Ibid., p. 431.

19.   Ibid., p. 432.

20.   Ibid.

21.   Ibid., pp. 432-33.

22.   Ibid., p. 432.

23.   Ibid.

24.   Derk Bodde, *China's First Unifier: A Study of the Ch'in Dynasty as Seen in the Life of Li Ssu* (Leyden, The Netherlands: Brill, 1938), p. 199.

25.   Ibid.

26.   Ibid., pp. 183, 201.

27.   Ibid.

28.   S. Y. Teng and John K. Fairbank, *China's Response to the West* (Cambridge, Mass.: Harvard University Press, 1954), p. 4.

29.   Marion J. Levy, Jr., *The Family Revolution in Modern China* (Cambridge, Mass.: Harvard University Press, 1949), pp. 22-28.

30.   Ibid., pp. 244-45.

31.   H. Franz Schurmann, *Ideology and Organization in Communist China* (Berkeley: University of California Press, 1966), p. 7.

32.   John H. Weakland, "Family Imagery in Passage by Mao Tse-tung," *World Politics* 10, no. 3 (April 1958), p. 399.

33.   Ibid.

34.   Ibid., pp. 399-400.

35.   Cyril Birch, "Fiction in the Yenan Period," *China Quarterly,* no. 4 (October-December 1960), p. 8.

36.   Ibid.

37.   "On the Victory of Smashing the Lin Piao Anti-Party Clique," *Peking Review,* nos. 35 and 36 (April 7, 1973), p. 19.

38.   Szu Hua-hung, "Lin Piao Anti-Party Clique: Sworn Enemy of the Dictatorship of the Proletariat," *Peking Review,* no. 52 (December 28, 1973), p. 7.

39. "Deepening Criticism of Lin Piao Through Repudiating Confucius," *Peking Review*, no. 5 (February 1, 1974), p. 3.
40. Yang Jueng-kuo, "Confucius—A Thinker Who Stubbornly Upheld the Slave System," *Peking Review*, no. 41 (October 12, 1973), pp. 5-6.
41. Schurmann, *Ideology and Organization*, p. 173.
42. Theodore H. E. Chen, *The Chinese Communist Regime: Documents and Commentary* (New York: Praeger, 1967), p. 117.
43. *The Constitution of the People's Republic of China,* adopted on January 17, 1975 by the Fourth National People's Congress of the People's Republic at its First Session (Peking: Foreign Languages Press, 1975).
44. Donald W. Klein, "Peking's Evolving Ministry of Foreign Affairs," *China Quarterly*, no. 4 (October-December, 1960), p. 29.
45. Ibid., p. 30.
46. Ibid., p. 35.
47. Ibid., pp. 37-38.
48. "Commemorate the 50th Anniversary of the Communist Party of China," *Peking Review*, no. 27 (July 2, 1971), pp. 6, 16.
49. Ibid., p. 18; see also Chalmers Johnson, "The Changing Nature and Locus of Authority in Communist China," in *China: Management of a Revolutionary Society,* ed. John M. H. Lindbeck (Seattle: University of Washington Press, 1971), pp. 70-76.
50. "Commemorate the 50th Anniversary," p. 19.
51. Arthur G. Ashbrook, "Main Lines of Chinese Communist Economic Policy," in *An Economic Profile of Mainland China*, vol. 1, Studies Prepared for the Joint Economic Committee, Congress of the United States (Washington, D.C.: U.S. Government Printing Office, 1967), p. 49.
52. Chou En-lai, "Report on the Work of the Government," *Peking Review*, no. 4 (January 24, 1975), pp. 23-24.

Chapter Three

Communist China's Basic Capabilities and Development Programs

As indicated in the introduction, national capabilities tend to be useful indicators of a nation's position in the world and of its broad tendencies in foreign policy and external behavior. A large part of a country's domestic and foreign activities can be viewed as efforts of the society to cope with its internal and external environments — to satisfy as many of the demands of the society as possible. Externally, a country requires, at the very least, access to basic resources that are not domestically available and security from invasion or intolerable outside coercion or deprivation. Internally, it needs, at the very least, to ensure subsistence for the greater part, if not for all, of its people and to maintain domestic order and cohesion at some minimal level. Often external goals can be pursued only at considerable internal cost and vice versa. The history of China over the last 2500 years can be described in terms of phases or cycles in Chinese ability to maintain this balance of internal and external forces. At times the country was integrated into a powerful and effective empire. At other times it broke down into petty kingdoms or warlord preserves on a regional basis. Many times it was overrun by outside forces. In the long run, however, China has always been able to reintegrate itself, to absorb the invader, and to preserve its integrity as one of the oldest cultures of human history.

For a country to achieve its basic goals at a minimal level is not sufficient for stability or operational effectiveness. If the state's survival is to escape jeopardy, there must be some margin of available resources above bare subsistence level, some margin of security from outside attack. From the viewpoint of national leaders, it frequently seems desirable to maximize these margins or at least some of them. In the late seventeenth and early eighteenth centuries the Chinese population — like populations in many other parts of the world — began to increase rapidly. However, the industrial revolution, which vastly enhanced the capacities of Western Europe, the United States, and, later, Japan for managing and harvesting the environment, was slow in reaching China. By the mid-nineteenth century, Chinese margins of domestic order, cohesiveness, productivity, and security from outside attack and infiltration were critically narrow, and the empire of the Ch'ing Dynasty could find no way to make these margins wider. The leadership — unlike Japanese elites during the latter part of the nineteenth century and the opening decades of the twentieth — had almost no notion of how to adapt to an industrialized, modernized world and the intricate challenges it had raised. As China's capabilities decreased, more effective powers — Great Britain, Tsarist Russia, Germany, France, and others — began to establish spheres of influence within the country and to acquire control of customs, tax collections, some legal jurisdictions, and other domestic functions.

In pursuing national interests, the leaders of a great power frequently try to achieve and maintain external capabilities greater than those of any other state in the system. Their efforts are constrained, however, by domestic needs and by limitations on the amount of the state's resources and on its ability to use those resources. Indeed, successful maintenance of a political system requires on the part of the leadership a balancing of demands and supports from the environment — including other states and their own constituencies. National leaders try to maximize their possibilities for maintaining power by meeting enough of these external and internal demands to ensure a balance of supports. If such demands should greatly exceed the level of support, however, the leadership runs the risk of losing its position. If the ability of a state to control, through its leaders, its external or internal environments (or both) falls below a certain threshold, there is likely to be a change in the leadership. And if this capacity falls below an even more critical threshold there is likely to be a revolution. In China the inability of the Ch'ing Dynasty to maintain even minimal control of the domestic and external environments brought about the collapse of the old empire in 1911 and a long period of fitful revolution, the emergence of regional warlord regimes, further foreign penetrations and encroachments, and moments of anarchy, war, and chaos.

Two new forces: the nationalists and the communists

Thus, during the 1920s there arose in China two forces, both influenced by Soviet Russia — the Kuomintang, or Nationalists, and the Chinese Communists — that developed rival claims and programs for reuniting the country. For a time they pursued an uneasy collaboration, but in fact they were bitter competitors for power and national leadership. During 1927 the Nationalists, under Chiang Kai-shek, drove the Communist leaders underground, or into remote enclaves in the mountains, and it looked as though the Kumintang might succeed in rebuilding China. The Kuomintang leadership then faced the problems of how to achieve and maintain some balance of control over external and internal environments, how to balance demands and supports, how to widen the margins of survival, and how to keep from falling below the critical threshold of power into revolution and perhaps chaos.

A discrepancy between the actual external condition of a nation-state and its preferred external condition gives rise to dissatisfaction or tension. Such dissatisfaction or tension, in turn, impels the leaders to select some activity calculated to alter the environment to one degree or another and thus reduce or eliminate the discrepancy and dissatisfaction. The discrepancy may be registered in absolute terms or, when one state is measuring itself against another state, in differential rates of change. Similarly, a discrepancy between the actual domestic condition of the nation-state and the preferred internal condition gives rise to dissatisfaction or tension and thus to the selection of some activity calculated to alter the domestic environment.

A country's domestic activities — a political revolution, an advance in technology, or rapid economic growth, for example — may alter its external relations in important ways. Conversely, a change in the external environment — loss of access to a critical resource, for example, or the threat of an enemy attack — may change in the external environment — loss of access to a critical resource, for example, or the threat of an enemy attack — may change a country's domestic activities in important ways. Often, the leaders must choose between allocating energy and resources for altering the external environment or allocating them for altering the domestic environment — sometimes a choice between "guns" and "butter." Since the revolution of 1911, responsible Chinese leaders among alternative domestic demands, requirements, and strategies of response.

For Chiang Kai-shek and his Nationalists, the discrepancies were often painfully evident. China had not advanced far economically, industrially, or agriculturally beyond where it had been under the late Ch'ing Dynasty. Much of the economy was still controlled by foreigners. At the same time, Chiang's regime was challenged domestically by unpacified, ambitious regional warlords and by a stubbornly resisting and growing Communist force, and externally, after 1931, by the encroachments of a militarist, expansionist, and aggressive Japan. Initially, Chiang Kai-shek accorded major priority to suppressing and, if possible, annihilating the Communists — even at the risk of Japanese encroachments. Later, as the Japanese aggression became more unmistakably lethal, and as it merged into World War II, the Nationalists and Communists undertook a new, uneasy alliance in efforts to stem the aggression. At the same time, they looked for their own positions after the war, each determined to emerge from the conflict stronger than the other.

By the close of hostilities in 1945, and increasingly thereafter, the Nationalists found it more and more difficult, indeed, impossible, to cope with inflation, black market activities, and problems of modernization while resisting the Communists. Thus, the inability of Chiang Kai-shek and the Kuomintang regime to maintain sufficient control of the domestic environment passed beyond a critical threshold during the 1945-1949 period and led to their overthrow by the forces of Mao Tse-tung and the Chinese Communists. The new leadership faced most of the same problems the Nationalists had struggled with, but it left no doubt about its determination to reintegrate China after a new, Maoist model, to modernize it as rapidly as possible, and to reestablish the nation as one of the great powers of the world. How have the Chinese Communists gone about it and to what extent have they been successful?

Elements of foreign policy

Many scholars feel that any country's foreign policies and actions are best accounted for in terms of its capabilities relative to the capabilities of other countries in the world system and other countries with which it frequently interacts. Strength in resources and overall capability often increases latitude of decision and action, making ambitious programs feasible and increasing probabilities of success. Weakness, on the other hand, limits independence and choice.

Considerable motivation for nation-state behavior seems to emerge from the tendency of a competing great power to measure itself against other great powers or for nations in a regional subsystem to compete with each other. Some nations — and China seems to be one of them — operate in a marginal, overlapping sphere between the great power system and a regional subsystem. Frequently, the strongest nation-state tends to measure itself against the second strongest nation-state, often in terms of comparative rates of growth; the second strongest nation-state tends to measure itself against the strongest and against the third strongest; and other nation-states tend to measure themselves, at least hypothetically, against the strongest nation-state, but more immediately against both the state that is next stronger and the one that is next weaker. Thus, an incremental lessening of the difference between the capacity of the strongest power in a system and the second strongest power in the same system may be an incremental indicator of dissatisfaction in the strongest power. On the other hand, an incremental increase in the difference between the capacity of the strongest power in the system and the second strongest power in the same system may be an incremental indicator of dissatisfaction in the second strongest power.

The next best explanation of a country's foreign policy and action may lie in the nature of its political leadership. To what extent are the national leaders satisfied or dissatisfied with things as they are? To what extent are they hostile or relatively benign in their attitudes? To what extent does their will, determination, or motivation tend to be strong or weak? Do the leaders appear to be active, dynamic, or do they seem passive and reluctant to innovate? In general, one would expect that the more dissatisfied, hostile, innovative, and dynamic the leadership, the more its nature and peculiarities might explain foreign policy and actions. Clearly, the nature of a given leadership may depend to some extent upon the nation's capability. Often the two factors are highly interdependent. Communist China seems to offer a case in point.

In general, we would expect the widening of the difference in capacity between a given nation-state and the next stronger power and the lessening of the difference in capacity between a nation-state and the next weaker power to give rise to dissatisfaction in that nation-state. However, if the difference in capacity (or rates of growth) is too great, if the geographical distance between the two nations is too great, if communications between them are too infrequent and low-keyed, or if the strategy of the states is not to compete for dominance, we would expect the likelihood of the generation of dissatisfaction to decrease. It must be kept in mind, however, that the time dimension is also important; that is, a nation-state may be motivated at least in part by grievances remembered from the past that may aggravate current dissatisfactions.

Depending upon their assessment of the international system, of which their country is a part, and upon their assessments of their country's own relative capabilities and other attributes, the leaders of a nation-state will tend to pursue some general strategy of operation in order to achieve or approximate their goals. In this volume we shall be concerned with the operational strategies that the Chinese Communist leadership has pursued and carried out.

We would expect that an upsurge in the internal growth of a state, whether or not it was part of a consciously conceived policy, might lead — indeed, if sufficiently vigorous, would almost certainly lead — toward an increase in the external activities of the state and a disturbance in the international equilibrium. This consideration suggests that the international system is always in a more or less dynamic condition with countries continually testing each other's capacities and displaying great lability of tensions in their relations with one another.

In order to challenge and overtake a stronger power or to defend its position against an encroaching weaker power, a nation-state may undertake any one of a number of strategies or a combination of two or more such strategies. For the most part, these strategies involve increasing the capabilities of the state or reallocating resources from one category of capability to another. The means may be essentially coercive and violent, or they may be economic, technological, diplomatic, or a combination. More specifically, a nation-state can increase its capacities through (1) internal growth (population growth or a growth in productivity); (2) trade; (3) acquisition of territory and population by conquest, purchase, discovery, or preemption; (4) increase of its military capabilities; (5) alliances; or (6) a combination of these developments.

However, an increase in population means an increase in consumption and in demands upon the resources and national product of the state. These are subsistence requirements. Beyond these, the technological capabilities of a population may require additional raw materials and markets if their production potential is to be realized. Thus, increases in population and productivity may, while contributing to the capacity of the nation, also raise additional demands for increasing foreign trade, or national control over or influence within the international environment, or a combination of these.

Other factors for explaining foreign policy and actors may include political institutions, political culture, and such considerations as the power struggles of domestic factions. It has been postulated that, after the capability factor has been analyzed, if dissatisfaction is low and will is weak, then political institutions, political culture, factional power struggles, and the like may be pertinent. With respect to China, however, it appears that capability, will, and dissatisfaction, along with political institutions and culture have all been important since the Chinese Communist leadership took power in 1949, and that over very recent years the struggles of party factions have also achieved significance.

It goes almost without saying that any in-depth consideration of contemporary China involves the development of a society that, over the better part of two millennia or more, created one of the great civilizations of human history. This depth of cultural background cannot be overlooked. Do we therefore view the People's Republic in terms of China's earlier historical continuity and cyclical evolution and perceive current developments as an emergence from a period of temporary confusion and the beginnings of another period of order and stability under a new dynasty? Or do we treat contemporary China as a new revolutionary regime that has broken entirely from its earlier history and institutions?

At first glance, the People's Republic stands out as a clearly revolutionary regime dedicated to destruction of the old order and the building of a new. It seems improbable, however, that, after some 2500 years of cultural lineage and continuity, even a revolutionary regime—even Mao Tse-tung himself—could throw off tradition altogether. Undoubtedly, the behavior patterns of the People's Republic are influenced by Marx, Lenin, and others (or by Chinese interpretations of Marx, Lenin, and others) but it is also quite probable that Confucius and the whole long lineage of China's past are also exerting persistent, if subtle, pressures and increasingly transforming the western part of the Chinese Communist heritage.

China's Place in the World
Economic Power Hierarchy

Leaders of great powers and of nations that aspire to great power status normally try to enhance national capabilities relative to other, competing nations and to acquire as much influence as possible over the external environment. In these respects the People's Republic of China is no exception: Chinese Communist leaders in Peking have made it clear on numerous occasions that they expect their country to achieve in the long run a position of prestige, military strength, industrial capability, and political influence and power. In this connection, indeed, qualified Western observers have asserted that the ultimate purpose of the Chinese Communist economic development program has not been economic growth per se,[1] but industrial and military strength and the achievement of political and military power in the shortest possible time at home and abroad. This kind of purpose is not peculiar to the People's Republic of China.[2]

Leaders of all powers, great and small, are constrained to one degree or another by capability limitations and domestic requirements. Since the establishment of their regime in 1950, Chinese Communist leaders have been working to increase the ability of their country to influence and control, to some degree at least, the external environment. In this regard, the Chinese People's Republic, like other regimes, has three possible courses: (1) the leaders can increase the basic capabilities of the society and state through economic and technological development; (2) they can reallocate resources—from the consumer sector into the industrial sector, for example, or from primarily civil concentrations to a military concentration; (3) they can pursue power and influence through alliance commitments. Most countries work for a combination of all three. As an emerging or developing state, the People's Republic of China might have been expected to place heavy emphasis upon economic and industrial development. As a communist state, it might have been expected to establish highly centralized, specialized, and pervasive political, social, and economic controls for fixing and shifting allocations. Also as a communist state, it might have been expected to align itself closely with the USSR and other socialist nations of the Communist bloc.

In this chapter and in the rest of this book we shall see how and to what extent the Chinese Communist regime has used these three major strategies, or combinations thereof, in the pursuit of basic capabilities, international influence, and power. The Chinese intent is to convert the country, step by step, from a backward, agricultural nation to an advanced, industrial state. This is a task that Mainland China shares with a number of other countries in the world that display essentially agricultural economies.

An anomaly among nations

In seeking to increase their capabilities and influence in the world, and also to safeguard the positions they already occupy, great powers and nations aspiring to great power status tend to compare themselves with other countries that are perceived as stronger or weaker but usually as being within the same order of magnitude with respect to overall capability. Just after the middle of the nineteenth century, Great Britain tended to compare itself with France. Later, from about 1890 until 1914, Great Britain and Germany tended to measure themselves against one another. Today the United States and the Soviet Union use one another as gauges of their capability, status, and prestige.

To a large extent, the behavior of great powers and of nations aspiring to great power status can be accounted for as efforts on the part of each to defend or improve its position in the international power hierarchy, or to secure or enhance national interests perceived as prerequisite to such defense or improvement of position in the international configuration of power.

Since 1950 Chinese economic growth and development have altered China's position in the world and have thus affected the country's foreign relations in important ways. At times, and especially in the mid-1950s, the Peking regime appeared to pursue greater power even at considerable cost to its people's standard of living. Overall, however, the People's Republic has placed major emphasis on raising the minimal level of economic well-being among the populace.

Where, within the current configuration of world power, should we place the People's Republic of China, and what comparisons should we make in order to obtain a clearer view of its current relationships and trends of development? Is China already a great power comparable to the United States and the USSR, or is it a second-level power such as Great Britain and France? Is it a lesser power even than these? On the basis of what criteria can we make a judgment? How does China rank in terms of such indicators of power as area, population, Gross National Product, and military capacity as compared with other nations? Against what countries can, and does, China measure itself? And to what extent can the foreign policies and behaviors of Communist China be explained in terms of the country's capabilities and position in the configuration of world power, as distinct from Marxist-Leninist-Maoist ideology and other considerations?

This chapter will be concerned with China's basic capabilities as measured in terms of area, resources, population, and productivity, and also with strategies selected by the leadership to improve China's position on these fundamental dimensions and to enhance its international prestige, power, and influence.

In order to improve its basic capabilities, a country can either seek to use more effectively whatever resources it already has, through improved methods of production, or it can seek to acquire new resources through trade, exploration, aid programs from other nations, conquest, or a combination of these strategies. This chapter will consider also to what extent the Chinese People's Republic has depended upon domestic technological development for improving production and upon assistance from the Soviet Union.

With respect to the international configuration of power, Mainland China has faced three possible strategies or combinations thereof for improving its position: increasing its economic and technological capabilities; extending its commercial, diplomatic, party, and other political ties externally; and enhancing its military capabilities. How has the People's Republic of China allocated its attention, resources, and activities in terms of these possible strategies? In order to approach this question intelligently, we need to consider first what kind of country Communist China is and where it belongs in the worldwide configuration of states.

During the first half of the 1960s, three collections and categorizations of data about national actors were made. Each was concerned with a different set of variables and designed to separate nations into clusters in terms of certain common characteristics. Russett et al. were concerned primarily with demographic and socioeconomic data.[3] Banks and Textor[4] and Banks and Gregg[5] dealt with political system characteristics. Ivanoff[6] developed indices of national power. Significantly, China did not appear similar to the same nations in any two, let alone all three, of these categories.[7]

In terms of demographic and socioeconomic indicators, China ranked among "traditional civilizations" in the second from the bottom stage of political and economic development. Other states in this category included Bolivia, India, Haiti, and South Vietnam. With respect to political system characteristics, the People's Republic emerged as "centrist" or totalitarian. In this group at the time were Spain, Portugal, all the communist states, and some of the authoritarian states among the developing nations. However, in the national power analysis, China appeared among "major international actors" in the second category from the top. Other states in this category included France, West Germany, the United Kingdom, and Canada. Thus, in a typology of states, China during the early 1960s was anomalous: it was the only underdeveloped major power.

Within any extensive typology of communist states, China also emerges in a category by itself.[8] In terms of modernization, the country tends to group with the least developed and culturally least Western among the communist states, such as North Korea, North Vietnam, Albania, and Outer Mongolia. On the other hand, in terms of attenuated ties to the Soviet Union, China resembles Rumania, Yugoslavia, Albania, and in some respects Czechoslovakia, but not North Korea, Vietnam, or Outer Mongolia.

Thus, even among nations of the so-called Communist bloc, China appears as something of an anomaly. With respect to national power ranking, however, China as far back as the early 1960s was surpassed only by the Soviet Union among communist states and—as noted above—was placed with advanced noncommunist nations of the industrialized West. So it appears that, however anomalous otherwise, China is clearly to be ranked in the higher levels of state economic capabilities.

There are other ways of approaching the problem of measuring and comparing China's economic strength. It can be argued that the power of a state derives from its area and natural resources; its population; levels of technology, industry, and production; trade; and military strength or potential.

The importance of development data for understanding Chinese Communist behavior has been suggested by Lucian Pye writing in the mid-1960s: "There is no major political system today about which we have less data and fewer meaningful facts than that of Communist China. Yet decisions which will shape our diplomacy, and more concretely our military establishment, for years ahead must be made in the light of what we now surmise to be the Chinese people's character and dynamics. Inescapably we fall back upon abstractions and gross generalizations."[9] On the other hand, "The more we give central attention to the modest but persistent patterns of domestic development, the more the extremes of Chinese behavior fade in significance. China thus appeared to have a calculated regime that was trying in a more or less intelligent fashion to build up slowly the basis for national unity and strength."[10] Much the same observations could be made about China today.

Area

In area the People's Republic ranks third (9,761,000 square kilometers), after the USSR (22,402,000 square kilometers) and Canada, with the United States in fourth place.[11] Thus China can be considered a great power to the extent that area is a criterion for such status. There is considerable evidence to remind us, however, that the Chinese Communist leaders, like Sun Yat-sen and Chiang Kai-shek before them, have been predisposed to measure the area of the People's Republic against the sum of territories governed or strongly influenced by the Chinese Empire at various points in its long history. Thus, while contributing to China's status in the world community, area may also provide a source of Chinese dissatisfaction and so contribute, in some measure, to China's external aspirations and behavior.

National area often provides a crude indicator of resources, depending on geographical location. There is likely to be a greater diversity of resources in an economy with a predominantly north-south extent as compared with one whose extent is largely east-west. Diversity is likely to be greater, also, if a north-south extent spreads between the temperate and tropical zones.[12] Situated as it is in the temperate zone, a neighborhood of general affluence as compared with the polar regions and tropics, China might be considered geographically rather well placed. In fact, the country is relatively endowed with respect to mineral wealth and is already a significant world producer of mineral products.

Resources

For generations prior to the establishment of the People's Republic, the mineral resources of China had been assessed by most Western experts as scanty, as in the case of oil, or generally low grade, as in the case of coal. Today, as a result of Maoist explorations, China ranks high in terms of energy resources. According to one assessment, China's energy resources are "definitely of the same order of magnitude as those of the USSR and the USA."[13] Indeed, hydroelectric and coal resources compare favorably with those of both the USSR and the United States.[14] In recent years, China has also emerged as a major world oil producer, ranking thirteenth in 1974, just behind Indonesia.[15]

Although the overall quality is low, China possesses large deposits of coal and now ranks third in the world, after the United States and the USSR as a coal producer. For the most part, the country's huge deposits of bituminous coal consist of gas coal and weak coking coal, but notable breakthroughs have been claimed in the use of anthracite for the production of steel.[16] The People's Republic has sufficient basic resources to become one of the world's largest steel producers. Iron ore, coal, and limestone are found in widespread localities, and there are large deposits of alloying materials such as manganese, tungsten, molybdenum, and vanadium.[17] In view of these and other resources, some specialists believe that, with favorable conditions of development, China could become an industrial giant.[18]

By the mid-1970s, indeed, Chinese media were reporting "an unending chain of overfulfilled quotas in coal mining, astonishing progress in oil drilling, and an amazing growth of power plant capacities." Thus, while many Western countries and Japan—dependent on uninterrupted flow of cheap energy—were "struggling to keep their technological societies afloat"—the People's Republic of China was watching with "uninhibited satisfaction and derision." For Peking, the energy crisis was one more proof of "the ultimate crisis of the capitalist system."[19]

Population

The size of a country's population is often used as an indicator of its capabilities—although large numbers of people may be a source of weakness, rather than strength, under some circumstances. It is well known that China, with up to 900 million people, has more inhabitants than any other country in the world.[20] After China, the next three nations in order of population size during the early 1970s were India (574 million), the USSR, (249 million), and the United States (214 million). China's population is also relatively young—more than a third being under fifteen years old.[21] Since a large population is often perceived as an attribute of national power, a certain status tends to be accorded to China on the basis of its very large numbers of people—perhaps a higher status than China's rank with respect to other indicators of power would properly warrant.

In fact, the actual population totals of the People's Republic remain something of a mystery and must be used with great caution. Year after year, the estimates vary greatly from source to source, even within China itself.[22]

In 1971 and again in 1972, a high-ranking Chinese official was quoted as saying that his government's supply and grain department used the number 750 million, the Ministry of Commerce 830 million, and the planning department 750 million. "Unfortunately, there are no accurate statistics in this connection," he asserted.[23]

Some years back, the annual percentage rate of increase was calculated at about 2.0, which ranked China number 65 among nations.[24] Under the Chinese Communist regime, the mortality rate was believed to have dropped from 40 to 50 per 1000 to between 15 and 25 per 1000, a consequence of bringing famine and pestilence under control. The birth rate, on the other hand, was thought to have remained at 40 to 50 per 1000. In itself, a 2.0 percent rate of population increase is not considered high. It becomes critically high, however, in terms of China's large population base and the country's relatively low level of technology and (estimated) per capita production. The large population is thus a source of difficult problems as well as a source of potential influence and power.

In the 1960s, the annual population increase was estimated to be about 16 million persons, a number that was almost equal to the total population of Canada. At that time, in other words, China, with an area of 9,761,012 square kilometers, had a population of probably something more than 700 million, whereas Canada, with approximately the same area (9,976,000 square kilometers), had a population of only a little more than 18 million. Today, there may be as many as 19 million additional inhabitants of China each year.

For some years, the Chinese Communist leaders refused to recognize a population problem in the People's Republic and referred to the numbers of people as a source of national strength. Since the early 1960s, on the other hand, the regime has taken numerous steps to control population growth. In recent years various claims have been made with regard to the effectiveness of the Chinese birth control program, but without consistent population data it is extremely difficult to accept such assessments with any high level of confidence.

Since there is no consensus about the size of China's population, we cannot be certain about any Chinese indicators that depend upon population numbers for calculation. All indicators of this kind are merely estimates, and hence they should not be taken too seriously.

Uncertainty about the size of China's overall population precludes a solid calculation for population density. Chinese population per square kilometer was estimated in the mid-1950s at 72 persons as compared with an estimated 138 persons per square kilometer in India at that time, 217 in West Germany, 254 in Japan, 305 in Taiwan, 348 in the Netherlands, and 3082 in Hong Kong.[25] If a current population total of 800 million is accepted, then China's density today would be about 85 persons per square kilometer. Many countries have higher densities of population than Mainland China. But the People's Republic faces special difficulties.

Overall population densities are misleading as a measure of population pressure on resources. This is particularly true with respect to comparing essentially agrarian countries such as China with highly developed industrial countries. Because of its technological capabilities, we do not think of the Netherlands, for example, as overpopulated, and it is now common knowledge how Japan's rapid technological development in recent generations has eased population problems in that country. In an industrialized nation, the productivity of the people allows them to convert domestic resources into energy more efficiently and, by specialization, to gain access through trade to resources that are not domestically available. But China combines high density on arable land with low industrialization and, therefore, tends to utilize available domestic resources inefficiently and to lack the specialized productivity for high levels of trade.

There is another, more favorable way of reviewing the problem, however. A highly industrialized society that provides its populace with private automobiles, well-heated houses, and arrays of energy-consuming gadgetries, generates very high product levels—and expectations for even higher levels. The United States presents the most spectacular example of such a consumer-oriented society. To date, on the other hand, the People's Republic of China has relied to a large extent upon labor-intensive, rather than capital-intensive technology and, while spreading the national product more evenly, has kept levels of private consumption at a generally modest level. It is thus worth noting that, in an era of energy and other resouce scarcities, the average United States citizen demands—and expects to receive—many times the resources demanded and expected by his Chinese counterpart.

The arable land to population ratio has presented China with a serious problem. There is great diversity in Chinese land productivity, so that vast areas of the country will support only a sparse population. The third largest country in the world, Mainland China, supports almost one-fourth of the world's population with only about 7 to 8 percent of the world's cultivated land.[26] As a consequence, large numbers of people are crowded into fertile areas and large cities. It has been estimated that the number of persons per square kilometer of cultivated land in 1967 approached 425 in India, 540 in Pakistan, and somewhere between 695 and 849 in China, depending upon the assumptions made as to the size of China's population.[27] These figures place China in a more disadvantageous situation than the overall Chinese density figure of 72-86 people per square kilometer would suggest.

Among agricultural countries of the world, China is one of the most densely populated farmlands. According to late 1960 estimates, the country's ratio of arable land to farm population was .191 hectares per capita as compared to .148 in South Korea, .241 in Japan, .476 in Thailand, .481 in India, and 15.119 in the United States.[28] These figures, like those for China's area and population, are impressive, but, like the others, they tend to be misleading. Not only are the statistics for China dubious at best, but, also, it must be remembered that the national product ranks low when divided by the total population.

Economic advances and constraints

Compared with most underdeveloped countries, China has made notable economic and social advances. Famine was endemic prior to 1950; millions of people died of starvation every year. During early years of the Maoist regime, famine was eradicated—partly through redistribution measures, partly by reorganization of production. Inflation had spiralled under the Nationalists; the Maoist leadership achieved an early stabilization. In terms of overpopulation and uncontrolled population growth, pre-Maoist China was perceived as sharing the plight of India. Today, the Chinese birth control program is attracting attention all over the world—even though, given the lack of reliable population statistics, the effectiveness of the effort remains in doubt. Prior to 1950, China was characterized by economic chaos. Today, the country is often put forward as a model of national economic growth. In terms of several indicators, the Chinese economy in 1952 was comparable to that of Meiji Japan and contemporary India. Yet, a decade later, the country had far outstripped India with respect to its industrial base and was overtaking Japan in certain sectors.[29]

Despite these noteworthy successes, however, Chinese development suffers serious constraints. Between 1949 and 1974 the country's industrial production is estimated to have grown at an average annual rate of 13 percent. But, whereas the annual growth rate for 1949-1950 has been calculated at 22 percent, the 1960-1974 annual rate was only 6 percent.[30] When viewed within a down-to-earth context of growing population, growing demands, aspirations, and expectations, and an unevenly advancing technology, it appears highly probably that the leadership of the People's Republic has been at once stimulated and constrained in its policies and activities by its basic attributes and by the country's position within the world community.

In terms of proportion of Gross National Product (GNP) attributable to agriculture, as compared with industry, China has tended to compare with countries such as Nigeria, Indonesia, Pakistan, and Ceylon. On the other hand, China's level of overall production places the country among leading industrialized nations of the world rather than among other developing, essentially agricultural countries. Chinese production also provides the country with a broad base for potential military as well as commercial development. But other countries have also undergone substantial growth in recent years, and it is not entirely clear to what extent China has improved its relative position on some dimensions. In terms of GNP, for example, China was ranked fifth ($46,256 million) in 1957, after the United States ($443,270 million), the USSR ($121,920 million), the United Kingdom ($61,379 million), and West Germany ($49,906 million). France, Canada, India, Japan, and Italy rank sixth, seventh, eighth, ninth, and tenth respectively. In 1957 the French, Canadian, Indian, Japanese, and Italian GNPs were $41,563 million, $32,291 million, $28,648 million, $27,844 million, and $25,003 million, respectively. The figure for China is considered accurate with ± 20 percent limits. If we were to deduct 20 percent, the People's Republic of China would rank sixth—behind France and Canada. If we were to add 20 percent, China would rank fourth, between the United Kingdom and West Germany. In a private memorandum of December 1968, John Gurley of Stanford University calculated for the People's Republic an actual GNP of $103 billion for 1957, $130 billion for 1960, and an estimated GNP of $147 billion for 1947.[31] Using 1960 data, on the other hand, Alexander Eckstein placed China eighth (after the United States at $551,800 million, USSR at $256,300 million, West Germany at $96,200 million, the United Kingdom at $91,500 million, France at $83,600 million, Japan at $77,000 million, and Italy at $52,800 million) with a GNP of $50,000 million.[32]

A source using 1973 data, ranked The People's Republic in sixth place ($180,000 million) as compared with the United States ($1,294,900 million), USSR ($624,000 million), Japan ($415,800 million), West Germany ($349,200 million), France ($257,400 million), United Kingdom ($172,476 million) and Italy ($136,980 million).[33] For the year 1974, another source estimates China's GNP at $223,000 million.[34]

In 1974 the world per capita GNP was estimated at $1414, that of the developed countries at $4377, and that of the developing countries at $382. Because of its low population and high national product, Kuwait ranked first among the countries of the world with a 1973 per capita income of $8178. Switzerland ($6565) ranked second, United States ($6154) ranked third, Japan ($3838) fifteenth, and the USSR ($2498) twenty-fourth. Against this background, China ($221) with a large population ranked ninety-second as compared with Ecuador ($375) seventy-third, North Korea ($364) seventy-fourth, and the Philippines ($262) eighty-fifth.[35]

Technological advancement in China involves three major aspects: (1) scientific laboratory industry; (2) urban industry comprising large-scale, centrally controlled basic and military industry, plus medium-scale industry controlled at the provincial and municipal level; and (3) rural industry.

China's scientific laboratory industry emerged from the Maoist principle that all research should be linked to production and "learning by doing." Thus, scientific institutes combine research and development with production. In the Physics Department of Tsinghua University, for example, students and teachers produce integrated circuits. Working largely by hand, they nevertheless use sophisticated photo-reproduction techniques, ultrasonic binding, and optical systems produced, in turn, by the Chinese Institute of Optics. The ability of the People's Republic successfully to pursue its nuclear research after the withdrawal of Soviet specialists serves as one indicator of the country's capacities for scientific research and development.

The main objective of large-scale urban industries is standarized output, and they are generally receptive to foreign technology that is likely to enhance that output. Their managements are more concerned with gradual product improvement, however, than with radical design or production-flow improvements. Often, such industries stand to benefit from the importation of whole plants, such as the integrated hot and cold steel-rolling mills that are to be built by West German and Japanese consortiums in Wuhan over the next few years. Small-scale, local industries are not centrally controlled or planned, but are coordinated and directed almost wholly at the county level.[36]

Between 1961 and 1965, during a period of comparatively open policy, the Chinese began looking to the West for modern steel and other related technologies. "Basic oxygen furnaces were imported from Austria and air separation plants from Japan and other countries. The production of alloys was greatly increased by expansion of the electrical steel capacity—mostly through imports of electric furnaces from Japan."[37] As noted by one Western observer, foreign technology "flows in only for industries at the top half of the pyramid, to the most advanced plants and activities. Even there, new equipment, processes and techniques are often used as much for training, education, and demonstrations, as for increasing output." Western visitors to Chinese plants, astonished by "the large number of seemingly redundant workers milling around the machinery," are often unaware that this seeming confusion is evidence of in-plant training and "advanced experience sharing," as well as the high labor/capital ratio that characterized Chinese industry.[38]

Perspectives for further development

China continues to rely upon agriculture for feeding its people and providing capital for industrialization. It is doubtful that patterns of past development in the countryside can be matched to the immediate future, however. Chinese agriculture will almost certainly continue to grow, but in a sense it is hampered by past successes: at present there are no obvious and gross inefficiencies in

China's agriculture that can be overcome in order to achieve spectacular new advances in the country's farm output.

Despite China's foreign exchange shortage and emphasis on policies of self-reliance, a certain amount of food will undoubtedly be imported. But importing grain and adopting agriculture technology from Western countries—although marginally significant in the short run—will not eliminate the long-term subsistence burden on Chinese agriculture. This consideration is certain to affect the country's foreign relations in important ways.[39] The further expansion of Chinese agriculture is not a simple matter of "digging more tube wells or pouring on more chemical fertilizer"—although such procedures will help. The possibilities for increasing the land under cultivation are limited, and large-scale development in the future will require the harnessing of China's northern rivers and probably also some new breakthroughs in the basic agricultural sciences. Such changes appear to be "well within the range of China's capacities," however, and in the somewhat longer run they are likely to be undertaken, if only for lack of other alternatives, the population being too large for the country to rely on massive food imports after the pattern of Europe or Japan.[40]

The need for foreign technology and equipment creates a difficult dilemma. With respect to steel production, for example, the "People's Republic has a choice between drifting toward greater dependence on imports of raw, semi-finished and finished steel production, or stressing imports of equipment and technology to bring domestic capabilities up to rising requirements. The former route runs counter to Peking's long-standing policy of self-reliance. . . . The latter policy runs up against the demands on foreign exchange. . . . China faces similarly difficult choices with respect to other aspects of industrialization."[41]

The distribution of production capabilities among the Chinese population is difficult to assess, but literacy rates offer something of a clue. The building of a modern industrial state requires more than resources and machinery; it also requires an educated populace. For most modernizing societies this presents a major problem, but China has made considerable progress in this respect over recent years. In the mid-1950s, with an estimated 47.5 percent of the population literate, China was ranked sixty-fifth. A 1973 estimate, by contrast, reports China in twenty-fourth place with an estimated 95 percent of the population literate.[42]

Public health and general welfare statistics offer another clue to Chinese successes in the distribution of production capabilities. From a low base line in 1950, the People's Republic has made impressive strides in these areas. Even many critics of the regime who have visited China in recent years attest to the general advancement. Despite such undeniable successes, however, the country still ranks relatively low in terms of many health and quality of life indicators such as infant mortality (47th); life expectancy at birth (53rd); population per hospital bed (109th); calories per capita (97th); and protein per capita (85th).[43]

By the early 1970s infant mortality in Iceland was 10 per thousand live births; in the United States it was 18; in China 55; India 139. At birth, a baby born in Denmark, Iceland, Luxembourg, Netherlands, or Norway might be expected to live for 74 years; life expectancy in the United States was 71 years; in China 62 years; in India 50 years. Population per hospital bed was 135 in the United States, 63 in Sweden, 1000 in China, and 1890 in India. The average caloric intake per capita was 3300 in the United States, 3410 in Ireland, 2170 in China, and 2070 in India. Protein intake per capita was 106 for the United States, 113 for Greece, 60 for China, and 52 for India.

The development *level* of a state's economic capabilities is important for current comparisons. The *rate* and *path* of its development are important for consideration of its future problems and prospects, while a nation's improvements or declines relative to other countries may be expected to affect its position in the world. China's agricultural change and industrialization have been closely interdependent from the start. Both of these paths of development, in turn, have involved large and complex political and economic, as well as technical, change. Indeed, the alterations have been so thoroughgoing that virtually no aspect of Chinese society has remained unaltered.

China as an Agrarian Society

The old agrarian order

Since the dawn of history, China has been essentially an agrarian society with social, economic, and political institutions appropriate to a land revenue system. Commerce has not been unimportant, even in ancient China, which traded up and down the east Asian coast, in central Asia, the Indian Ocean, along the east coast of Africa, and with the Roman Empire. Nevertheless, the Chinese Empire depended largely on land revenue for its income and economic power. During the nineteenth and early twentieth centuries, China's status as an agricultural society with a large population and underdeveloped technology made it vulnerable to penetration and exploitation by various Western powers and Japan.

The economy inherited by the Chinese People's Republic from the old regime was little short of chaotic. From the collapse of the Manchu Empire in 1911 until the Communist takeover in late 1949, large parts of the country had been torn by revolution, civil war, foreign invasion, warlordism, famine, and flood.[44] In major cities of China proper, commerce and industry had come very nearly to a standstill,[45] while the industrial base in Manchuria had been stripped by the USSR of more than $2 billion worth of industrial plants, machinery, and equipment. Railroads had been cut by contending armies, public works were in a state of disrepair, the population was disorganized.[46] The country had been subject to galloping inflation.[47] In fact, during later phases of Nationalist rule, "China no longer constituted an integrated unit from the economic point of view."[48]

Under these circumstances it seems safe to conclude that as long as the Chinese Communists were destroying, or promising to destroy, the old and faltering order, they had many social, economic, and political forces working for them. Along with the expulsion of exploiting foreign interests, the Chinese Communist program proposed, through centralized control, the demolition of the old order, so to speak, and the step-by-step rebuilding of the social, economic, and political systems.

From the start, a major and frequently proclaimed purpose behind the agrarian program and the acceleration of industrial development was the attempt to overtake the United Kingdom and Japan—although the target date has been postponed a number of times over the years. "Twenty years in a day" was one slogan that was put forward. In 1958, during the Great Leap Forward, Chinese leaders asserted their determination to overtake Britain in fifteen years. More recently, spokesmen in Peking have conceded that more time will be needed to overtake the major powers industrially.

Developing agriculture as a
base for industrialization

A major constraint on Chinese modernization has been the shortage of capital. In order to overcome this difficulty, the People's Republic from the start relied heavily on agricultural development and the increase of farm output. The means used were simultaneously political, economic, and technological.

In general, Chinese social, economic, and political institutions were outcomes of the agrarian properties of the society and were not appropriate to or adequate for the building of a modern industrial state. Moreover, the Nationalist regime, "though increasingly identifying itself with the interests of the urban capitalists, nevertheless failed to develop a social framework within which a healthy capitalist system could thrive."[49] Through 1949, agriculture, accounting for about 75 percent of the population, contributed approximately 40 percent to the national product. An additional 10 percent of the population living in rural areas but engaged in nonfarming tasks accounted for 20 percent of the total national output. "Thus it took three out of four Chinese workers to feed the country (and supply a modest margin of agricultural exports) as opposed to one out of seven in the United States, and one out of two in Japan and the Soviet Union."[50]

The rapid development of heavy industry was intended to provide a material base for self-defense, for the well-being of the populace, for further increases in industrial capacity, and for the improvement of China's position in the world.[51] This was to be accomplished over a span of fifteen or twenty years (after about 1958), in part by investing surplus capital from agriculture in the industrial sector and in part through early assistance from the USSR. There were powerful social and political pressures for land redistribution—the expropriation of landlord holdings and their distribution among the landless peasantry. Indeed, these pressures had provided much of the political and military dynamics for raising the Chinese Communist leadership to power over the mainland. However, the Chinese People's Republic was unavoidably and crucially concerned with land productivity and dividing landlord holdings into small, private plots would not, in the long run, solve that problem.

China was caught in something of a vicious circle. National income was too low to provide for significant accumulation of capital. Without such accumulation, however, it would not be possible to industrialize and achieve rapid growth of national income. The basic problem confronting Mao Tse-tung in his plans for the economic development of China was how to breach this circle. With four-fifths of the country's population engaged in agriculture, it was natural for Chinese leaders to look in that direction for the saving of a considerable part of the capital needed for industrial advancement.[52]

Prior to the Communist seizure of power, land in China had been both privately held and unequally distributed. About 10 or 15 percent of the farm population owned 53 to 63 percent of the land. According to W. W. Rostow, however, outright tenancy, although it had been increasing over the decades, was not as prevalent as generally believed.

> *In 1947 only about one-third of the farm population were tenants, one-quarter were part owners, and about 40 to 45 percent were full owners. Therefore, agrarian unrest in China was primarily compounded of interacting influences generated by the pressure of population and low productivity rather than the extent of tenancy. High population densities, particularly pronounced in South China, led to an intense competition for land; this land hunger of the peas-*

> *antry—based on scarcity—opened the way for exploita-*
> *tion and abuse as illustrated by insecurity of tenure,*
> *high rents varying from 40-70 percent of the crop,*
> *and, for Szechwan at least, collections of rent for*
> *years ahead.*[53]

In view of these considerations, Mao Tse-tung and his colleagues proposed to attack political aspects of the agrarian problem in two main stages: first, the expropriation of landlord holdings and distribution of land to those who tilled it, and, later, the collectivization of agriculture. This sequence, long established in Maoist theory, had been practiced on local levels in parts of Kiangsi province during the early 1950s and later in Yenan and elsewhere.

An agrarian reform law of 1950 had the broad objective of setting free productive forces, the developing of agricultural production, and preparing for the industrialization of a new China. The "struggle against the landlord" was a primary means: his land, draft animals, farm implements, and surplus grain were confiscated. Fundamental to the redistribution process was the policy of allotting requisitioned land to the peasants who had actually been tilling it.[54] People's tribunals were established in every *hsien,* or county, to ensure that the land reform measures were carried out.[55]

Political aspects of the agricultural revolution progressed much faster than many outside observers had foreseen. The redistribution of land to peasant tillers had been scarcely completed before collectivization began. During 1955-1956 the peasants were rapidly organized into cooperatives.[56] Then, during the course of a few months in 1958, more than seven-hundred-thousand collective farms were transformed into a total of twenty-six-thousand rural communes.

The land redistribution and collectivization programs had economic, as well as political, implications at every step. But the Chinese leadership was concerned also with many of the more technical problems associated with increases in rural production. During the 1950s, agricultural policymakers used "the massive application of an essentially traditional technology" in order to achieve increased farm output. Millions of peasants were mobilized in order to improve old irrigation and drainage systems, to construct new ones, to consolidate fragmented plots of land, and to expand multicropping.

In the late 1950s and early 1960s, bad weather was combined with ineffective management during the Great Leap Forward, and farm output dropped by 20 percent and more. Reorganization of the commune and improved weather significantly improved production, and by 1962 output was approaching levels that characterized the mid-1950s. Then, beginning about 1964, large-scale use of chemical fertilizer and new techniques of water management contributed steady and substantial increases in farm output.[57]

Industrialization: The Soviet model and Soviet aid

During the 1950s, the People's Republic of China largely patterned its economic strategy after that of the Soviet Union, although with many Chinese variations and special applications. As Mao Tse-tung told the Eighth Congress of the Chinese Communist party in September 1956, "We must be good at learning from our forerunner, the Soviet Union." It was only with the emergence of the Sino-Soviet conflict in the late 1950s that the Chinese began to depend more on self-reliance and less on Soviet tutelage.

The state or socialized sector of the Chinese economy had the basic function of helping to bring about the transition to a socialist society by gradually broadening the sphere of domestic planning and control.[58] It seemed evident, however, that the success of the total program depended not only upon the reorganization of Chinese society through land reform, the accumulation and reallocation of capital, and domestic efforts at industrialization but also upon outside assistance, from the USSR particularly, and also from other relatively developed countries of the Communist bloc. In these terms, domestic policy and effort seemed to be critically linked with an important sector of foreign affairs—the interactions between the Chinese People's Republic and other nations with communist regimes.

To some Western observers, the initial credits extended by the Soviet Union to the Chinese People's Republic looked "niggardly,"[59] amounting to less than one might have expected a powerful, highly developed communist country to make available under the circumstances. On the other hand, the level of Soviet assistance was probably vital. Indeed, as suggested by Doak Barnett, it is doubtful that "the Chinese Communists could have implemented their first Five Year Plan without Soviet technical assistance, which has been of extraordinary importance in crucial sectors of the Chinese economy."[60]

Through the Sino-Soviet treaty and agreements of February 14, 1950 and trade pacts signed that spring, the USSR advanced $300 million in credits.[61] On April 20 the USSR and the People's Republic signed a series of economic agreements providing for exhanges of commodities, Soviet loans for the purchase of machinery by China, and the establishment of Sino-Soviet joint corporations for a variety of purposes including the exploitation of mineral resources in Sinkiang over a period of thirty years.[62]

Under a series of agreements beginning in 1950, the Soviet Union agreed to transfer to the People's Republic of China in the course of three Five Year Plans (1953-1967) a total of 300 industrial plants, a large proportion of the "whole spectrum of Soviet technology, and the administrative techniques and skills required for the running of a modern technology."[63] In September 1953, the USSR agreed to help the People's Republic build 141 key industrial plants, including joint iron and steel plants, coal-mining enterprises, power plants, nonferrous metallurgical enterprises, petroleum processing plants, motor vehicle factories and machine-building factories.[64]

During the autumn of 1954, N. A. Bulganin and N. S. Khrushchev agreed in Peking to a second Soviet loan amounting to $130 million and a total of $100 million in supplies and equipment in addition to previous commitments.[65] The Soviet Union also agreed to sell all its shares in the Sino-Soviet joint stock companies to China. At the same time plans were laid for the joint construction of a new railway linking China and the Soviet Union by way of Sinkiang.

In the course of a visit to China early in 1956, A. I. Mikoyan promised Soviet support for an additional 55 projects involving $625 million in supplies and equipment. Altogether, during the first Five Year Plan, the USSR instituted 211 China aid projects.[66] Soviet deliveries of complete plant installations "constituted the very heart" of the first Five Year Plan and the Great Leap Forward.[67]

Early in 1958 Chinese Communist authorities asserted that about 7,000 Soviet experts had worked in the People's Republic up to that time. Some responsible sources have estimated, however, that "there may have been as many as 10,000 to 20,000 (and if military experts were included the figure would probably be higher)."[68] Prior to 1950 the share of Soviet trade with China amounted to about 5 percent of total Chinese trade; by 1959 the Soviet share was approximately 50 percent. By the later date, Soviet exports to China were as large as all Soviet exports to the underdeveloped countries of the world combined.[69] One-sixth of all Soviet exports machinery and nearly three out of every four complete industrial plants sent abroad by the USSR had gone to China.[70] According to agreements concluded during the 1950s, "By the end of 1967, Communist China was to have 300 modern steel mills, electric power plants, machine-tool plants, aircraft plants, chemical plants, electronics plants, and agricultural machinery plants. All these plants would be dove-tailed together as suppliers and customers of one another."[71] In fact, complete plant imports increased almost tenfold between 1952 and 1960—and then dropped off dramatically.[72]

The evidence thus suggests that, if Soviet aid to the People's Republic of China was less than many Western observers had expected, it was nevertheless of enormous importance in its implications. Under their arrangements with the Soviet Union, Chinese Communist planners "were in the enviable position of skipping the costs and delays in (a) research and development, (b) design and blueprints and (c) testing and evaluation."[73] According to one Western specialist, "History gives no parallel example of a nation being offered a complete industrial system on a platter."[74] This indicates that the USSR rendered the Chinese People's Republic enough assistance to provide means for substantially narrowing the gap between population and productivity.

Throughout the 1950s the large transfer of Soviet capital goods helped the Chinese to achieve a high rate of domestic investment in plants and equipment. Between 1952 and 1959 investment was growing at an average annual rate of 27 percent. If Soviet assistance had continued at a commensurate rate, China, as viewed by careful observers in the mid-1960s, might have come very near to solving its population-productivity imbalance by 1968 or at least by the early 1970s. This would have been a critical contribution on the part of the USSR, even though the Russians expected the Chinese to pay them back. Against this background, it was all the more difficult to understand, at the time, why the Chinese had allowed the Sino-Soviet dispute to reach the point where Soviet technicians were recalled and Soviet assistance all but withdrawn. In retrospect, there seems to have been another side to the issue, however. By pursuing a policy of self-reliance, China has undoubtedly enhanced its position and influence in the world since the early 1960s.

The relative success of the Peking regime in rehabilitating the economy during this initial period can be explained, in part at least, by three major factors: (1) fighting on the Chinese Mainland had ceased for the first time in a dozen years; (2) in this new environment, Chinese Communist efforts at curtailing wartime inflation were generally successful; and (3) the relative and perhaps unexpected mildness of the 1949 Common Program put forward by the Maoist leadership "succeeded in relieving the urban population's feelings of anxiety and uncertainty toward the Communist regime."[75] There was support for the regime from many commercial and other distinctly noncommunist sectors of society.

Changes effected by the Maoist regime during the 1950s were not achieved without severe cost to some groups in the society. During 1952 the Peking regime undertook the "3-Anti" campaign against corruption, decay, and bureaucracy. The purpose appears to have been to achieve cleaner and more efficient government, to carry on aggressive class struggle against elements considered inimical to Chinese Communists interests, and to cleanse the party of undesirable personnel.[76]

While employing the 3-Anti movement within the party and government, the Chinese Communists also launched the "5-Anti" struggle against bribery, tax evasion, theft of state assets, cheating, and theft of state economic secrets. During this campaign it was alleged that many party members, on moving from rural to urban environments, had fallen victim to the corrosion and fierce attacks of the bourgeois class, which must therefore be held basically responsible for all corruption, mismanagement, and subversion in Communist China. The lawbreaking merchants now replaced corrupt officials as the chief target of attack.[77]

In pursuing its struggle against the corrupt bourgeoisie, the People's Republic issued statutes that ranked cases according to seriousness and the willingness of the accused to confess. Five forms of punishment were proclaimed: surveillance by government organs, reform through labor service, imprisonment for a fixed period, life imprisonment, and death. Penalties for corruption and waste in governmental and party service ranged from dismissal to labor reform prison terms, and death. The 3-Anti and 5-Anti campaigns demonstrated ways in which a centralized regime with carefully worked out strategies and tactics in the social, economic, political, and psychological spheres would pursue revolutionary aims in a governmentally regulated context over a period of years and through interlocking stages of development. The 3-Anti and 5-Anti campaigns amounted to Maoist class warfare, planned and executed by the sovereign leadership of the People's Republic—protracted warfare against domestic class opponents.

The first five year plan

During the second stage of the Chinese Communist undertaking—the period of the first Five Year Plan (1953-1957)—the central government began the establishment of forced-draft industrialization after the Soviet model. Emphasis was placed upon rapid expansion of Chinese capacity and output in basic industrial commodities. The plan emphasized overall state planning, agricultural collectivization, the socialization of commerce and industry, tight controls on consumption, a high level of investment in industry, and a rapid rate of growth.[78] In the course of this five-year period, Chinese Communist industrial production probably doubled again, reaching a level more than four times that of 1949—although the rate was slower and less steady than it had been during the period of economic rehabilitation.[79]

A high priority was assigned to the development of electric power during the 1953-1957 period. The most important of various power projects under the first Five Year Plan called for fifteen large thermal plants with capacities of more than 50,000 kilowatts to be constructed in Manchuria, northwest China, and southwest China.[80] By the end of the first Five Year Plan, Chinese Communist authorities asserted that total power output had been raised from a 1952 level of 7.26 billion kilowatts to 19.03 billion kilowatts in 1957, surpassing the 15.9 billion kilowatt target of the Plan.[81] High priorities were also assigned to coal, steel, pig iron, cement, petroleum, chemicals, rubber, nonferrous metals, and machine building.[82]

China's petroleum industry was in a particularly backward state. Prior to the first Five Year Plan, the People's Republic focused on the rehabilitation and restoration of existing facilities. Imports from the Soviet Union accounted for 50 to 70 percent of Chinese consumption during these years, but crude oil production increased from 121,000 tons in 1949 to 436,000 tons in 1952. The first Five Year Plan placed major emphasis on exploration, and proved reserves increased from less than 30 million tons of natural crude to 100 million tons in 1957. China's first modern petroleum refinery was build during 1956-1959 at Lanchou with expertise and equipment supplied by the Soviet Union.[83]

The steel industry was in a shambles when the People's Republic was established in 1949. Domestic production had dropped from a 1948 high of 1,800,000 tons of pig iron and 900,000 tons of steel to 250,000 tons and 160,000 tons, respectively, in 1949. Immediately after the end of World War II, the USSR had stripped away as war booty much of the machinery that had served the Japanese, and other plants were gutted during the post-war civil struggle between Nationalists and Communists. With Soviet aid, however, the People's Republic immediately began to rebuild its steel industry: by 1952 production had already surpassed pre-Communist peak levels, and over the next five years pig iron output tripled, and the output of steel increased fivefold. Over the span of two and one-half decades, Chinese production of crude steel increased from 606,000 tons in 1950 to 23,800,000 in 1974—a truly spectacular advance.[84]

It had been the intention of the Chinese Communist leadership to extend the policies of the first Five Year Plan (1953-1957) with a second Five Year Plan (1958-1962). By the end of the first Five Year Plan, however, Communist China was still confronted by a lag in agricultural output, and the implications of this inadequacy were exacerbated by a continuing population growth[85] and a slackening of the country's rate of industrial growth.

Chinese industrial personnel were beginning to outgrow earlier, somewhat naïve expectations that somehow Soviet institutions, advanced technology, and massive investment could rapidly eliminate all obstacles to industrialization.[86] The regime was thus facing a wide range of managerial problems, and there was the necessity of paying the USSR back for credits that had been advanced. Under these circumstances, the Chinese Communist leadership, while pleased with the rapid growth of the economy, may have realized at the same time that achievements under the first Five Year Plan had been small compared with China's urgent needs. Under these circumstances they may well have chafed "under the brick by brick approach of their Soviet mentors."[87]

The Great Leap Forward

Sometime during the autumn of 1957, the Peking regime decided upon a radical new approach.[88] The second Five Year Plan was superseded early in 1958 by the Great Leap Forward, which amounted to a complete turnabout in Chinese Communist economic policy. The Great Leap was described by Western economic specialists as "an ill-conceived scheme to drive the Chinese economy ahead at a much faster pace" by doubling and redoubling agricultural and industrial output in a few short years.[89] If it was a disaster, and it may well have been, nevertheless we would be in error to dismiss it as an unqualified disaster, since much progress was made in a number of sectors.

At first the reports from pilot projects in various parts of the country were highly enthusiastic and promising. Targets everywhere were seemingly being fulfilled and often overfulfilled. To practiced observers on the outside, however, it soon became evident that the announced increases could not be accepted as true. And in August 1959, the first of many drastic downward revisions appeared. Outside observers began to view the Great Leap Forward as a "statistical fiasco."[90]

During the Great Leap Forward political pressures in Communist China gave rise to a massive but largely uncoordinated program of investment. The leadership in Peking exerted powerful pressures on party members at local levels, on directors of communes, on managers of local enterprises, and on other responsible party and nonparty personnel to expand production "at a pace practically impossible to achieve."[91] New factories were set up "without much consideration of whether their products were vitally needed. Old plans were revised upwards constantly. A 30 percent expansion of capacity in one area would be turned into a 100 percent expansion. The result was chaos."[92]

The effect on the farm sector of collectivization in general and the establishment of communes in particular was judged by many Western observers to have been uniformly unfavorable at the very least. Farm production declined sharply, and the inadequate supply of agricultural raw material slowed down important elements of the industrial sector.[93] The trend in industry was toward the substitution of quantity for quality, and by 1960 that sector also began to falter.[94] The whole economy suffered a setback and did not begin to recover until 1962.

It appeared to some Western observers that "The talents of the leadership that had been military virtues on the Long March to Yenan—and in the final conquest of the mainland—were not fully transferable in running a large centrally planned economy."[95] Despite seemingly overwhelming odds, Mao Tse-tung's guerrilla-style political and economic strategies and tactics, as well as his military strategies and tactics, had worked well as long as he was tearing down the old order and dividing landlord holdings among land-hungry peasants. But whether these styles of attack were appropriate for building a modern technological society now came up for serious questioning.

In view of this development, doubts were raised not only about the appropriateness of Mao's domestic policies and methods but also about those aspects of his foreign policy that bore on Chinese relations with the USSR. As suggested by one Western observer:

> The surest way of ultimately attaining status as the third superpower was to remain under Soviet tutelage at least until 1967; that is, through three 5-year plans. By 1967, the entire 300 major industrial plants would have been completed; the Chinese would have been the beneficiaries of important atomic technology which the Soviets could find no compelling reason to refuse; the training of millions of industrial workers, technicians and scientists would have been finished; and the Chinese would have had sufficient experience to run their own planning and statistical systems. All the Chinese Communists needed was patience, a virtue that Chinese are supposed to possess in ample measure. With patience Communist China by about 1967 would have been very largely self-sufficient.[96]

Difficulties were compounded in July 1960, when the USSR suddenly withdrew its large corps of experts from China. With their departure, the Chinese found themselves unable to operate many of the key industrial plants built as Soviet aid projects, and numbers were forced to close down.[97] In the words of Chinese Communist economic planner, Po I-po, this sudden withdrawal was like "taking away all the dishes when you have only eaten half a meal."[98]

In retrospect, it appears that some of the more negative assessments of the Great Leap Forward and its consequences may have been overdrawn. An examination of Chinese industrial production indexes in time series (1949-1974) tends to smooth over what looked like a disaster at the time. True, the rate of growth, "which had surged to 45 percent in 1958, dropped to 22 percent in 1959, and was only 4 percent in 1960 as the Great Leap Forward began to collapse." Yet growth continued, even though much of it, according to one Western viewpoint, would have occurred "without a Leap Forward."[99]

In line with Great Leap policies in other branches of industry, China had focused for a time on the development of small and shallow oil fields. Nevertheless, during the 1958-1962 period the proved reserves of oil doubled, reaching 200 million tons in 1959-1960, and dependence on imports began to decrease substantially. By 1963 the Peking government began to describe the country as basically self-sufficient in oil. Exploratory drilling was undertaken about the same time in order to ascertain offshore reserves. A basis had not been established for China's emergence as an oil exporter.[100]

During the period of retrenchment that followed the Great Leap Forward, most of the small iron and steel plants were closed down, and steel production dropped from 18.67 million tons in 1960 to 8 million tons a year later.[101] As viewed by two Western observers, "The withdrawal of Soviet technicians in mid-1960 had a great impact on the steel industry. Not only did the technicians leave the Chinese with two major unfinished plants—Wu-han and Pao-t'ou—but they also took with them the managerial and technical know-how that was in extremely short supply. The People's Republic was fortunate to have a sufficient number of Soviet-trained managers and technicians to keep major plants in operation and to finish the Wu-han and Pao-t'ou plants, but shortages of "finishing capacity in these two new plants remain a problem to this day [1975]."[102]

Only the buildup of a considerable technical force over previous years enabled Communist China to stave off a complete collapse after the withdrawal of Soviet assistance in 1960.[103] The economic crisis probably was at its worst in 1961.[104] By then the Peking regime had already undertaken what it termed a "readjustment program" and what outside observers referred to as a "painful retrenchment."[105] This led to something of a recovery, which the regime identified as the "upsurge" of 1964-1965.

A part of this modest success was attributable to new support from outside. The Soviet Union and the communist countries of Eastern Europe provided credits to ease China's balance-of-payments difficulties. In 1961 the Soviet Union extended $46 million in credit to finance Chinese importation of about 500,000 tons of Cuban sugar. The People's Republic also acquired $320 million long-term credit from the USSR to fund the bulk of its accumulated clearing debt.[106] By 1965 heavy industry had largely recovered—although the annual growth rate had fallen from 20 percent per year in 1953-1957 to 8 or 9 percent per year.[107]

Despite this aid from the USSR in 1961, the Great Leap Forward marked a break with dependency upon Soviet technology and Soviet industrial bureaucratic models of organization, and the beginning of a concerted effort in the direction of Chinese self-reliance and self-assertion. There were several difficulties ahead, however.

A major assumption underlying the Great Leap Forward was that China's vast population, contrary to the Malthusian theories of bourgeois economists, could be turned into an economic asset rather than a liability, that human beings should be viewed as producers rather than consumers. The more people, the more hands there were to build socialism by means of labor-intensive technologies.[108] From the viewpoint of many Western economists, of course, this thesis "could hardly be more in error in a country pushing hard against the limits of existing agriculture to obtain food."[109]

A commonly professed Marxist-Leninist view had been that a country or a region is "overpopulated only because of a gap between the technological level of the society and the appropriateness and effectiveness of the political and economic systems." The population difficulty in a capitalist society had been perceived by Marxists as rooted inevitably in the conflict between capitalist production relations—how the economic system is organized—and the labor or productive force. Marxists had believed that this collision between capital and labor must inescapably give rise to a state of relative underemployment and overpopulation, and that the sole solution for the population problem of a capitalist country would be the seizure of state power by the proletariat.[110]

There is a great deal to be said for the view that "appropriate and effective political and economic systems" can do much to solve unemployment and related problems associated with overpopulation in technologically advanced societies. What is often overlooked in both capitalist and socialist societies, however, are the considerations that advanced technologies tend to generate higher demands for energy and other basic resources and to stimulate growing demands for consumer goods that, in turn, cause pollution and require large amounts and varieties of resources for their production.

But what about population in a noncapitalist, preindustrial society such as China? A critical question there was whether or not the effectiveness of the political and economic systems could be improved sufficiently without some degree of control over population growth. According to Chinese Communist authorities in the late 1950s, Mao Tse-tung and his colleagues, once having seized power, had been able to attack the population problem by altering the proportional shares of the different sectors of the economy. Thus, the state sector was made significantly larger than the private sector, and the industrial sector was increased relative to the agricultural sector. Under these conditions, it was claimed, productivity could be raised and the living conditions of the people, even the living conditions of a rapidly expanding population, could be steadily improved as larger and larger numbers of people were put into productive work.[111]

Without doubt the Chinese Communist regime had achieved a great increase in Chinese industrial production and consumption. But the gap between technological capability and the needs of a growing population was still wide and perhaps becoming wider. According to Colin Clark, writing in 1965, in no post-World War II year had the Chinese people been able to obtain as much to eat per capita "as they had even in the 1930's."[112]

Could the Chinese close the gap between the growing population and the developing—but still too slowly developing—economy? According to a Western view, "If the Malthusian trap were not to close, industrialization had to be achieved without delay, had to be conducted on a tremendous scale, had to be simple to administer, and had to be achieved at low cost measured in terms of the food and raw materials China would have to export. The Soviet-sponsored industrial program met all these criteria."[113] But now the Chinese were virtually on their own.

In the meantime, however, Chinese Communist attitudes toward population and birth control had begun to change. With the collapse of the Great Leap Forward, Peking authorities had undertaken a campaign against early marriages and the discouragement of too many children in early years as indirect approaches to the problem of birth control.[114] Later, here the regime moved cautiously toward abortion and sterilization. By the early 1970s the Peking government was distributing Chinese-developed birth control wafers in large quantities.

During 1966 and 1967 China's economic problems were complicated by the controversies of the Great Proletarian Cultural Revolution, which brought about serious disruptions in agriculture and industry in many parts of the country and caused great political confusion. For months Maoist and anti-Maoist forces were locked in ideological and sometimes violent struggle, and for some years it was not clear what the outcome would be. From the viewpoint of an outside observer it appeared quite possible that these disruptions in economic and technological development, coming in the wake of the Great Leap Forward, might turn out to be fatal for the progress that Mao and his colleagues had been trying to achieve.

The third Five Year Plan (1966-1970) was overshadowed, in many respects, by events of the Cultural Revolution. The turmoil of this period resulted in serious coal shortages and transportation tie-ups that produced another downward turn in steel production, and in some plants there were work stoppages during the anti-Confucius campaign of 1974. Compared to the Great Leap Forward, however, these setbacks were minor and temporary. During the Cultural Revolution, large numbers of high-ranking Party and government leaders lost their jobs. But with the exception of a few riot-torn cities, which captured the attention of the outside world, "the day-to-day activities of the economy — the collection and carrying out of financial transactions — continued undisturbed on the basis of the institutional roots established over the first 17 years of Communist rule."[115] Although the Chinese growth rate was substantially lower than it had been (8 percent per annum between 1960 and 1974 as compared with 22 percent per annum during the 1949-1960 period), industrial production increased steadily throughout the years of the Cultural Revolution — and faster thereafter.[116]

By 1970 the disruptions of the Cultural Revolution had subsided, and the Chinese economy was undergoing a new surge of expansion. Both imports and exports increased more rapidly than during any earlier period. At the same time, China's national product grew substantially, so that foreign trade began to represent only a small part of the GNP. Quantitatively, China's reliance on foreign trade was now considered marginal.

In the autumn of 1970 Premier Chou En-lai announced that a fourth Five Year Plan for 1971-1975 had been drafted, and many leading Party bureaucrats who had been deposed during the Cultural Revolution — notably Party Secretary Teng Hsiao-ping — began to reappear. Then, toward the middle of 1973 a new political controversy revealed that the struggle between moderates and radicals had by no means been settled. In the course of what was known as the "anti-Confucius, anti-Lin Piao" campaign, attacks were leveled against reliance on material incentives, foreign technology, and the leadership of rehabilitated bureaucrats.[117] As during the seemingly more acute struggles of the Cultural Revolution, however, the index of Chinese industrial production continued to rise.[118]

The Peking leadership had placed emphasis upon the concept of self-reliance for many years, especially since the renunciation of Soviet tutelage, but early in 1974 a renewed campaign of exhortation was initiated in the press.

A major aspect of the Chinese concept of self-reliance involves resource mobilization. The drive to use local resources as a substitute for reliance on imported resources has been applied not only with respect to foreign technology, but also in an effort to limit local demands for capital allocated from Peking.[119] In these terms, an important purpose behind this new call for self-reliance was believed by outside observers to be an effort to exert ideological and social pressure upon industrial managers "to get them to rely as much as possible upon the resources of their own enterprises or localities, and thus to reduce the clamor for imported technology."[120]

As viewed by the Chinese leadership, however, self-reliance on the national level is not meant to suggest complete self-sufficiency. On the contrary, foreign trade has reached unprecedented levels since 1971.[121] For China, self-reliance means avoiding dependency. Foreign technology will be required in the short-run, to be sure, but as a means for reducing the need for some of these imports in the long run — *and not to provide any foreign interest with a social, ideological, economic, political, or military foothold.*[122]

Trends in Chinese Trade

In spite of its large size, the People's Republic does not yet rank as a major trading nation. Increasingly, however, foreign trade is constituting an important means of facilitating and accelerating the country's modernization. As a state monopoly, commercial relations provide an effective tool for transforming Chinese society into a modern industrial state.[123] To a greater extent than for many other countries, the foreign trade of the People's Republic has been shaped by its foreign policy objectives[124] — although the Chinese need for trade has probably influenced the country's foreign policy, as well. Diplomatic relations involving the People's Republic, the USSR, the United States, and Japan are likely to be influenced by trade patterns in a number of important ways.

Overall trends in the development of China's trade have fluctuated considerably since 1950. In terms of United States dollars, Chinese trade expanded steadily from 1950-1959, with a slight decline in 1952, which may have been an outcome of the 5-Anti campaign and a Western embargo on strategic goods, and another decline in 1957, attributable to overinvestment and shortages of agricultural products. In 1958, trade volume rose sharply because of import demands for capital goods to support the Great Leap Forward. A 1959 peak was followed by a declining trend reflecting the economic crisis triggered by the Great Leap and the deterioration of relations with the Soviet Union. Trade revived gradually during 1963-1966, but remained below the earlier peak. The Cultural Revolution was accompanied by mild declines, but since 1970 both exports and imports have tended to rise.[125]

Chinese trade during the 1950s was oriented toward the USSR and other countries of the Communist bloc. From 1950 to 1959 the total turnover of trade between China and the Soviet Union increased more than fivefold from $320 million to a peak of more than $2 billion. Sino-Soviet trade accounted for more than half of China's total trade during 1952-1955 and more than 40 percent during 1956-1960. With the exacerbation of the Sino-Soviet conflict, however, trade between the two countries began to decline to $45 million in 1970, which was approximately 2 percent of the 1959 peak. In 1971 Sino-Soviet trade recovered somewhat, but the USSR was China's fifth largest trading partner in 1972, eighth in 1973, and tenth in 1974. Except for Albania and Yugoslavia, China's trade with East European countries has generally followed the Sino-Soviet pattern.[126]

Following President Nixon's visit to the People's Republic (February 1972) and the rapprochement between the two countries, Sino-United States trade, "Which had been nonexistent in 1970, rose to $805.1 and $933.8 million by 1973 and 1974, respectively, with wheat sales, jet transport exports, and a number of other major contracts highlighting this unexpectedly rapid development."[127] As an outcome of Chinese purchases of American agricultural commodities, by 1974 the United States had become China's number two trading partner. By that time Japan had become the People's Republic of China's leading trade partner, accounting for about 20 percent of China's foreign trade turnover and demonstrating a substantial complementarity between the two economies.[128] On the one hand, Japan requires raw materials for its modern industrial economy, and Japanese industrial leaders consider the People's Republic a logical supplier. Chinese foreign trade planners, on the other hand, need the machinery, equipment, and industrial manufactures that Japan can export. Also, the short, relatively cheap water transport between Japan and China makes the partnership attractive.[129]

With respect to trade, as in other aspects of its economic policy, the People's Republic continues to stress the concept of self-reliance — avoiding economic and/or political dependency on any other power. The regime is determined to preserve its independence, avoid reliance on foreign assistance, limit any foreign presence, and forestall outside meddling with its economy. Trade must be carried out solely on the basis of equality and mutual benefit,[130] and foreign interests must not be allowed to penetrate the Chinese economy.

Notes

1. Edwin F. Jones, "The Role of Development Policies and Economic Organization in Innovation and Growth: Communist China," in *An Economic Profile of Mainland China*, vol. 2, Studies Prepared for the Joint Economic Committee, Congress of the United States (Washington, D.C.: U.S. Government Printing Office, 1967), p. 676.

2. Arthur G. Ashbrook, Jr., "Main Lines of Chinese Communist Economic Policy," in *An Economic Profile of Mainland China*, vol. 1, p. 17. See also Alexander Eckstein, *Communist China's Economic Growth and Foreign Trade* (New York: McGraw Hill, 1966), p. 1.

3. Bruce M. Russett, Hayward R. Alker, Jr., Karl W. Deutsch, and Harold D. Lasswell, *World Handbook of Political and Social Indicators* (New Haven, Conn.: Yale University Press, 1964).

4. Arthur S. Banks and Robert B. Textor, *A Cross-Polity Survey* (Cambridge, Mass.: MIT Press, 1963).

5. Arthur S. Banks and Phillip M. Gregg, "Grouping Political Systems: The Q-Factor Analysis of a Cross-Polity Survey," *The American Behavioral Scientist* 9, no. 3 (November 1965), pp. 3-6.

6. Dimitri Ivanoff, *International Environment Evaluation System*, Douglas Missile and Space, Systems Division, Report SM-51925 (Santa Monica, Calif., January 1966).

7.   Davis B. Bobrow, "Old Dragons in New Models," *World Politics* 19, no. 2, (January 1967), p. 310.

8.   Ibid., p. 313.

9.   Lucian W. Pye, "Coming Dilemmas for China's Leaders," *Foreign Affairs* 44, no. 3 (April 1966), p. 387.

10. Ibid., p. 389.

11. Ruth Leger Sivard, *World Military and Social Expenditures 1976* (Leesburg, Virginia: WMSE Publications, 1976), pp. 21-22. The area of Canada and the United States are 9,974,000 square kilometers and 9,363,000 square kilometers, respectively. Compare these figures with Russett, et al., *World Handbook,* p. 139.

12. Charles P. Kindleberger, *Foreign Trade and the National Economy* (New Haven, Conn.: Yale University Press, 1962), pp. 32-37.

13. John Ashton, "Development of Electric Energy Resources in Communist China," in *An Economic Profile of Mainland China,* Vol. 1, p. 299.

14. Bobby A. Williams, "The Chinese Petroleum Industry: Growth and Prospects," in *China: A Reassessment of the Economy* (Washington, D.C.: U.S. Government Printing Office, 1975), p. 225.

15. Vaclav Smil, "Energy in China: Achievements and Prospects," *China Quarterly,* no. 65 (March 1976), p. 55.

16. Alfred H. Usack, Jr. and James D. Egan, "China's Iron and Steel Industry," in *China: A Reassessment,* p. 270.

17. Ibid., p. 266.

18. K. P. Wang, "The Mineral Resource Base of Communist China," in *An Economic Profile of Mainland China,* Vol. 1, p. 169. See also K. P. Wang, *The People's Republic of China: A New Industrial Power with a Strong Mineral Base,* United States Department of the Interior, Bureau of Mines (Washington, D.C.; U.S. Government Printing Office, 1976).

19. Vaclav Smil, "Energy in China," p. 54. See also V. Smil, "Exploiting China's Hydro Potential," *International Water Power and Dam Construction* 28, no. 3 (March 1976), pp. 19-26.

20. Arthur G. Ashbrook, Jr., "China: Economic Overview, 1975," in *China: A Reassessment,* p. 23.

21. Ibid.

22. Dwight H. Perkins, "Constraints Influencing China's Agricultural Performance" in *China: A Reassessment,* p. 352.

23. Foreign Broadcast Information Service *Daily Report,* December 10, 1971 by radio station KYODO (Tokyo), August 23, 1972, as quoted by Leo A. Orleans, "China's Population: Can the Contradictions be Resolved?" in *China: A Reassessment,* p. 71. *PRC: Handbook of Economic Indicators,* CIA, 1976 cites the population as over 950 million in 1976.

24. Russett, et al., *World Handbook,* p. 47. India ranked 54 (2.2), the USSR 73.5 (1.8), and the United States 77.5 (1.7). Kuwait was 1 (15.1) and Sarawak 2 (5.1).

25. Russett et al., *World Handbook,* p. 138. In the United States, the population per square kilometer is twenty, in the USSR it is ten, and in Canada it is two. See also John S. Aird, "Population Growth and Distribution in Mainland China," in *An Economic Profile of Mainland China,* vol. 2, pp. 372-73.

26. Marion R. Larsen, "China's Agriculture Under Communism," in *An Economic Profile of Mainland China,* vol. 1, p. 199.

27. See John S. Aird, "Population Growth and Distribution in Mainland China," in *An Economic Profile of Mainland China,* vol. 2, p. 373. Aird presents numbers of persons per square mile.
28. Perkins, "Constraints Influencing China's Agricultural Performance," p. 354.
29. Eckstein, *Communist China's Economic Growth,* pp. 3, 11.
30. Robert Michael Field, "Civilian Industrial Production in the People's Republic of China: 1949-74," in *China: A Reassessment,* p. 149.
31. Russett et al., *World Handbook,* p. 152.
32. Eckstein, *Communist China's Economic Growth,* p. 249.
33. Sivard, *World Military and Social Expenditures,* pp. 21-22.
34. Ashbrook, "China: Economic Overview, 1975" in *China: A Reassessment,* p. 23.
35. Sivard, *World Military and Social Expenditures,* p. 20.
36. Hans Heymann, Jr., "Acquisition and Diffusion of Technology in China," in *China: A Reassessment,* pp. 691-96.
37. Usack and Egan, "China's Iron and Steel Industry," p. 277.
38. Heymann, "Acquisition and Diffusion of Technology in China," p. 696.
39. John P. Hardt, "A Summary," in *China: A Reassessment,* p. 16.
40. Perkins, "Constraints Influencing China's Agricultural Performance," p. 350.
41. Usack and Egan, "China's Iron and Steel Industry," p. 284.
42. Sivard, *World Military and Social Expenditures,* p. 26.
43. Ibid, p. 15.
44. Ashbrook, "Main Links of Chinese Economic Policy," p. 18.
45. A. Doak Barnett, *Communist Economic Strategy: The Rise of Mainland China* (Washington, D.C.: National Planning Association, 1959), p. 4.
46. See, for example, "Red Army 'War Booty' Removals from Manchuria" and "General Summary of 'Report on Japanese Assets in Manchuria'," *United States Relations with China* (Washington, D.C.: Department of State Publication, 1949), pp. 596-604. For a description of the pre-1949 Manchurian economy, see Eckstein, *Communist China's Economic Growth,* pp. 13-14.
47. Yuan-li Wu, *An Economic Survey of Communist China* (New York: Bookman, 1956), p. 64.
48. Ibid., p. 341.
49. Ibid., p. 64.
50. W. W. Rostow, *The Prospects for Communist China* (New York: Wiley, 1954), p. 224.
51. Robert Michael Field, "Chinese Communist Industrial Production," in *An Economic Profile of Mainland China,* vol. 15, p. 271.
52. Ygael Gluckstein, *Mao's China: Economic and Political Survey* (Boston: Beacon, 1957), p. 31.
53. Rostow, *Prospects for Communist China,* pp. 233-34.
54. Mao Tse-tung, "Report to the Central Committee of the Communist Party of China, June 6, 1950," *Current Background,* no. 1 (June 13, 1950), p. 3.
55. Mao Tse-tung, "The People's Tribunals: Instruments of Agrarian Reform," and "Regulations Governing the Organization of People's Tribunals," *Current Background,* no. 151 (January 10, 1952), pp. 1, 4-6.

56. Liu Shoa-ch'i, "Political Report," New China News Agency (NCNA), Peking, in English, Morse to Europe, September 16, 1956. See also, *Current Background,* no. 412 (September 28, 1956), p. 10.
57. Perkins, "Constraints Influencing China's Agricultural Performance," pp. 351-353.
58. Rostow, *An Economic Survey,* p. 197.
59. Gluckstein, *Mao's China,* p. 67.
60. Barnett, *Communist Economic Strategy,* p. 80.
61. Robert M. Slusser and Jan F. Triska, *A Calendar of Soviet Treaties 1917-1957* (Stanford, Calif.: Stanford University Press, 1959), p. 270.
62. Gluckstein, *Mao's China,* pp. 64-75.
63. Ashbrook, "Main Lines of Chinese Economic Policy," p. 22.
64. Gluckstein, *Mao's China,* p. 66, quoting from New China News Agency (September 15, 1953).
65. "Communique on Negotiations Between China and the Soviet Union," October 12, 1954, *Survey of China Mainland Press,* no. 906 (October 12, 1954) pp. 1-9.
66. "Sino-Soviet Communique of April 7, 1956," *Survey of China Mainland Press,* no. 1265, p. 30; Gluckstein, *Mao's China,* p. 67.
67. Eckstein, *Communist China's Economic Growth,* p. 105.
68. Barnett, *Communist Economic Strategy,* p. 26.
69. Robert L. Price, "International Trade of Communist China, 1950-1965," in *An Economic Profile of Mainland China,* vol. 2, p. 592.
70. Ibid.
71. Ashbrook, "Main Lines of Chinese Economic Policy," p. 22.
72. Eckstein, *Communist China's Economic Growth,* p. 105.
73. Ashbrook, "Main Lines of Chinese Economic Policy," p. 22.
74. Ibid.
75. Ta-Chung Liu, "The Tempo of Economic Development of the Chinese Mainland, 1949-65," in *An Economic Profile of Mainland China,* vol. 1, p. 54.
76. "Overcome the Corrosion of Bourgeois Ideology: Oppose the Rightist Trend in the Party," *Current Background,* no. 163 (March 5, 1952), p. 58.
77. "The Communists and the Bourgeoisie," *Current Background,* no. 166 (March 14, 1952), p. 2.
78. A. Doak Barnett, *China After Mao* (Princeton, N.J.: Princeton University Press, 1967), p. 11.
79. Field, "Chinese Communist Industrial Production," p. 275.
80. Barnett, *Communist Economic Strategy,* p. 22.
81. Ibid., p. 23.
82. Eckstein, *Communist China's Economic Growth,* p. 108.
83. Williams, "Chinese Petroleum Industry," p. 244.
84. Usack and Egan, "China's Iron and Steel Industry," pp. 273-76.
85. Barnett, *Communist Economic Strategy,* p. 35.
86. Thomas G. Rawski, "China's Industrial System," in *China: A Reassessment,* p. 184.
87. Ashbrook, "Main Lines of Chinese Economic Policy," p. 26.
88. Barnett, *China After Mao,* p. 14.
89. Ashbrook, "Main Lines of Chinese Economic Policy," p. 26.
90. Liu, "Tempo of Economic Development," p. 67.
91. Ibid., pp. 66-67.

92. Dwight H. Perkins, "Economic Growth in China and the Cultural Revolution (1960-April 1967)," *China Quarterly,* no. 30 (April-June 1967), p. 46.
93. *An Economic Profile of Mainland China,* Foreword, vol. 1, p. x.
94. Eckstein, *Communist China's Economic Growth,* pp. 52-53.
95. Ashbrook, "Main Lines of Chinese Economic Policy," p. 27.
96. Ibid., p. 26.
97. Field, "Chinese Communist Industrial Production," p. 276.
98. Quoted by Price, "International Trade of Communist China," pp. 591-92.
99. Field, "Civilian Industrial Production in the People's Republic of China: 1949-74," p. 151.
100. Williams, "Chinese Petroleum Industry," pp. 230-33.
101. Usack and Egan, "China's Iron and Steel Industry," p. 277.
102. Ibid.
103. Chu-yuan Cheng, "Scientific and Engineering Manpower in Communist China," in *An Economic Profile of Mainland China,* vol. 2, p. 544.
104. John Philip Emerson, "Employment in Mainland China: Problems and Prospects," in *An Economic Profile of Mainland China,* vol. 2, p. 445.
105. Edwin F. Jones, "The Emerging Pattern of China's Economic Revolution," in *An Economic Profile of Mainland China,* vol. 1, p. 79.
106. "Communist China's Balance of Payments, 1950-1965," report from Central Intelligence Agency, in *An Economic Profile of Mainland China,* vol. 2, p. 631.
107. Perkins, "Economic Growth in China," pp. 42-43.
108. See Liu Shao-ch'i, "The Present Situation, the Party's General Line for Socialist Construction and Its Future Tasks," Second Session of the Eighth Congress of the CCP, May 26, 1958, in *Current Background,* no. 507, (June 2, 1958), pp. 1-25.
109. Ashbrook, "Main Lines of Chinese Economic Policy," p. 27.
110. Robert C. North, "Communist China and the Population Problem," in Stuart Mudd (ed.), *The Population Crisis and the Use of World Resources* (The Hague: Junk, 1964), pp. 176-87.
111. Wang Ya-nan, "The Post-Liberation Population Problem of China," *Extracts from China Mainland Magazines,* no. 84 (May 27, 1957), p. 2.
112. Colin Clark, "Economic Growth in Communist China," *China Quarterly,* no. 21 (January-March, 1965), p. 148.
113. Ashbrook, "Main Lines of Chinese Economic Policy," p. 25.
114. See "Early Marriage Is Harmful, Not Beneficial," *Survey of China Mainland Press,* no. 2757 (June 13, 1962), p. 11; "A Problem That Deserves Consideration by Unmarried Young People," ibid., no. 2745 (May 24, 1962); and "What is the Most Suitable Age for Marriage," ibid.
115. Ashbrook, "China: Economic Overview, 1975," p. 27.
116. Field, "Civilian Industrial Production in the People's Republic of China: 1949-74," p. 149.
117. Ashbrook, "China: Economic Overview, 1975," pp. 27-28.
118. Field, "Civilian Production in the People's Republic of China: 1949-74," p. 149.
119. Heymann, "Acquisition and Diffusion of Technology in China," p. 690.

120. Ibid., p. 696.
121. Ashbrook, "China: Economic Overview, 1975," p. 32.
122. Heymann, "Acquisition and Diffusion of Technology in China," p. 690.
123. Nai-Ruenn Chen, "China's Foreign Trade, 1950-74," in *China: A Reassessment,* pp. 617-18.
124. Young C. Kim, "Sino-Japanese Commercial Relations," in *China: A Reassessment,* p. 600.
125. Chen, "China's Foreign Trade, 1950-74," pp. 619-20.
126. Chen, "China's Foreign Trade, 1950-74," pp. 628-29.
127. William Clarke and Martha Avery, "The Sino-American Commerical Relationship," in *China: A Reassessment,* p. 501.
128. Kim, "Sino-Japanese Commercial Relations," p. 600.
129. Ibid.
130. Clarke and Avery, "Sino-American Relationship," p. 510.

Chapter Four

Military Capabilities of the People's Republic of China

Among possible activities available to a country in protecting its territory, safeguarding its sovereignty, and enhancing its influence abroad are building and maintaining its armed forces, issuing warnings and threats on the basis of these forces, and making military, naval, air, and missile commitments of force. The level of armed capability is often used as an indicator of a nation's power, and a country's relative position in the international hierarchy of military capability can often account for — along with its basic industrial capabilities — important aspects of its external behavior. We may expect the military capabilities of a country — relative to the military capabilities of other countries — to be a critical factor in its foreign relations. Where, in these terms, does the People's Republic of China fit into the hierarchy of the world's military powers?

It seems safe to assert that the Chinese Communist armed forces are not like any other armed forces in recorded history, nor, perhaps, are any other contemporary armed forces as difficult to assess in terms of relative capability or potential. It is also true that the military activities of few countries have been as obscure as those in China since 1950. Overall, however, the military policy of the People's Republic has provided for large conventional forces combined with small but steadily growing nuclear deterrent capabilities. While thus combining elements of traditional and modernized military capabilities, the regime has generally sought to keep expenditures under close control or, as suggested by one outside observer, to develop "the biggest bang for their bucks" — although the Chinese have "still found it necessary to spend a significant share of the "bucks" that have been available.[1]

Historical Evolution of Chinese Military Power

The history of Chinese Communist armed forces reveals their central role in policy and accounts for some of the peculiarities in their current status, which statistical comparisons cannot reveal. Over the years, Mao Tse-tung and other Chinese Communist leaders have boasted that the strength of their armed forces lies less in their weapons, equipment, and military training and discipline than in their political and ideological indoctrination, determination, ingenuity, and commitment. These are difficult qualities for the Westerner to assess, particularly insofar as they are put forward by Chinese Communist leaders as weaponry more powerful, in the long run, than even missiles and nuclear warheads. But an examination of Chinese Communist military history will reveal an emphasis on human factors of morale, political training, discipline, ideological education, and thought reform; it will reveal a concentration on guerrilla tactics, people's warfare, and the permeation of the army by politics and of the people by the army. It is this almost wholly alien emphasis that is all the more striking to Americans, whose military tradition is shot through with an equally extraordinary focus on the material factors of military technology — equipment, weapons, and weapon systems.

The Chinese Communists have used a variety of titles for their armed forces: the Workers' and Peasants' Red Army, beginning in 1927; the Eighth Route Army, following the Japanese attack in 1937; the New Fourth Army, an additional force established in 1938; and the Chinese People's Liberation Army, with the beginning of the civil war against the Nationalists in 1946.[2]

Throughout the greater part of his political career, Mao Tse-tung consistently placed major faith in armed force, particularly his own special variety of guerrilla armed force. His rise to power within the Chinese Communist movement depended heavily upon his success at building and deploying the Red Army, and it should be remembered that during the years when these forces were being organized and enlarged he was often out of favor with the top party hierarchy and operating on its fringes, at best. Power, Mao asserted, comes out of the barrel of a gun. The history of the Chinese Communist rise to sovereignty — first through the Kiangsi Soviet in the early 1930s, then in Yenan, and finally over the mainland of China — is inseparable from the history of the Chinese Red Army. According to a 1928 resolution drawn up for the Second Party Conference of the Hunan-Kiangsi border area, "the existence of a regular Red Army of adequate strength is a necessary condition for the existence of Red political power."[3] In Mao's words, "An independent regime must be an armed regime."[4]

During the late summer and autumn of 1927 the Chinese Communist party, under instructions from Moscow, undertook a series of abortive insurrections against Nationalist and warlord forces. After the collapse of these undertakings, various retreating revolutionary elements including left-wing defectors from Kuomintang forces, communist-organized miners and other labor groups, peasant guards from Hunan villages, and cadets from a Nationalist training regiment withdrew to Chingkangshan, a former bandit stronghold in the mountains of the Hunan-Kiangsi border. It was from these disparate elements that the first units of the Chinese Red Army were formed. Their numbers were augmented, over succeeding years, by deserters and prisoners of war from Nationalist, warlord, and provincial armies and by dissatisfied peasants.

Life was precarious at the Chingkangshan base. Supplies were short and the troops had neither food nor clothes in sufficient quantities. Anticommunist forces were strong around the periphery and supply routes were closed off. Often the Workers' and Peasants' Army had to fight for barest survival. "Cold as the weather is," Mao wrote in late November 1928, "many of our men are still wearing two suits of clothes of single thickness."[5] The troops became inured to hardship, however, and according to Mao all shared alike with respect to both hardship and reward. "Everybody from the army commander down to the cook lives on a daily fare worth five cents, apart from grain. In the matter of pocket money, if two dimes are allotted, it is two dimes for everybody; if four dimes are allotted, it is four dimes for everybody."[6]

The Red Army, in view of its bare-bones condition of material life and its seemingly never-ending battles, could "sustain itself without collapse," Mao said, only because of its "practice of democracy," which was to say that the officers did not beat the men, officers and men received equal treatment, soldiers enjoyed "freedom of assembly and speech," cumbersome formalities and ceremonies were done away with, and military account books were "open to inspection by all."[7] Under these conditions, captured soldiers and deserters who were not brave "in the enemy army yesterday" became "very brave in the Red Army today."[8]

Mao saw clearly the importance of combining guerrilla warfare with class struggle. If the Red Army were to succeed, it was necessary to gain the support of the poor peasants and alienate no more of the upper-class elements than was unavoidable at any given stage of the long-range conflict. "The deepest source of the immense power of war," Mao wrote in 1938, "lies with the masses of the people." By "the people" he meant the revolutionary classes, primarily the workers and poor peasantry.

There were special difficulties with respect to training the Red Army. Mao noted that in conventional armies the average soldier requires six months or a year's training before he can fight, but Red Army soldiers, "though recruited only yesterday," had "to fight today with practically no military training to speak of."[9] These circumstances required special training methods. But there were other difficulties. Mao conceived of the Red Army as a revolutionary social and political force as well as a military force. As pointed out by Alexander George, "the Chinese Communists learned from their rich experience in guerrilla warfare that an army fights best when discipline and the performance of military duties rest at least in part on genuinely voluntaristic motives and are not extracted solely through fear of punishment for disobedience."[10] The problem was how to devise a training program that would transform the attitudes and motives of Red Army recruits.

Over the years, conscious efforts were made to create "a type of social organization consonant with the revolutionary aspirations of the Chinese Communist leaders." New recruits were not only trained for military duty, but, in fact, "resocialized for participation in a new way of life" both in the armed forces and afterwards as well.[11] The Red Army became the laboratory and testing ground for methods of training that were applied in later years to many other sectors of the populace under ideological remolding or thought-reform movements. The effort was not only to create an effective soldier but also to "alter important aspects of the individual's personality, attitudes and behavior in order to make a 'good communist soldier' out of him."[12] These methods of training and ideological transformation — often referred to by Westerners as "brainwashing" — have become notorious in recent years, but frequently they are misunderstood and the results exaggerated. Some understanding of them is essential if one is to have a sense of Maoist organization and behavior.

The methods of thought reform were essentially a means of transforming the traditional beliefs and value structures of larger numbers of soldiers as well as civilians through a blend of coercion and persuasion. According to a resolution written for the Fourth Army of the Red Army in December 1929, various nonproletarian ideas were greatly hindering the carrying out of the party's correct line among the soldiers. The source of these various incorrect ideas lay in the peasant and petty bourgeois origins of the men, but the ability of the party to wage "a concerted and determined struggle against these ideas" and to rectify them was an important cause of difficulty.[13] Among these incorrect ideas and tendencies were the purely military viewpoint, extreme democratization, nonorganizational viewpoints, absolute equalitarianism, subjectivism, individualism, and adventurism.

The *purely military viewpoint* regarded military work and political work as opposed to each other and often subordinated the organs of political work to those of military work. Rectification included political education of officers and men and programs of reciprocal criticism between party and purely military organs.

Extreme democratization included such "erroneous proposals" as to carry out democratic centralism in the Red Army from bottom to top, to "ask lower levels to discuss first, then let higher levels decide." This attitude was considered dysfunctional in a military organization. Rectification included strict enforcement of the "democratic way of life under centralised guidance." The proper course involved decisionmaking by a leadership that kept itself in close touch with the rank and file, absorbing and abstracting the needs of the rank and file and then acting on the basis of these needs within a Marxist-Leninist-Maoist framework.

Nonorganizational viewpoints referred to insubordination of the minority against the majority. Party discipline required minority obedience to the majority. Rectification included intensive inner party criticism and inculcation of self-discipline.

Absolute equalitarianism was manifested by such absurdities as denying the necessity for officers to ride horses and demanding absolute equality of officers and men. *Subjectivism* referred to the tendency to analyze political situations and develop work guidelines from a subjective rather than a party viewpoint. Rectification required education of officers and men in order to raise their thought "to a political and scientific level, instilling an ability utterly to merge self-interest with the interests of the party." *Individualism* involved vindictiveness (for example, being criticized inside the party by a soldier comrade and then seeking to retaliate outside the party), forming cliques, taking a mercenary view, and hedonism (constantly hoping to march on big cities with the hope of finding pleasure). Rectification included ideological education and strict discipline.

Adventurism included acting blindly regardless of objective and subjective conditions, slack military discipline especially in defeat, unnecessarily setting fire to houses, corporal punishment, and shooting of deserters. Rectification consisted of ideological work, inculcation of self-discipline, and strict enforcement of army regulations.

Whenever soldiers or platoon, company, or battalion commanders of the enemy forces were captured, indoctrination was immediately carried on among them. First they were divided into those who wished to stay and those who wished to leave. The latter were given traveling expenses and set free. "This immediately shatters the enemy's calumny that 'the Communist bandits kill everyone on sight'," Mao wrote. The former were reeducated by thought-reform procedures. "The Red Army is like a furnace," Mao wrote, "in which all captured soldiers are melted down and transformed the moment they come over."[14]

According to Mao, writing in the late 1920s:

> *The tactics we have worked out during the last three years in the course of the struggle are indeed different from any employed in ancient or modern times, in China or elsewhere. With our tactics, the struggles of the masses are daily expanding and no enemy, however powerful, can cope with us. Ours are guerrilla tactics. They consist mainly of the following points:*
>
> *Disperse the forces among the masses to arouse them, and concentrate the forces to deal with the enemy.*
>
> *The enemy advances, we retreat; the enemy halts, we harass; the enemy tires, we attack; the enemy retreats, we pursue.*
>
> *In an independent regime with stabilized territory, we adopt the policy of advancing in a series of waves. When pursued by a powerful enemy, we adopt the policy of circling around in a whirling motion.*
>
> *Arouse the largest numbers of the masses in the shortest possible time and by the best possible methods.*
>
> *These tactics are just like casting a net; we should be able to cast the net wide or draw it in at any moment. We cast it wide to win over the masses and draw it in to deal with the enemy. Such are the tactics we have applied in the past three years.*[15]

These and other Maoist styles of military operation were applied, tested, and refined not only in the late 1920s and early 1930s against Nationalist and warlord forces in Kiangsi, but also later against both Nationalist and Japanese units in Yenan and after World War II in the civil war for control of the mainland. The emphasis was clearly upon indoctrination, training, harnessing peasant discontents and hostilities, and shrewd guerrilla tactics combined with highly mobile, somewhat more traditional warfare. It is worth noting that the Red Army "never used tanks until 1946, nor military aircraft until 1949."[16] Although difficult to measure, as compared with weapons and numbers of troops, Maoist methods of organization, indoctrination, and political struggle are important factors in assessing the effectiveness of the People's Liberation Army, even today.

Recent Status of Chinese Forces

During the Korean War Chinese Communist armed forces probably reached a peak strength of about seven and one-half million men. After 1954 the army was reduced to about half its 1949-1954 size. Since then the standing military force has probably fluctuated between two and one-half and something over three million men. As estimated by outside observers, the Chinese armed forces in the mid-1970s (about 3.1 million men) were comparable to those of the United States (3.1 million) and the USSR (3.5 million.)[17] The number would be much larger if all Chinese militia categories were included. (In parts of China, at least, membership in militia organizations may include virtually all inhabitants of a locality able to carry a rifle.) In terms of estimated military expenditure as a percent of GNP, China (at less than 10 percent) was comparable in the early 1970s to the United States (6 percent) and the USSR (6 percent); much lower than the highest ranking country, Israel (48 percent); but somewhat higher than the United Kingdom (5 percent), France (3 percent), India (3 percent), West Germany (3 percent), and Japan (1 percent).[18]

Such statistics must be used with great caution, however. As indicated in chapter two, estimates of GNP, population levels, and levels of military expenditure are all subject to considerable error. The attempt to calculate China's expenditures on defense as a percentage of GNP is particularly hazardous, since a large, relatively nonmodernized army is not necessarily an undue expense to the People's Republic; indeed, it may represent a net cost "roughly equivalent to zero."[19] A force of two or three million men in the army represents only about one-half of one percent of the total labor force and does not represent much loss of national income. In addition, the Chinese Communist armed forces have maintained a tradition of self-production and supply and have frequently been turned out to assist in planting and harvesting. They are thus, in part, a work force. Military officers and units have also been used for the carrying out of political and economic administration in various parts of the country. And finally, the People's Liberation Army carries substantial domestic police and border guard responsibilities.[20] In view of these considerations, then, the size and capabilities of the Red Army may be considerably greater than budget allocation as a percentage of GNP may seem to suggest.

With respect to modern armaments and supporting services such as naval and air power, however, China ranks far below the major superpowers with annual defense expenditures totalling "less than one-fifth those for the United States and the Soviet Union and less than one-half those of the NATO countries combined." From these estimates — especially when juxtaposed to the country's large population — it follows that China's gap with respect to defense expenditures per man in the armed forces is even wider as compared with like expenditures by other leading powers.[21]

Military modernization tends to compete directly with economic growth, and this consideration has undoubtedly served as a constraint on certain lines of development within the PLA.[22] Where resources are scarce, competing demands are likely to be made on them. Chinese Communist leaders have had to decide at every step how various limited resources should be allocated — how much for the improvement of agriculture, consumer goods, building machines and tools, heavy industry, military forces, and so forth. As suggested by a Western analyst, "Resources devoted to military equipment production represent economic growth foregone; resources devoted to investment goods represent military modernization foregone."[23] Mao-Tse-tung and some of his colleagues, probably through their long years of guerrilla experience, learned how to develop vast semiconventional, modified guerrilla-type forces at very low cost. On the whole, with the significant exception of nuclear development, Chinese Communist leaders seem to have opted for economic growth rather than military modernization, but not without considerable intraparty controversy.

The Problem of Military Modernization

A number of interrelated disputes within the armed forces and also between military officers and the party have been revealed over the years by official Chinese Communist publications. These disputes, over the desirability (in principle and in terms of opportunity and cost) of military modernization, have arisen from a number of sources and issues, including: (1) differences in viewpoint between professionally oriented officers, themselves party members, and dominant party members; (2) disagreements with respect to the speed of technical modernization and the relative priority to be assigned to socialist as opposed to national defense construction; (3) the need for acquiring modern weapons abroad and for acquiring foreign military experience; and (4) the desirability of "a tightly disciplined, hierarchical military organization, as opposed to reversion to the 'unity of officers and men' in order to preserve the 'glorious tradition' of the PLA."[24] There are strong indications, too, that issues of modern weaponry lay near the heart of Sino-Soviet estrangement.[25]

During the mid-1950s party leaders and officers of the Liberation Army became increasingly aware of critical deficiencies in military equipment and in the ability of both officers and men to operate electronic, chemical, biological, and nuclear weapons. Without modern technical equipment and without the combined operation of various military arms with high technical capacities, the courage of men alone could not achieve victory in war. "At present," the head of the General Political Department conceded, "our knowledge of military science, technology and modern command is not much but very little, and the weakness of technology is still a main problem in connection with army-building. We must with our maximum efforts overcome this backwardness."[26] By mid-1955, members of the Chinese Communist General Staff were urging the regime to build and maintain well-equipped and modernized forces, including a more powerful air force, and to coordinate economic and defense policies more effectively. This could not be undertaken, however, except at a certain cost in overall Chinese development, and the inclination of political leaders was to subordinate military modernization to basic economic and industrial planning.

The Sino-Soviet dispute

It is difficult to determine how much the controversy over military modernization contributed to the Sino-Soviet dispute and how much, conversely, the Sino-Soviet dispute contributed to the controversy over military modernization. Undoubtedly the relationship between the two phenomena was deeply interactive.

Sino-Russian disagreements over the correct use of Soviet ICBM capacity can be dated from the Twentieth Congress of the Communist Party of the Soviet Union (CPSU) in February 1956. On that occasion Khrushchev and other Soviet leaders asserted that advances in nuclear weaponry were rendering large-scale warfare unfeasible in that not only the imperialists but also civilization as a whole, including socialist societies, ran the risk of destruction. The triumph of world communism, they stated, must be accomplished without recourse to massive violence.

The successful testing of a Soviet ICBM and the orbiting of a Russian satellite in the autumn of 1957 persuaded the Chinese Communists that the world balance of power had shifted decisively in favor of the USSR and its allies. The Chinese expectation under these circumstances seems to have been that this Communist bloc superiority ought to be exploited through a more militant and aggressive policy in support of national liberation wars in various parts of the world.[27] The Russians agreed that a shift in the world balance had taken place: the Communist world was no longer encircled by the imperialists, whose far-flung empires were rapidly disintegrating. Possibly with a new awareness of nuclear potentialities, however, they were apprehensive of local wars that might escalate to a nuclear level. The Russian inclination was to use the new balance of power as justification for what the Soviet leadership referred to as competitive coexistence.

In spite of these differences, on October 15, 1957, the two countries signed an agreement with respect to new technology and national defense under which the USSR was to provide the People's Republic with a sample of a nuclear bomb and technical specifications for its manufacture. The outcome, however, was quite different from what might have been expected.

At the time of the Moscow Conference during November 1957, the Chinese Communists still seem to have expected to acquire a higher level of Soviet assistance in nuclear weaponry. In January 1956 a new military training program was proclaimed on the basis of Chinese strategic policy, the peculiarities of Chinese terrain, the "glorious traditions" of the army, training experience of recent years, and "the development of modern military techniques and military science," into which "Soviet advanced experience would also be incorporated. A major task involved the coordination of the various branches of the army in combat under the modern conditions of atom bombs, chemical warfare, and guided missiles."[28]

This program was never implemented or even heard of again. Between January and April high officials and leading publications put forward an entirely new military line "which represented a hundred and eighty degree switch from that which had prevailed only a few weeks previously."[29] Precisely what happened to Sino-Soviet relations immediately before, during, and after the Great Leap Forward period is not at all clear. It may be that the Russians were reluctant to assist the Chinese in achieving nuclear capability. At least one Western observer has suggested that "sometime in 1958, perhaps on the eve of the Formosa Straits crisis, the Chinese may have outrightly asked the Russians for nuclear warheads; the Russians, it appears from later Chinese charges, refused — unless they maintained control over the weapons."[30] Peking's decision to go it alone may have been influenced also by what, from a Chinese viewpoint, looked like a Russian unwillingness to allow the People's Republic to achieve some of its major objectives in Formosa and elsewhere. It may also have been a Chinese response to the price Soviet Russia demanded in return for advanced scientific and military assistance. Soviet demand may well have included joint control of nuclear weapons and advanced delivery systems that were being projected.[31]

In any case, a year later, on June 20, 1959, the Russians, according to Chinese charges, unilaterally tore up the agreement of October 1957.[32] It was despicable, Chinese leaders proclaimed, to rely on foreign countries, foreign military experts, and foreign military textbooks and "to despise one's own military heritage." What counted were men, not weapons. It was more important to revolutionize an army than to modernize it. Mao's principles of guerrilla warfare were still applicable. The nation in arms — organized in communes and with a vast militia — was the best form of organization for total war.[33] Communist China, moreover, would develop its own rockets and nuclear weapons.

Professionalism and politics

A major concern in Communist China at this time was the "Red-Expert" issue — the question of the proper balance between ideological "redness" (political mobilization, revolutionary dedication, and activism) on the one hand, and expertise (scientific training and research professionalization, specialization, and technical skill) on the other. In agriculture and industry the issue involved a prolonged struggle between those who proposed to solve economic and industrial problems by a kind of guerrilla approach, relying heavily on political organization, social discipline, ideological exhortation, ingenuity, and improvisation, and those who, on the other hand, were predisposed to emphasize scientific, engineering, and technical knowledge and application. In the military sphere, this controversy emerged to some degree as a struggle between those supporting increased army, navy, and air force professionalism, and those predisposed toward a manpower army available for performing ideological and political functions, flood and disaster duty, and economic reconstruction work. This description is an oversimplification, however; the reality was much more complex.

Viewed in retrospect, the 1958 decisions — capsuled in such slogans as "politics in command" and "the party commands the gun" —

marked a setback for professionalization of the armed forces together with an effort to combine continued reliance on revolutionary strategy and people's war with the allocation of substantial resources for developing nuclear weapons.[34]

In many respects, the decision to check professionalization and delay army modernization can be explained as an effort to make a virtue out of what Maoist leaders perceived as a necessity.[35] The economy could not support industrialization, the development of modernized conventional military forces, and the building of a nuclear base all at the same time. In retrospect, it appears that the first and third considerations were emphasized at the expense of the second. Large numbers of troops were put to work on construction projects. Local, low-cost militia forces were expanded enormously. Methods of "close war," involving guerrilla tactics and largely defensive weapons, were stressed as opposed to "distant war" preparations involving more advanced military technology. The professional officer corps was put at a disadvantage and kept off balance through regulations requiring them to serve at least a month each year as common soldiers in menial tasks and even hard labor.[36]

Controversy between elements in the armed forces and the party reached a peak in September 1959, when a major shift was undertaken in the Chinese Communist high command.[37] Marshal P'eng Teh-huai, a member of the Politburo, active head of the Military Affairs Committee of the Central Committee of the Chinese Communist Party, minister of national defense, and a Red Army veteran with a record extending back to Kiangsi Soviet days, was relieved of his military and politico-military posts.[38] Both P'eng and General Huang K'o-ch'eng, chief of the General Staff and a member of the Central Committee and the Military Affairs Committee, were charged with political crimes against party leadership and possibly, in the case of P'eng, with carrying grievances to Khrushchev. The two were accused also of representing the military line of the propertied class and supporting an erroneous or false line with respect to Maoist ideology.[39]

During 1960, full-scale rebellions broke out in parts of China, and near-starvation was widespread. In the view of some careful observers in the West, the survival of the regime was at stake. Under these circumstances the Peking leadership, dependent upon the army for quelling insurrections and restoring social order, found itself compelled to make important concessions by restoring somewhat the balance between professionalism and political consciousness. After the restoration of domestic order, however, the party "placed an even lower value on the professional army while giving even more stress to its political and economic roles."[40] Politics was still in command.

Chinese Communist leaders sensitive to the country's lack of nuclear weapons and the superiority of the United States in nuclear capabilities, placed major emphasis upon will, determination, long-range American instabilities, and the certainty that revolutionary China would prevail in the end. Maoist leaders apparently considered that the delay in military modernization would render China somewhat vulnerable until a nuclear program could be made effective. Falling back on long experience with disadvantage, Maoist leaders renewed their emphasis upon party discipline, hard work, good organization, determination, iron will, national unity, and shrewd maneuvering. It was asserted over and over again that the current of history was on China's side and that, in the long run, fatal contradictions would weaken and destroy the imperialist camp. The thought of Mao Tse-tung was presented as China's most powerful weapon.

Weapons production

One should not be misled by these exhortations, however, nor by the undeniable restraints on Chinese Communist military development. Certainly the Soviet withdrawal of assistance in the latter part of 1960 presented Mao Tse-tung and his colleagues with a serious dilemma. Military modernization depends largely upon what the Chinese Communists call their metal-processing industry. It depends upon highly trained scientists, engineers, technicians, and craftsmen in addition to critical metals. With the withdrawal of Soviet support in this sphere, it became painfully evident that military modernization, drawing heavily upon these scarce elements, was in direct and crucial competition with Chinese economic growth.[41]

Chinese production of conventional arms practically ceased in the wake of the Great Leap Forward and the mid-1960 withdrawal of Soviet military assistance. Since then there has been a generally upward trend—with periods of rapid growth in 1964-1966 and 1969-1971, each followed by a sharp decline. The first of these declines was an outcome of the Cultural Revolution; the second may have been associated with civilian military tensions generated by Lin Piao's fall from leadership in 1971 or by underlying disputes over economic priorities and budgetary allocations within the government—a feeling that in the long run Chinese security depended more on a strong economy than on military build-ups.[42] Given the intense competition for chronically scarce resources, current military expenditures may be viewed as maintaining the minimum necessary utility required in the present state of world affairs.[43]

Although the military modernization program may have been slowed down rather seriously, it has continued to claim a considerable share of the output of the Chinese metal-processing industry. Indeed, programs for the production of military equipment may have been stepped up in order to adjust for the loss of Soviet military assistance.[44]

During 1959, moreover, new research institutes were established to intensify the Chinese Communist program, and jet propulsion was identified as one of twelve major tasks, ranking next to developing peaceful uses of atomic energy.[45] During that year alone an estimated one-half of the three million workers, technicians, and engineers in Chinese machine-building industries were engaged in defense-oriented projects. By 1964 more than 400 senior scientists were reportedly engaged in nuclear physics in the Institute of Atomic Energy in the Chinese Academy of Sciences and in a number of Chinese universities.[46] And by the end of 1965 at least five of the eight ministries of machine-building industries were devoted to defense purposes.[47] Meanwhile, too, the Chinese Communist nuclear program was under development. One source estimates this program to have involved an annual investment of approximately $100 million and an annual operating cost of about $30 million.[48]

In the late 1960s it was estimated that the development of a French-type nuclear *force de frappe* would cost the People's Republic about $1 billion a year or—depending on the rate of exchange at which this sum is converted to yuan—something more than half the Chinese Communist defense budget in 1965.[49] On the other hand, official budget figures probably understate military expenditures, so that a modest nuclear strike program might absorb as little as 25 percent of the military budget, or an allocation of perhaps 2 or 3 percent of the Chinese GNP.[50] At best, such a program would entail "a quite sizable diversion of resources for an underdeveloped country with scarce technical manpower and a modest industrial base."[51] But Communist China appears to be both willing and able to make such diversions in pursuit of effective nuclear capability. The consequences with respect to the world power configuration and the probabilities of war and peace are not easy to assess.[52]

On November 18, 1971 in the atmosphere at its Lop Nor site in Sinkiang, the People's Republic conducted the twelfth in a series of nuclear tests dating from October 1964. Estimated to have been in the 20 kiloton range (equivalent to 20,000 tons of TNT), this explosion was considerably smaller than the previous one of October 1970, which was believed to have had the explosive force of 3 million tons of TNT. Another test at about the 20 kiloton level was completed on January 7, 1972, and three months later—on March 18 of that year—a test at a level somewhere between 20 and 2,000 kilotons was conducted.[53] Most of these tests have been tower releases, but some have been gravity drops from aircraft. It is widely assumed that these tests mark important steps in the Chinese program for developing an intercontinental ballistic missile system.[54]

A further indicator of China's progress in technology was the launching on April 24, 1970 of her second satellite, which, according to the Hsinhua News Agency, "successfully sent back scientific data on various experiments."

The Cultural Revolution's
Effects on the PLA

The People's Liberation Army, like the earlier Chinese Red Army, has always been closely tied to domestic political events and the fortunes of the people at large. If the Great Proletarian Cultural Revolution increased the power and influence of the PLA and raised Lin Piao to second place in the political hierarchy, it also had the longer-range effect of diffusing, even fragmenting, power throughout the Chinese polity and producing a pluralism that was somewhat reminiscent of the Kuomintang era but unprecedented under the People's Republic. Tensions and conflicts seem to have developed within the Party and government in Peking as well as between the central authority and groups in the provinces.

During the autumn of 1970 and the spring of 1971 the PLA became subject to considerable criticism. Increasing emphasis was placed upon the study of Marxism, Leninism, and Mao Tse-tung's thought among units of the PLA. Comrades in the military were accused of relying on empiricism at the expense of revolutionary theory and with insufficiently understanding "the important meaning of conscientious reading."[55] Units of the PLA were exhorted not to "rest on past laurels, but to carry out revolution more cautiously and attentively"—eliminating the "baggage of glory and merit," guarding against arrogance, conceit, complacency, stagnation, and inertia.[56]

In the autumn of 1971, Lin Piao, who had been officially designated as principal deputy and successor to Mao, suddenly disappeared. At the time there was no public warning or any explanation. Almost simultaneously the chief of staff of the People's Liberation Army and several other officials of top rank fell from sight. Later, in December 1971, the commanders of the eleven military regions, all of whom had been associated with Lin, were shifted to other positions. Subsequently it was announced that Lin, a conspirator and arch-traitor, had died in a plane crash while fleeing from an unsuccessful attempt to assassinate Mao.[57]

During the anti-Confucius, anti-Lin Piao campaign that ensued, bitter attacks were levelled against reliance on military incentives, foreign technology, and the leadership of rehabilitated bureaucrats.[58]

The Chinese Army in the Mid-1970s

The existence of the Chinese People's Liberation Army, even in its nonmodernized state, has exacted a powerful influence upon Asian affairs and possibly even upon world affairs. Despite its underdeveloped aspects, the Chinese economy "is capable of providing Communist China with a military potential which can, and indeed has, significantly altered the power balance on the Asian continent."[59]

In terms of its manpower and weapons characteristics, the PLA could be described as a defensive, rather than an offensive force—although what is defensive and what is offensive tends to be a subjective judgment depending very much on the observer's interests and perspectives. In any case, we expect that the Asian, if not the world, balance will be altered even further as the People's Republic progresses with the development of its nuclear warhead and missile capabilities.[60]

With somewhere between 2.9 and 3.5 million men under arms, the People's Liberation Army in the mid-1970s was second only to the Soviet Red Army in terms of manpower. About four-fifths of the PLA manpower appears to be concentrated in the ground forces, which were organized into approximately 160 divisions in 1975.[61] By that year, the number of armored divisions had increased from five in 1971 to seven, and the number of cavalry divisions from three to four. According to some authorities, the number of airborne divisions had increased from two to six, but these may have been essentially air transportable units. Among outside observers there was a widespread consensus that, with respect to modernity and quality, Chinese armed forces lagged significantly behind those of the United States and the Soviet Union.[62]

Among some United States and other military observers in the mid-1970s, there was an inclination to believe that there had been an overall slowdown in the production of Chinese weaponry—especially aircraft.[63] In any case, according to 1975 estimates something over 3,000 fighter aircraft were believed by Western observers to maintain responsibility in the air for the strategic home defense of the People's Republic.[64] Consisting of about 135,000 personnel in 1975, China's tactical air force, as assessed by the International Institute for Strategic Studies in London, is built largely around obsolescent Soviet-built aircraft, including about 1,500 MIG-17, 1,500 MIG-19, some 200 MIG-21, plus a few F-9 which are a Chinese derivation of the MIG-19. These and other fighter-interceptor aircraft were believed to lack all-weather capability, air-to-air missiles, and equipment for facilitating accurate ground strikes.[65]

China's naval manpower was estimated in 1975 by the International Institute for Strategic Studies at something less than 250,000, including land-based personnel. At that time, the fleet consisted of about 680 patrol boats and 20 escort vessels and destroyers. Officially, the Chinese navy ranked as the world's third largest, after those of the United States and the USSR, but it remained essentially a coastal defense force. Seriously vulnerable in antisubmarine warfare and related sensing techniques, the People's Republic had already launched a submarine expansion program that provided, by the close of 1975, an inventory of about 50 boats. It was generally agreed that China would be hard pressed to counter the Soviet Pacific fleet.[66]

By the mid-1970s the People's Republic had developed nuclear weapons for delivery by bombers and by medium- as well as intermediate-range ballistic missiles (IRBMs and MRBMs) which encompassed most of Asia within their range. Submarine-launched ballistic missiles and longer range land-based missiles were also believed to be under development, as well as a nuclear-powered attack submarine.[67] In 1975 the number of Chinese nuclear weapons in hand was estimated to be something between 20 and 30 IRBMs (deployed in permanent sites with a range of about 1500 nautical miles) and about 50 MRBMs.[68]

Up to 1975 there had been no detected effort to produce an ABM system in China. SAM sites were limited in number but increases had been noted in common antiaircraft weapons. As delivery vehicles, China has deployed about 60 Tu-16 medium bombers with a combat radius of 1500 miles and part of a 400-strong Il-28 force, with a combat radius short of 1000 miles. But the core of Chinese deterrent capability has been a land-based ballistic missile force of about 30 intermediate-range ballistic missiles of 1250 miles range and about 50 medium-range ballistic missiles with a 700-mile range. A 3500-mile-range ballistic missile has begun operational deployment tests. The development of a submarine-launched missile capability may already be underway.[69]

In the mid-1970s the People's Republic maintained a domestically produced air defense radar system and a ballistic missile early warning system "giving 90 percent coverage against Soviet missiles." The chairman of the United States Joint Chiefs of Staff referred to China's air defense system at this time as "outmoded."[70]

As viewed from a conventional Western perspective, the military capabilities of the People's Republic have been somewhat limited. China has been able to provide significant military aid to neighboring communist countries such as North Korea and Vietnam. Its volunteer forces turned the tide during the Korean War. Chinese troops successfully invaded India. The People's Republic has effected more limited operations such as the capture of Hainan Island (1950), the take-over of Tibet (1950-1951), a series of military exchanges in the Taiwan Straits (1954 and 1958), continuing action against Soviet troops along the border (1960s and 1970s), and the take-over of the Paracel Islands (1974).[71] The regime has been able to infiltrate noncommunist countries with guerrilla units and has applied large-scale pressure on the borders of India and other neighboring countries. Increasingly, the Chinese have been exporting arms to other countries.[72] Most significantly, however, the People's Liberation Army and Chinese nuclear development have had the overall effect, since 1950, of discouraging whatever serious intrusions into Mainland China may have been contemplated by Nationalist China, the United States, the Soviet Union, India, or any other country. In addition, these capabilities have raised China to a position the whole world must reckon with.

As assessed during the mid-1970s, the People's Republic could not mount a full-scale war against major targets such as the United States or the Soviet Union, although it could fight a conventional war against these powers on its own territory or close to its own borders. China has been viewed by outside observers as threatening to dominate East and South Asia on land by its military potential; this possibility has undoubtedly been enhanced by the withdrawal of United States troops from Southeast Asia.

From its own perspective, the Soviet Union, while expanding its interests in the Mediterranean, Africa, and the Middle East, has tried to stabilize the military situation in South and Southeast Asia by increasing its stake in Vietnam and, recently, in India and by moving naval forces into the Indian Ocean and South China Sea. As viewed by Peking, such extensions of Soviet influence amount to a flanking of China on the south as well as the north. The uncertain balance of the early and middle 1970s could change very rapidly, however, if China were to make rapid strides in its nuclear and missile-delivery capability. It appears that the post-Maoist leadership has every intention of pursuing this course. Only a few weeks after Mao's death, China conducted, on November 17, 1976, its fourth nuclear test of the year—the largest yet undertaken. The test was described as a complete success—although quantities of fallout were subsequently reported as far away as the eastern coast of the United States. To the extent that the Chinese are successful in their nuclear and other military efforts, the whole world balance of military power might be altered in ways that, in view of the lack of historical precedent, are difficult to identify or foretell.

Notes

1. Robert F. Bernberger, "The Economic Consequences of Defense Expenditure Choices in China," in *China: A Reassessment of the Economy*, (Washington, D.C.: U.S. Government Printing Office, 1975), p. 468.

2. See Lt. Colonel Robert B. Rigg, *Red China's Fighting Hordes* (Harrisburg, Pa.: Military Service, 1951), p. 13.

3. Mao Tse-tung, *Selected Works*, vol. 1 (New York: International, 1954), p. 66.

4. Ibid., p. 79.

5. Ibid., p. 82.

6. Ibid.

7. Ibid., pp. 82-83.

8. Ibid., vol. 2, p. 239.

9. Ibid., vol. 1, p. 81.

10. Alexander L. George, *The Chinese Communist Army in Action* (New York: Columbia University Press, 1967), p. 25.

11. Ibid., p. 26.

12. Ibid., p. 32.

13. Mao, *Selected Works*, vol. 1, p. 105.

14. Ibid., p. 83.

15. Ibid., p. 124.

16. Rigg, *Red China's Fighting Hordes*, p. 10.

17. "Economic Consequences of Defense Expenditure," p. 467.

18. Sydney H. Jammes, "The Chinese Defense Burden, 1965-74," in *China: A Reassessment*, p. 466.

19. J. G. Godaire, "Communist China's Defense Establishment: Some Economic Implications," in *An Economic Profile of Mainland China*, vol. 1, Studies Prepared for the Joint Economic Committee, Congress of the United States (Washington, D.C.: U.S. Government Printing Office, 1967), p. 161; and Jammes, "Chinese Defense Burden, 1965-74," p. 460.

20. Godaire, "Communist China's Defense Establishment," pp. 161-62.

21. Jammes, "Chinese Defense Burden, 1965-74," p. 468.

22. Godaire, "Communist China's Defense Establishment," p. 164.

23. Ibid.

24. Ralph L. Powell, *Politico-Military Relationships in Communist China*, U.S. Department of State, Bureau of Intelligence and Research, October 1963, p. 2.

25. Harold P. Ford, "Modern Weapons and the Sino-Soviet Estrangement," *China Quarterly*, no. 18 (April-June 1964), p. 160.

26. T'an Cheng as quoted in Alice Langley Hsieh, *Communist China's Strategy in the Nuclear Era* (Englewood Cliffs, N.J.: Prentice-Hall, 1962), p. 57. Text in *Current Background*, no. 422 (October 18, 1956), pp. 13-21.

27. Ellis Joffee, "The Conflict Between Old and New in the Chinese Army," *China Quarterly*, no. 18 (April-June 1964), p. 132.

28. "New Training Programme Promulgated by the General Department of Supervision of Training," *Liberation Army Daily*, January 16, 1958, in *Survey of China Mainland Press*, no. 1786, p. 808.

29. Ford, "Modern Weapons," p. 162.

30. Joffee, "The Conflict Between Old and New," p. 132, quoting from the *New York Times,* September 14, 1963.
31. See Hsieh, *Communist China's Strategy,* pp. 98-109.
32. *Peking Review,* no. 33 (August 16, 1963), p. 14.
33. Ibid.
34. Morton H. Halperin and John Wilson Lewis, "New Tensions in Army-Party Relations in China (1965-1966)," *China Quarterly,* no. 26 (April-June 1966), p. 58.
35. John Gittings, "China's Militia," *China Quarterly,* no. 18 (April-June 1964), pp. 100, 110.
36. "Resolution Made by the Enlarged Meeting of the Military Affairs Commission of the Central Authorities of the Chinese Communist Party on Strengthening Political and Ideological Work in the Army," Peking, October 20, 1960, *Bulletin of Activities of the People's Liberation Army,* no. 3 (January 7, 1961), in J. Chester Cheng (ed.), *The Politics of the Chinese Red Army* (Stanford, Calif.: Hoover Institution, 1966), p. 67.
37. Powell, *Politico-Military Relationships,* p. 2.
38. Ibid., p. 1.
39. "Resolution Made on Work in the Army," in Cheng, *The Politics of the Chinese Red Army,* p. 67.
40. Halperin and Lewis, "New Tensions in Army-Party Relations," p. 59.
41. Godaire, "Communist China's Defense Establishment," p. 164.
42. Jammes, "Chinese Defense Burden, 1965-74," p. 464.
43. Angus H. Fraser, "The Utility of Alternate Strategic Postures to the People's Republic of China," in *China: A Reassessment,* pp. 457-58; see also Fraser's *The People's Liberation Army: Communist China's Armed Forces,* National Strategy Information Center, Inc. (New York: Crane, Russak and Company, 1973), pp. 17-25.
44. Alexander Eckstein, *Communist China's Economic Growth and Foreign Trade* (New York: McGraw Hill, 1966), pp. 164-65.
45. Chu-yuan Cheng, "Scientific and Engineering Manpower in Communist China," in *An Economic Profile of Mainland China,* vol. 2, p. 544.
46. Ibid.
47. Ibid.
48. Eckstein, *Communist China's Economic Growth,* p. 262, quoting Dwight Perkins.
49. Ibid.
50. Ibid., p. 263.
51. Ibid., pp. 262-63.
52. For comparisons of the conventional and nuclear capabilities of various countries, including the People's Republic of China, see *SIPRI Yearbook of 1975, World Armaments and Disarmament,* Stockholm International Peace Research Institute (New York: Humanities Press, 1976).
53. Jonathan D. Pollack, "Chinese Attitudes Toward Nuclear Weapons, 1964-69," *China Quarterly* (April-June 1972), p. 271.
54. *New York Times,* November 19, 1971, p. 1.
55. Peking, *Kuang-ming Jih-pao,* March 14, 1971, in *Survey of China Mainland Press,* no. 4867 (March 29, 1971), pp. 1-5.
56. Peking, *Jen-min Jih-pao,* April 6, 1971, in *Survey of China Mainland Press,* no. 4883 (April 23, 1971).
57. Fraser, "Utility of Alternate Strategic Postures," p. 452.

58. Arthur G. Ashbrook, Jr., "China: Economic Overview, 1975" in *China: A Reassessment,* p. 27.
59. Eckstein, *Communist China's Economic Growth,* p. 251.
60. Fraser, *The People's Liberation Army,* pp. 13-16.
61. *Strategic Survey* (London: The International Institute for Strategic Studies, 1975), p. 101.
62. Fraser, "Utility of Alternative Strategic Postures," p. 444; see also Fraser, *The People's Liberation Army,* pp. 4-16.
63. Fraser, "Utility of Alternate Strategic Postures," p. 446.
64. Ibid.
65. *Strategic Survey,* pp. 101-102.
66. Ibid., p. 101.
67. Jammes, "Chinese Defense Burden, 1965-74," p. 459.
68. Fraser, "Utility of Alternative Strategic Postures," p. 447.
69. *Strategic Survey,* p. 102.
70. Ibid., p. 446.
71. Ibid., p. 442.
72. For world patterns in the selling of arms, see Stockholm International Peace Research Institute, *The Arms Trade with the Third World* (Stockholm: Almqvist and Wiksell, 1971).

PART 2

Describing and
Projecting Chinese
Communist Foreign
Policy

Chapter Five

Chinese Foreign Relations: Overview of the first decade and a half

Many Western observers have tended to examine Chinese Communist policy and behavior largely in terms of Marxist-Leninist-Maoist ideology. Previous chapters have suggested, however, that Chinese history, custom, and tradition, the capabilities of China, its position in the world configuration of power, and levels of dissatisfaction with the status quo are extremely important factors.

It would be useful to begin with a discussion of how Chinese foreign policy is made and how decisions in foreign affairs are reached. The available documentation does not provide many clues in this sphere, however, and inferences are not easily drawn. Throughout the course of Chinese Communist development since the early 1920s, there have been repeated efforts to analyze both domestic and foreign policymaking in terms of contending Party cliques. With the emergence of the Sino-Soviet conflict, outside observers have often tried to analyze policies and decisions according to the prominence of leaders and cliques and their supposed tendencies in the past to take a rightist, leftist, or center position on major issues and to connect these tendencies, in one way or another, with attitudes toward the Soviet Union and the United States. This approach has led to some useful insights and numerous predictions, a few reasonably accurate. But good analysis depending on the observation of leadership cliques requires long experience on the part of the observer, a great deal of intuition, much speculation, and a certain amount of luck. Generally, the usefulness of this approach is limited at best.

Unquestionably, Marxist-Leninist-Maoist ideology goes a long way toward shaping Chinese Communist views of the world and human history and has a profound influence on what Chinese Communist leaders expect other countries to do. Ideology has also been of central importance in organizing the national will, guiding policy and disciplining its implementation. Sometimes there has been a tendency in the West to view ideology as the single overriding determinant in Chinese affairs and the foreign relations of the People's Republic as part of a vast Marxist-Leninist-Maoist plot — largely hostile, aggressive, expansive, and even irrationally belligerent. But evidence produced by Chinese Communist behavior since 1950 strongly suggests that (within limits shaped, in part at least, by ideological considerations) the leadership of the Chinese Communist party has been rather pragmatic on issues of foreign policy, as well as domestic policy, basing decisions on "a continuing calculation of the world balance of power" — although with other considerations also playing their parts. The Sino-Soviet conflict, in particular, suggests that when the Peking leadership has perceived that Chinese interests and the power of the People's Republic are at stake, these considerations have overridden ideological loyalties. In retrospect, moreover, the overall policy of the People's Republic appears to have been more rational, less aggressive, more concerned with self-defense, and more selective in its policies of growth than many outside observers had expected.

Nevertheless, two diametrically opposed views with respect to many aspects of Communist China have been widely held: one, that "there is no new thing under the sun"; the other, that "the former things are passed away; behold, all things are become new." The first view tends to be held by those who consider historical trends and predispositions of Chinese history and Chinese culture more lasting and significant than Marxism-Leninism or other influences from the outside. This suggests that indigenous factors of the past are the most significant clues to the future, that in the long run disturbing influences from the outside will be overshadowed by the persistence or reassertion of Chinese values and ways of doing things. On the other hand, the second view is often held by those who see communism, extended form Moscow, as the central determining factor that has overridden virtually all other considerations in Chinese revolutionary developments over recent decades.

In more specific terms, although some Westerners expected Mao Tse-tung and his colleagues to establish a relatively mild, Tito-style government, others predicted extreme Chinese Communist militancy and expansionism. So far, reality seems to have emerged somewhere in between — but not where almost anyone expected. To date, then, there is no firm evidence for choosing definitely between these polar views, "nor for the assumption that the truth lies nearer the middle than the extremes." With respect to many, if not most, Chinese Communist considerations, the "question is still open," although we can scarcely avoid putting forward certain propositions and assessments.[1] In general, however, the People's Republic, despite many characteristics that have set it apart from other countries, appears to have based its foreign policies upon certain fundamental principles that are normally pursued by sovereign states.

Like most other countries, the People's Republic of China is concerned with the defense of its borders and the preservation of its integrity as an independent, sovereign actor. Moreover, as an outcome of its long history of economic, political, and military penetration by Western powers and Japan, the Maoist regime has been persistent in its determination to expel outside interests from within its boundaries and to maintain control over its domestic institutions, policies, and processes. These tendencies go a long way toward explaining the relationships of the Peking regime with the USSR, as well as with the United States, Japan, the Republic of China on Taiwan, and a number of other countries.

The various Taiwan Straits crises are largely attributable to these major elements of policy. In retrospect, it is also evident that much of the militancy and expansionism that seemed to characterize Chinese foreign policy, especially during the 1950s, could be attributed to the intent of the regime to reestablish at least the more prominent historical boundaries of the old empire. To a large extent the absorption of Tibet, the Korean intervention, the Sino-Indian border dispute, and aspects of the Sino-Soviet conflict can be explained in similar terms. In this connection, it must be noted that in spite of current accommodations with the status quo, the People's Republic still maintains that Taiwan and Hong Kong rightfully belong with the Mainland regime. In addition, the People's Republic also asserts a right to considerable territories within the USSR that were once a part of the old empire, although there is no current evidence that Peking has any intention of acting on these claims in the foreseeable future.

Although the People's Republic provided some assistance — especially in the 1950s and early 1960s — to dissident movements in the Congo, Burma, Indonesia, and elsewhere in Asia, Africa, and Latin America, the Peking regime has supported the general principle that revolution cannot be successfully exported from one country to another. Furthermore, the desire for relations with newly established governments in the Third World has increasingly inhibited Chinese support to revolutionary factions in those regimes. According to Maoist views, a revolutionary regime such as the People's Republic can advise and assist a foreign revolutionary movement, but the main dynamics must emerge within the other country as a result of internal contradictions and conflicts. In line with the Panch Shila, or Five Principles, proclaimed by China and India in 1954, however, the People's Republic has maintained the proposition that "all countries, big or small, should be equal and that the Five Principles of Peaceful Coexistence should be taken as the principles guiding the relationship between countries." According to these Principles, the people of each country have the right "to choose the social system of their own country" and "to protect the independence, sovereignty, and territorial integrity of their own country."[2]

A still different perspective is obtained when one examines broad statements of Chinese foreign policy made over the years by leaders and official spokesmen of the Peking regime. Admittedly, the actual foreign policies and activities of a country may diverge considerably from the principles enunciated by its leaders, but often much can be learned by a comparison of the two — foreign policies as they are professed and foreign policies as they are actually carried out over a period of time. Although the People's Republic has seemed to diverge from their professed policies in a number of specific instances, overall, from a current perspective, there appears to be a considerable correlation between the two.

This chapter will be concerned with the overall development of China's foreign relations during the first decade and a half after the establishment of the People's Republic. Subsequent chapters will deal with China's relations with the United States, the USSR, Europe, other Asian countries, Africa and South America since the mid-1960s.

The Varied Nature of Chinese Communist Foreign Policies

In operational terms, the Peking regime has been relatively more modest in putting forward territorial claims than some of its aggressive policy statements might have led observers to expect. Specifically, the active policy claims of the Chinese People's Republic have been confined so far to China proper, Taiwan, Manchuria, Inner Mongolia, Sinkiang, Tibet, and the Paracel and Spratly Islands in the South China Sea. More ambitious

claims to territory in the USSR, Southeast Asia, south of the Himalayas, and elsewhere have not been translated into active policy. The
Chinese People's Republic moved quickly to reintegrate Tibet into
national territory — largely by force of arms. In general, however,
the new regime was less aggressive in its lateral expansion than many
outside observers had expected. Hong Kong, which Great Britain
annexed in 1842, was not molested by the new regime — in part,
perhaps, because of the Crown Colony's role as the single largest
earner of foreign exchange among noncommunist sources. Macao,
for the time being, was allowed to remain in the posession of
Portugal.

Specific Chinese Communist foreign policy goals seem to include
(1) maintenance of the security and integrity of the Chinese People's
Republic, (2) efforts to seize Taiwan, (3) the unification under the
Peking regime of outlying or alienated territories that the leadership
considers to be rightfully integral parts of the Chinese People's
Republic, (4) the (outward) adjustment of Chinese boundaries in the
Himalayas and elsewhere, (5) the protection and enhancement of
Chinese Communist power and influence, especially in adjoining
regions of Asia, and also in competition with the USSR, and (6) the
development of "bargain basement" methods of influencing Asian,
African, and even Latin American countries by economic and technical assistance and by advice on guerrilla warfare and political and
economic policy.

Chinese Communist implementations of foreign policy have
ranged over a wide spectrum from nonviolent instrumentalities
through various levels of violence — including incidents at Quemoy,
Matsu, and elsewhere involving relatively low levels of force, an invasion of (and withdrawal from) Indian territory, and war in Korea.

Among nonviolent instrumentalities are the normal negotiations,
diplomatic exchanges, information arrangements, and cultural programs more or less common to all contemporary nation-states. Also
included is the more specialized people's diplomacy that applies
Marxist-Leninist-Maoist principles and styles to propaganda and cultural programs. These are aimed, for the most part, at militant
nationalist and dissatisfied minority groups and leftist or potentially
revolutionary organizations that the People's Republic hopes to
influence.[3]

Upon achieving power in 1949, the general tendency of the
Chinese Communist leadership was to seek normalization of diplomatic relations with most other nations of the world. In appealing
for general diplomatic recognition, however, the People's Republic
made explicit that it would enter into formal relations only with
those governments that had severed relations with the Nationalist
government and that stood ready to adopt a friendly attitude to the

new Communist regime.[4] Mao and his colleagues announced that they would examine all treaties concluded by the Nationalist government and recognize, revise, renegotiate, or abrogate them according to their contents.[5] In fact, most of them were allowed to lapse.

Over ensuing months, all communist countries — including Yugoslavia — recognized the Chinese People's Republic, as did the United Kingdom, Switzerland, the Scandinavian countries, Israel, and six Asian neutrals (Afghanistan, Burma, Ceylon, India, Indonesia, and Pakistan). The new regime reciprocated in all cases except with respect to Yugoslavia, which did not receive recognition from Peking until five years later.

At first it was not clear whether or not the United States would recognize the People's Republic of China, there being strong predispositions in both directions by sectors of the American populace. However, a series of incidents threatening the lives or property of American citizens and consular representatives in Manchuria and China proper, the doubts and tensions raised by the investigations and accusations of communist influence in the State Department by Senator Joseph McCarthy, the activities of the pro-Nationalist China lobby in the United States, and the militant behavior of the Chinese Communists themselves — especially with the outbreak of the Korean War — combined to strengthen the influence of those who were in strong opposition to recognition of the new regime.

The Chinese People's Republic also laid prompt claim to China's permanent seat on the Security Council of the United Nations. In this effort the regime was blocked by the Republic of China on Taiwan and by a majority of members in the United Nations General Assembly, especially by the United States. Over subsequent years, the United Nations-sponsored police action in Korea, increasing United States commitment to Chiang Kai-shek's Nationalist regime, the fact that Nationalist China was a permanent member of the Security Council, and a variety of other factors tended to harden the lines of resistance, especially on the part of the United States and many smaller countries dependent on United States military and economic assistance, to Peking's admission to the international body.

The rights and wrongs of the situation are difficult to establish, but the following generalizations can be made with some confidence:

1. The Chinese Communist regime tapped a tremendous reservoir of dissatisfactions — peasant dissatisfaction with the land system, dissatisfactions on the part of many intellectuals with the Nationalist regime, animosities on many levels generated by the interventions in and exploitation of China by European powers and by Japan, tensions stimulated by a large and growing population coupled with an inadequate technology, and so forth.

2. Many people in the United States experienced deep anxieties and fears because of the establishment of a new communist regime

over the most populous country on earth. In some instances, what had formerly been a vague fear of "yellow peril" took more specific form as anti-communism. There was also a tendency in some quarters to feel a particularly deep-seated and subtle resentment arising from the fact that a people whom American missionaries had been trying to convert to Christianity for several generations, sometimes on "little brown brother assumptions," had ended up in the camp of "Godless, atheistic communism."

3. Chinese feelings of resentment and hostility and American feelings of challenge, uncertainty, fear, anxiety, and perhaps a desire to chastise, tended to feed the conflict and encourage both sides toward suspicion, hostility, intransigence, and the defense of dubious positions.

Meanwhile, the Peking regime appeared to be forging strong ties with the Soviet Union. Within two months after his proclamation of the Chinese People's Republic, Mao Tse-tung was on his way to Moscow in order to negotiate an alliance with Stalin. He arrived in the Soviet capital in December 1949 and stayed eight weeks. A major outcome was the thirty-year Treaty of Friendship, Alliance and Mutual Assistance signed February 14, 1950.[6] It is now well known, of course, that good relations between the two countries were short-lived.

Crises Involving Peking

Jan F. Triska has identified at least twenty-three crises between 1949 and 1965 in which the Chinese Communists were directly involved (see Table 5.1).[7] Of these crises, three (the Sino-Soviet of 1960, the Soviet-Albanian of 1961, and the Sino-Soviet of 1963) were essentially political confrontations. Insofar as the Chinese People's Republic was a party, the Vietnam crisis of 1954 largely involved material aid to the Democratic Republic of Vietnam (DRV) and threats against the French. The Sino-Japanese crisis of 1958 was also essentially political, but there were incidents of minor force. The Sino-Burmese crisis of 1955 included threats and troop movements but not much overt violence. The Laotian crisis of 1960-1961 also involved troop movements but not a high level of overt violence. The Indonesian crisis of 1959 included clashes between local Chinese and the Indonesian government, but the Chinese People's Republic was not directly, or at least overtly, involved in the violence. The Sino-Indian border dispute of 1959 and the Kashmir crisis of 1965 included clashes of troops. The other thirteen crises involved varying amounts of force — especially, of course, the Korean fighting, which was a full-scale war.

Table 5.1 Crises involving the Chinese People's Republic—1949–65

Legend:
CPR   Chinese People's Republic
DRK   Democratic Republic of Korea (North Korea)
DRV   Democratic Republic of Vietnam (North Vietnam)
KMT   Kuomintang (Nationalist China)
ROK   Republic of Korea (South Korea)
ROV   Republic of Vietnam (South Vietnam)

DATE	CRISIS	PARTIES	OUTCOME
1949	Vietnam	KMT, French government in Vietnam vs. CPR	Peking successfully kept KMT out of Vietnam; Viet Minh launched first successful assault against Saigon forces
1950	Tibet	CPR vs. Tibet, India	China reasserted suzerainty over Tibet; India made concessions
1950	Korea (Chinese intervention)	U.S./U.N., ROK vs. COR, DRK/USSR	Protracted conflict without apparent resolution
1950–51	Taiwan Straits	U.S. vs. CPR	No invasion of Taiwan; U.S. limited material and diplomatic support of Taiwan
1950–51	Full Chinese offensive in Korea	CPR/DRK/USSR vs. U.S./ U.N., ROK	Compromise and delayed withdrawal
1954	Vietnam	U.S. vs. CPR/DRV	China derived communist-dominated government in Vietnam received diplomatic recognition through presence at Geneva Conference as one of Five Great Powers
1954–55	Offshore islands	CPR vs. U.S./Republic of China	CPR deterred U.S.-sponsored KMT invasion of Mainland, isolated U.S. from allies on Taiwan issue; U.S. forced to reassert for KMT regime; CPR gained several offshore islands

DATE	CRISIS	PARTIES	OUTCOME
1955–56	Sino-Burmese border	CPR vs. Burma	Limited but significant territorial gains for China; increased image of CPR as strong but magnanimous; closer ties between two nations
1958	Quemoy	CPR vs. KMT/U.S.	Quemoy and Matsu remain in KMT hands; political status of Taiwan not altered; U.S. forced to commit itself to defense of Quemoy-Matsu; KMT forced to abandon plans to invade Mainland; crisis probably increased tension in Sino-Soviet relations
1958	Friction with Japan	CPR vs. Japan (KMT participating)	Trade loss for both nations; loss of CPR prestige among neutrals; hardening of Japan's nonrecognition policy; failure of Peking to influence Japanese elections; sacrifice of previous gains in Sino-Japanese rapprochement
1959	Tibet	Khamba tribesmen (India an interested party) vs. CPR	CPR repressed rebellion after some 65,000 rebels killed; retained and increased control over Tibet
1959	Sino-Indian border	CPR vs. India	Temporary, de facto settlement; limited territorial gains for CPR; Five Principles of Peaceful Coexistence tarnished; loss of CPR prestige in Third World; wavering of Indian neutrality; heightened Indian preparations; Indian disillusionment with Sino-Indian harmony
1959–60	Indonesia	Indonesia vs. CPR	Treaty of 1955 signed with political gains for both sides; China made most concessions; 40,000 Chinese nationals returned to China; curtailment of position of Chinese population in Indonesia

DATE	CRISIS	PARTIES	OUTCOME
1960	Sino-Soviet conflict: Bucharest	CPR vs. USSR	CPR made tactical retreat, lost prestige and economic assistance; shows of solidarity in pro-Soviet ranks
1960	Sino-Soviet conflict: Moscow	USSR vs. CPR	Stalemate; USSR may have gained slight edge; CPR gained Albania as ally
1960–61	Laos	Laotian rightists with U.S. support vs. CPR with USSR and DRV	Geneva Conference accepted CPR's demand for a neutral Laos; CPR preserved leverage in Laos through military base area in that country; Pathet Lao retained control of Laos highlands, keeping supply routes open into South Vietnam
1961	Soviet-Albanian dispute	USSR vs. Albania (with CPR support)	Albania suspended from pro-Moscow international socialist movement; CPR assured of a continuing ally
1962	Taiwan Straits	U.S./KMT vs. CPR	Temporary de facto settlement; no territorial or political gains to either side; U.S.-KMT relations further strained; KMT again restrained from invading Mainland
1962	Sino-Indian border	India (only in technical sense goaded by CPR) vs. CPR	Minor territorial gains for CPR; humiliating defeat for India; subsequent taxing Indian defense expenditures
1963	Sino-Soviet conflict	CPR vs. USSR	Failure of CPSU–CPC talks; shift from euphemistic polemics to public acrimony; stalemate in ideological dispute; further Chinese failure to discourage test-ban treaty
1964	Gulf of Tonkin	U.S./ROV vs. DRV/CPR	Direct and immediate Sino-U.S. confrontation avoided; basis for increased U.S. intervention in Vietnam

DATE	CRISIS	PARTIES	OUTCOME
1965	U.S. bombing of DRV	U.S./ROV vs. DRV/CPR	Response of CPR remained essentially verbal, although bombing led to increases in CPR support to DRV; CPR forced to redefine and restrict criteria of intolerable U.S. "aggression"
1965	Kashmir conflict	Pakistan (CPR) vs. India (U.S., USSR, U.N. participants)	Tashkent Agreement, January 1966, provided status quo ante; CPR lost prestige; Pakistan evinced gratitude for CPR assistance

All of the crises in which the Chinese Communists used overt force were more or less concerned with attempts to seize territory held by the Nationalists, the repelling of Nationalist attacks, and the reestablishment or (from Peking's viewpoint) the defense of China's borders. For example, in October 1950 Chinese Communist forces invaded Tibet and established military and administrative headquarters. Units of the People's Liberation Army entered the country on October 7, 1950. By the end of November these and other Chinese Communist forces had gained wide control over the eastern regions and had secured a footing in the west. These actions antagonized, India, which according to a public statement by Prime Minister Nehru, had never recognized Chinese suzerainty over Tibet. Through an exchange of notes, the Indian Government asserted that the Chinese invasion was entirely without justification, whereupon Peking accused New Delhi of being under the influence of foreign powers hostile to China. In the end, the Indian government gave way, recognizing Chinese suzerainty and disclaiming any desire to interfere in China's domestic problems. Tibet appealed to the United Nations, but discussion was postponed indefinitely, the member states being preoccupied with Korea.[8]

In Tibet and elsewhere in territory claimed by the People's Republic, conflicts tended to develop over ensuing years when the Chinese incorporated non-Chinese peoples, who frequently (sometimes through their own Communist party organizations) vociferously charged the Peking regime of "Great Han imperialism."

Undoubtedly, the Chinese Communist leaders would have preferred to implement their policies by methods short of war. It has always been a central tenet of both Maoist policy and guerrilla strategy and tactics to invest little or no energy in actual confrontations of armed force for the attainment of objectives that can be achieved by alternative means. On the other hand, the Chinese Communists, when they have had violent instruments available, have tended not to hesitate to use them under circumstances that have seemed appropriate.

Early Encouragement of Armed Struggle

As early as 1926 a spokesman for the Communist International in Moscow had predicted the defeat of Japan in a major war, to be followed by the transformation of the conflict into a vast liberation movement of Asian countries oppressed by foreign imperialism. Under these circumstances, a liberated China was to develop into a major power in the Pacific and serve as a magnet for drawing together all peoples of the yellow race in Asia as a threat to the capitalist world of three continents.[9]

From 1947 to 1951, the Chinese Communist leadership followed a policy of encouraging armed struggle beyond China's borders. The effort seems to have been less for the purpose of acquiring new territory (except along doubtful borders) than to encourage the establishment of new, communist-dominated regimes. During late 1949 and early 1950, the Peking regime, with confidence in its ability to capture Taiwan, made preparations for what was to be the biggest campaign in the history of modern Chinese warfare." But in June 1950 the United States, responding to the Korean crisis, neutralized the Taiwan Straits and thus prevented the Chinese Communists from achieving their purpose. Peking accused the United States of turning Taiwan into a colony and a military base for attacking the mainland.[10]

Since 1947 the Chinese Communist leaders had been exhorting other Asian communist movements to follow the way of Mao Tse-tung by advancing armed struggle. In November 1959 the World Federation of Trade Unions met in Peking. Major speeches and much discussion were devoted to problems of armed rebellion in various parts of Asia. Even today, the direct, practical connections between the Peking meetings (and the years of Chinese Communist espousal of armed rebellion) and various insurrectionary movements in Asia during the late 1940s and early 1950s are difficult to assess: conditions were favorable for revolution in most of the areas, and Chinese Communist encouragement was perhaps not a prerequisite for armed rebellions. There can be little doubt, however, that Chinese Communist example and influence had a powerful impact on armed uprisings that took place in Burma, India, Indonesia, Malaya, the Philippines, and elsewhere.

Not all Asian communists were in favor of what were sometimes viewed as uncritical adaptations of Maoist theory and practice. In July 1949 the editorial board of the Bombay *Communist* attacked the pro-Peking wing of the Communist party of India for drawing parallels between Asian revolutionary activities and the experience of Mao Tse-tung. In fact, they said, Mao had placed too much emphasis on the peasantry, to the neglect of the proletariat: "We must state emphatically that the Communist party of India has accepted Marx, Engels, Lenin, and Stalin as the authoritative sources of Marxism. It has not discovered new sources of Marxism beyond these."[11] Later, however, on July 27, 1950, the Cominform publication *For a Lasting Peace, For A People's Democracy* used a quotation from Liu Shao-ch'i to reprimand the Bombay editors: "The path taken by the Chinese people in defeating imperialism and its lackeys and in founding the People's Republic of China should be taken by the people of many colonial and dependent countries in their struggle for national independence and the people's democracy."[12]

The Early Basis for
Sino-American
Disputes in Asia

One aspect of communist armed struggle in Southeast Asia involved a rebellion of the Viet Minh against France. As Chinese Communist rule was extended to China's southern border after Maoist victories on the mainland, the Peking regime began giving large-scale assistance to the Viet Minh.[13]

Vietnam had first been brought into the Chinese orbit as far back as the third century B.C.; in 207 B.C. a Chinese general, having served as imperial delegate to the delta region, declared himself king of Nam Viet (Southern Land). This was the first of several similar states to be formed, to disintegrate, and to be reformed over the next two thousand years in that particular sphere of Chinese influence. In ancient times, a major Chinese goal was to inhibit development in the delta region of too strong a state near China's southern frontier. The Chinese also wanted a privileged position there in order to flank trade routes to India and the Mediterranean. And, finally, it was useful to have a buffer there between the empire and barbarians in Southeast Asia. At least some of these goals are probably relevant today. As suggested by Doak Barnett, almost all strong Chinese governments have regarded Vietnam as a strategic buffer and also as a natural sphere of Chinese influence.[14]

With the fall of France and the Low Countries to Nazi Germany during the early phases of World War II, Japanese leaders began to speculate about the disposition of French and Dutch colonial possessions in Asia.[15] Particularly, they were afraid that Germany might obtain political control of French Indochina and the Netherlands East Indies.[16] In efforts to avoid what they perceived as encirclement by the United States, Great Britain, and other powers, Japan was hoping to achieve a monopoly over the rubber, tin, and rice of Indochina and to use the French colony as a base for attacking Malaya and Indonesia.[17] The Japanese occupation of southern Indochina in 1941 threatened all of Southeast Asia; the Japanese thrust into northern Vietnam was aimed specifically at China. Ultimately, the result of World War II for Vietnam, as for other parts of Asia and for China itself, was the weakening of imperialist influences from both Europe and Japan—a weakening that set many of the conditions for revolt and revolution during the 1950s and 1960s. Chinese interests would be served best if a pro-Chinese, or at the very least a neutral, regime were established over the whole of Vietnam with a minimum of outside influence other than that of China itself.

In 1949, on the basis of three years of armed conflict between Vietnamese nationalist forces and French troops trying to restore order, France began to organize a Vietnamese national army and an autonomous Vietnamese state. These hostilities led into a combined civil war and an anti-imperialist war against French forces.[18] In November 1949—not long after Chinese Communist troops, in clearing southern China of Nationalist forces, had first reached the Vietnamese border—Liu Shao-ch'i asserted in a speech before the World Federation of Trade Unions conference in Peking that the "war of national liberation" in Vietnam had "liberated" ninety percent of Vietnamese territory.[19] A crisis developed at about this time when Nationalist Chinese units, fleeing from the People's Liberation Army, began crossing the frontier into Vietnam. Peking claimed the right of hot pursuit and issued allegations, threats, and warnings to French authorities, but refrained from military action. The crisis came to an end with French assurances to Peking that the Nationalist Chinese troops were being disarmed and interned.

The Chinese People's Republic recognized the Democratic Republic of Vietnam—established by the Viet Minh—early in 1950 and began providing it with sustained military support.[20] In the course of a telegram exchange by Mao and Ho Chi Minh, the Chinese leader stated that China and Vietnam were "meeting on the front line" of an anti-imperialist struggle for the liberation of the two peoples.[21] In short order, the above-mentioned arrival of Chinese Communist forces at the Vietnamese border had transformed the struggle in Vietnam into a consideration of international importance. What had often been interpreted in many Western quarters as a local, somewhat leftist, but essentially nationalist guerrilla struggle tended now to be viewed in the United States and some other Western countries as a threatening front in the worldwide conflict with international communism.

The Chinese People's Republic especially wanted to protect the railway that joined Yunan province with Hanoi and Haiphong and with mineral deposits along the Sino-Vietnamese border. In line with past history, moreover, Chinese Communist leaders sought special relations with Vietnam as a base for a sphere of influence in Southeast Asia.

Early Chinese Relations with Japan

Chinese attitudes toward Japan were influenced by the record of Japanese aggressions against China during the 1930s and World War II and also by the presence of United States military forces in that country and on neighboring islands. The People's Republic refused to recognize the validity of the San Francisco Peace Treaty of 1951, though Japan renounced title to Taiwan without specifying to whom the sovereignty was transferred, and also a 1952 treaty by which Japan made peace with Chiang Kai-shek's Republic of China and thus implicitly recognized Nationalist title to Taiwan.[22] With the Korean War, Peking made whatever efforts it could to counteract the San Francisco settlement and reduce the value of Japan as a military base and as an ally of the United States. The People's Republic also hoped that the USSR would make the establishment of Soviet relations with Japan conditional upon the establishment of normal relations between Tokyo and Peking, but in this they were disappointed.

Perceiving Japan as a powerful economic competitor and, over the long run, a possible military rival, Chinese leaders were predisposed toward obstructing that country's ties with the United States and other countries of the West. But Japan's diplomatic recognition of Nationalist China required the Peking regime to rely heavily on Japanese leftist groups in order to exert pressure on the Tokyo government.

In 1957, with Japanese elections in the offing, the Peking regime tried to make the China question a Japanese campaign issue. Hence, a provision was placed in one of the trade proposals to the effect that Chinese Communist trade missions in Japan should have the right to fly the flag of the People's Republic. In response to Nationalist Chinese resentment, Premier Kishi reasserted his policy of nonrecognition, and on May 2 a Chinese Communist flag was torn down at the Chinese trade mission in Nagasaki. Four days later the Chinese Communists seized a number of Japanese fishermen in the Yellow Sea and announced thereafter that a bilateral fishing agreement between the two countries would be allowed to lapse. On May 30, after Kishi's reelection, Peking withdrew general permission for the entrance of Japanese vessels into Chinese ports. Then, in August, in protest of Japan's fingerprinting of foreign visitors, Peking cancelled a number of projected trade fairs, and in October ongoing trade talks were adjourned. Later, Tokyo modified the fingerprinting regulations, and trade negotiations were resumed.

Cognizant of socialist gains in the recent elections, Peking began pressing for normalized relations with Japan. A joint Sino-Japanese Socialist statement called for diplomatic recognition of the People's Republic, a bilateral peace treaty, and neutralization of the western Pacific.[23] In the spring of 1960, Peking extended a vociferous welcome to demonstrations in Japan against ratification of the revised security treaty with the United States.

The signing of a Sino-Japanese fisheries treaty on November 9, 1963 was an important step toward more normal relations between Japan and the People's Republic. However, progress was inhibited by the fact that Peking appeared to view the Japanese Communist party to be the true leader of the Japanese people's movement, and also by the growing Sino-Soviet controversy, which tended to put ·the USSR and the People's Republic in competition for influence within Japan.

The Sino-American Dispute

Taiwan, Korea and Indochina

In the aftermath of World War II, Korea—liberated from Japanese control—had been left divided by American and Soviet zones of occupation. United Nations efforts to reunite the country were not successful, and with the withdrawal of occupying forces, two rival governments emerged, each claiming overall sovereignty. In the wake of Mao Tse-tung's visit to Moscow in December 1949, the North Korean regime (the Democratic People's Republic of Korea) began to receive military support from the USSR and Communist China.

Initial United States support for South Korea (the Republic of Korea) was limited,[24] but world events were scarcely conducive to peace of mind among United States leaders. The USSR seemed dedicated to the extension of its power and influence along its western European, southern European, and Middle Eastern perimeters. Since the end of World War II there had been Soviet-American contests of will and capability in Iran (1946), Greece (1947-1948), and Berlin (1948-1949). Then, in August 1949, the USSR successfully exploded its first atomic bomb. Under these circumstances, it was perhaps not surprising that many Americans saw events in China, Korea, and Southeast Asia as further extensions of monolithic Soviet power and world revolutionary purpose.

Despite this chain of events, President Truman and his advisers were generally reluctant to involve the United States too deeply on the Asian mainland—often to the bitter frustration of their critics. In 1949 General Douglas MacArthur had by implication excluded South Korea from the defense perimeter of the United States: "The Pacific has become an Anglo-Saxon lake," he asserted, "and our line of defense runs through the chain of islands fringing the coast of Asia. It starts from the Philippines and continues through the Ryukyu Archipelago which includes its broad main bastion, Okinawa. Then it bends back through Japan and the Aleutian Island chain to Alaska."[25] Following a policy of letting the dust settle in Asia, the United States reduced its commitment to the Chinese Nationalists. On January 5, 1950, President Truman asserted that the United States did not have any intention of utilizing its armed forces to intervene in the China situation then current. Nor would the government pursue a course that would "lead to involvement in the civil conflict in China," or "provide military aid or advice to Chinese forces on Formosa." The emphasis would be on economic assistance, wherever appropriate.[26]

Later, the same month, Secretary of State Dean Acheson went even further, excluding Taiwan and the East Asian mainland from United States responsibility. "The defense perimeter" of the United States in the Pacific included "the Aleutians, Japan, the Ryukyus, and the Philippines," but as far as the military security of other areas in the Pacific was concerned, "it must be clear that no person can guarantee these areas against military attack. . . . Should such an attack occur . . . the initial reliance must be on the people attacked to resist it and then upon the commitments of the entire world under the Charter of the United Nations."[27]

The whole situation was suddenly altered with the North Korean attack on South Korea on June 25, 1950. The attack precipitated a decision on the part of President Truman to interpose the United States Seventh Fleet between Taiwan and the mainland on the grounds that a Chinese Communist occupation of the Nationalist-held island would threaten United States forces in the Pacific. The invasion of South Korea reset United States policy in Asia for the next two decades, partly by catalyzing critics of the administration who had been challenging American noninvolvement on the Asian mainland as appeasement, softness toward communism, or even outright treason, and partly by presenting to Washington what President Truman and many other Americans saw as a direct threat to American interests.

Soviet and North Korean perceptions and purposes are still not entirely clear. Probably Stalin and other communist leaders expected North Korean forces to absorb South Korea and unify the country with minimal resistance and cost to themselves. It is quite possible that United States policy assertions about noninvolvement on the east Asian mainland contributed to the Soviet and North Korean decisions.

The intentions of the People's Republic of China are also obscure. In retrospect, it appears that the entrance of Communist China into the Korean War was cautious, even reluctant. It may be that their involvement would have remained quite limited—comparable to their involvement in the Vietnamese conflict of that time—if they had not come to perceive, however inaccurately, that the United States intended to invade Manchuria.[28]

Acting through the United Nations, the United States promised immediate military support to the Republic of Korea, the United States Seventh Fleet began patrolling the Taiwan Straits, and American troops were ordered into combat on the Korean front. As General Douglas MacArthur set off for Taipei as United Nations commander, large units of the People's Liberation Army moved into new positions in Shantung province and in northeastern China. This decision on the part of the United States, together with Chinese Communist counter-moves, set the stage for many of the Sino-American conflicts and confrontations of the next two decades.

By September 1950 the Democratic People's Republic of Korea was suffering serious setbacks. On October 7, United Nations forces advanced beyond the thirty-eighth parallel into North Korea—despite warnings from India that entry of United States troops would bring overt Chinese Communist intervention. By mid-October Chinese People's Volunteers were crossing the Yalu River from Manchuria and taking up positions on North Korean territory. A communist counteroffensive soon gained momentum, and presently United Nation forces were falling back rapidly.

As is now common knowledge, the Korean War became a see-sawing, long drawn-out, essentially stalemated struggle in which neither side seemed able to effect a victory. After two major but unsuccessful Chinese offensives in April and May 1951, truce talks began at Soviet Russian initiative along lines that, as Peking seems to have anticipated and feared, tended to leave major Chinese demands unsatisfied.

In an effort toward facilitating an armistice in Korea, the Eisenhower Administration in February 1953 unleashed Chiang Kai-shek or, more specifically, removed the restraint on Nationalist Chinese operations against the Chinese mainland. However, the signing of a Korean truce in June 1953 provided a new measure of stability in northeast Asia; even earlier, in 1952, the Chinese Communist leadership had begun to abandon reliance on armed struggle and to cast about for an alternative policy. But in Indochina, Ho Chi Minh had intensified his campaign against the French, and the People's Republic of China began sending him supplies. (For these and other reasons it was some time before Peking's new policy—characterized, in due course, as the Bandung spirit, discussed later in this chapter—became clearly operational.) Meanwhile, as Peking increased its program of military aid to North Vietnam, the United States began stepping up its diplomatic and military support of the French effort, although there was no direct American intervention.

The first indication of a change in Chinese Communist policy was the willingness of the Peking regime to accept a settlement of the Indochina crisis that fell short of demands put forward by the Viet Minh. In September 1953 the Chinese People's Republic announced its interest in a negotiated settlement for Indochina, possibly based on an armistice after the Korean model. Both Ho Chi Minh and the French seemed to favor peace talks, and in Berlin on February 18, 1954 the Foreign Ministers of the Big Four agreed to hold a conference at Geneva on the Indochinese and Korean wars.

By mid-March 1954 French forces were under seige at Dien Bien Phu. At this point the United States agreed to provide air power in order to counter Chinese air interventions, whereupon the Chinese Communists began to complain of the military encirclement of China. Meanwhile, Chinese Communist deliveries of artillery and antiaircraft pieces to the Viet Minh had begun to tip the balance in Indochina. Secretary of Defense John Foster Dulles warned that the United States would bomb Chinese staging bases if the Chinese Communists were to intervene directly. United States aircraft carriers began moving from Manila toward Indochina. France rejected a proposal by Dulles to use nuclear weapons. The Chinese Communists made it clear that they were watching the moves of the United States with great vigilance and would not take it lying down if threatened with further intervention. Dien Bien Phu fell on May 7—the day before the Geneva Conference turned its attention to the Indochina question.

Under the Geneva agreements it was stipulated that none of the countries of Indochina should join any military alliance, and neither of the two Vietnamese regimes was to receive outside military aid except on a replacement basis. Ho Chi Minh's regime was to withdraw its forces from Vietnam south of the seventeenth parallel, from Laos, and from Cambodia. A small French military mission was to remain in Laos. Three international control commissions—each chaired by India and including Canada and Poland as the other members—were to supervise these military arrangements. Vietnam, in effect, was partitioned at the seventeenth parallel, but general elections were to be scheduled for July 1956, and it was widely assumed that voters would give the whole country to the communists.[29]

At the Geneva Conference, Chinese Communist representatives played a major role in negotiating the truce formula that led to the division of Vietnam and the incorporation of North Vietnam into the Communist bloc.[30] Thereafter, the Chinese People's Republic made important allocations of resources in order to build North Vietnam into an ally, providing economic assistance, developing communications and industry, and helping in the expansion and equipment of armed forces.[31]

The United States did not sign the Geneva agreements, but issued a unilateral declaration to the effect that it would not disturb the arrangements.[32]

The Taiwan Straits crises

From the beginning of the Korean War the United States had been increasing its support of the Chiang Kai-shek regime. These circumstances gave rise to a series of confrontations with Nationlist forces and with the United States during the 1950s and early 1960s.

Over the years, according to Charles McClelland, the Chinese Communists became increasingly practiced and proficient at waging acute international crises. When confronted by strong military-political resistance and the need to disengage, McClelland concluded from a detailed study of Taiwan Straits crises, the Peking regime allows its interactions to drift off and to decline in frequency and intensity, and it tapers off its acts of violence. "The more acute crises it experiences," however, "the more the Communist Chinese government resembles other governments in crisis behavior by rapidly 'peaking' and then eroding its sequence of crisis acts and by employing wider and more varied ranges of acts from its total inventory."[33]

During 1954, in the wake of the Korean War, the United States, further increasing its support for the Kuomintang regime, began to endow the unleashing of Chiang with something more than token force by increasing American military aid to the Nationalists and encouraging them to seize and occupy islands just off mainland shores. Sino-American tensions were further aggravated by a Chinese Communist attack on planes of the Seventh Fleet that were searching for survivors of a British airliner shot down off Hainan Island, and there was a sharp exchange of notes. On August 17 President Eisenhower told correspondents that a Chinese attack on Taiwan would have to run over the Seventh Fleet.

Soon after signing the Geneva agreements, Peking—freed somewhat from its preoccupation with Korea and Vietnam—undertook a powerful propaganda campaign focused on the "liberation" of Taiwan, and Red Army artillery began bombing Quemoy on September 3, 1954. At this juncture, a Soviet delegation headed by Nikita Khrushchev arrived in Peking and thus raised apprehensions in the United States that the Soviet Union was prepared to lend its direct support to the People's Republic in the current crisis. What actually took place may have been a foreshadowing of the Sino-Soviet conflict that surfaced a few years later.

One of Khrushchev's major purposes may have been to gain support for his effort to unseat Malenkov from the premiership and replace him with Bulganin, who was a member of the delegation visiting Peking. It may be inferred that Khrushchev, in order to encourage Chinese support, was prepared to make concessions provided they did not threaten Soviet Russian security. In any case, a joint communiqué issued October 11 provided—not for Soviet support of China in the Straits crisis—but for: (1) a second Soviet credit, $130 million, to the Chinese People's Republic; (2) Soviet Russian withdrawal in the spring of 1955 from Port Arthur; (3) a joint, peaceful approach to international relations, especially with respect to Asia; (4) a willingness to establish normal relations with Japan despite the relatively conservative and pro-American disposition of its government; (5) transfer of the joint stock companies, with compensation to the Soviet Union, to Chinese ownership at the beginning of 1955; and (6) Soviet scientific and technical aid to the CPR, including, as became evident in retrospect, the completion of new, connecting railway lines, already under construction, between the two countries by way of Sinkiang and Outer Mongolia, and also assistance in basic nuclear research.[34] Significantly, Khrushchev made no public commitment to Peking on the issue of Taiwan.

Chinese Communist shore batteries began the systematic shelling of Quemoy Island on September 3, 1954, and the Nationalists undertook air and naval raids on the mainland. Secretary of State Dulles announced that the United States would defend Quemoy to the extent that it was necessary for the defense of Taiwan. In early January, Chinese Communist forces captured Yikiang Shan Island and prepared to attack Iochen. President Eisenhower, sought, and was granted, emergency authorization from the United States Senate to defend Taiwan with United States forces. Air and naval reinforcements were dispatched to the Straits.

The outcome of the crisis was a de facto settlement. The United States had thwarted Peking's effort to seize the offshore islands as stepping stones to Taiwan; the Chinese Communists, on the other hand, had succeeded in deterring a United States-sponsored invasion of the mainland.

Toward the end of 1954 the United States signed a treaty of alliance with the Nationalist government, and in January 1955 Congress— through the Formosa Resolution—authorized the President to commit United States forces in defense of Quemoy and Matsu if he concluded a Chinese Communist attack upon them to be part of an attack on Taiwan itself.

During the spring of 1955 the People's Republic eased its pressure on Quemoy and Matsu, and the United States tried unsuccessfully to persuade the Nationalist government to evacuate two offshore islands. Between 1955 and 1958, however, the conflict of Communist, Nationalist, and American interests over Taiwan, the offshore islands, and the Straits remained relatively quiet, although there were Kuomintang harassments of the mainland from time to time. A 1957 agreement between the United States and the Nationalist government provided for surface-to-air missile installations on Taiwan, and thus the military capabilities of Quemoy and Matsu were substantially advanced.

During the summer of 1958 Peking launched a new propaganda campaign proclaiming Chinese Communist readiness to liberate Taiwan by any means at any moment. Chinese Communist shore batteries began bombarding Quemoy and Matsu on August 23, and radio transmissions from the Chinese coastal regions warned of an early assault on Taiwan. The United States responded by dispatching air, marine, and naval reinforcements to Taiwan. Secretary of State Dulles warned against interference with United States convoys. Peking then proposed ambassadorial talks, and on September 15 representatives from the United States and the Chinese People's Republic began meeting in Warsaw. In the meantime, heavy exchanges of artillery fire were maintained by shore batteries on the mainland and on Quemoy and Matsu.[35] Finally, on October 6, Peking proposed a unilateral cease-fire that was continued for two weeks and then altered to provide for firing on odd-numbered days. Again, the outcome was not definitive. Quemoy and Matsu remained in Nationalist hands, Taiwan was forced to abandon its plans for invading the mainland, and the United States broadened its commitment to include the defense of the two offshore islands as well as Taiwan.

A third crisis took place in the Taiwan Straits during June and July 1962, when the Peking regime accused Chiang Kai-shek, "with the support and encouragement of U.S. imperialism," of preparing an invasion of coastal areas of the mainland.[36] The United States reacted by sending an additional $90 million worth of military aid to Taiwan together with eight-inch howitzers, capable of firing atomic shells, for deployment on Quemoy.

There had been evidences of increased tension in several parts of Asia since early spring of 1962. On May 15 the United States had announced its intention of sending troops to Thailand in response to new revolutionary disturbances in Laos. Elements of the Indian army were reported to be moving their outposts closer to the military highway built by the Chinese but considered by the Indians to extend across their territory to Ladakh. Chiang Kai-shek's Republic of China on Taiwan appeared to be preparing an invasion of the mainland. And the USSR was believed to be supporting—or at least encouraging—dissident, non-Chinese elements in Sinkiang.

During the latter half of May 1962 Chiang Kai-shek's Nationalist government issued new calls for an invasion of the mainland. The People's Republic responded with assertions that such an invasion would be resisted and warned the United States not to undertake military action. Large Chinese Communist forces began moving into Fukien Province and Soviet jets were moved to southern Chinese bases.

There were further exchanges of threats between Taiwan and the mainland until, on June 27, President Kennedy announced that the United States would neither support a Nationalist invasion of the People's Republic nor allow Chinese Communist forces to attack Quemoy, Matsu, or Taiwan. Nationalist troops on Quemoy exchanged artillery fire with Communist units on the mainland. Khrushchev announced that an attack on the People's Republic would be interpreted as an attack on the Soviet Union, while Peking charged that the United States was intruding on Chinese Communist air space and territorial waters.

Aerial fighting and artillery exchanges continued intermittently into October, at which point the conflict subsided into another prolonged impasse. The outcome was a new de facto settlement.

Vietnam

During the late 1950s and early 1960s Chinese Communist conflicts or potentials for conflict with the United States were building up, increment by increment, in Southeast Asia. It was during months and years immediately following the Geneva Conference that the United States made a number of relatively small decisions that nevertheless significantly deepened the commitment of that country to a concern for shaping the outcome of affairs on the Asian mainland and thus paving the way for involvement during the 1960s in the war in Vietnam.

Refusing to sign the Geneva declaration on July 24, 1954, the United States had pledged itself to be of assistance in seeking a just and honorable settlement. Then, on October 23, President Eisenhower promised South Vietnamese Premier Diem considerable United States support in building a strong and viable state capable of resisting subversion or aggression. The Geneva declaration had included a call for elections during the summer of 1956 for the reunification of Vietnam. The Diem government, which was not a signatory, refused to be bound by this election provision. Charging interference from the North, Diem and other South Vietnamese leaders on October 26, 1955 declared South Vietnam to be an independent republic. The United States then provided economic and military assistance, including some 600 military advisers, to help the Diem government subdue guerrilla resistance and put down other opposition.

The intent of the 1954 Geneva Conference was to remove Laos from contention in the cold war. French troops, with minor exceptions, and Viet Minh forces were to be withdrawn, the introduction of new troops or arms was prohibited, the Royal Laotian government and the Pathet Lao were expected to collaborate in administering provinces that had been in conflict, and responsibility for treaty implementation was accorded to the International Control Commission. However, in the United States, the tendency was to view the settlement as a communist victory, and Washington, refusing to be bound by the agreements, responded by establishing the Southeast Asia Treaty Organization (SEATO). Moreover, the merging of territory held by the Pathet Lao under Royal Laotian sovereignty did not take place.

Toward the end of 1960 the Soviet Union, at the request of neutralist Premier Souvanna Phouma, had begun to dispatch arms by airlift to the Pathet Lao and to neutralist forces under Kong Lae. In December rightist forces under United States sponsorship occupied Vientiane and established a new government. The Chinese People's

Republic expressed serious concern and supported Soviet-North Vietnamese proposals for a reconvening of the Geneva Conference. The Pathet Lao rapidly expanded its control over much of the country, and Peking threatened retaliation if SEATO forces intervened.[37] In May 1961, the United States agreed to the reconvening of the Geneva Conference, which acceded to Communist China's demand for a neutral Laos. Peking managed to retain a military base area, and the Pathet Lao continued to retain control of highland areas that facilitated the movement of supplies from North Vietnam into South Vietnam.

While the Chinese Communists were expanding their influence in the province of Phong Saly, the USSR had undertaken an airlift in support of revolutionary forces in Laos. The Chinese People's Republic cooperated in this airlift, which passed over Chinese territory, until it came to an end in early 1962. The undertaking seemed to enhance Soviet influence on the Pathet Lao and thus to increase somewhat the influence of the USSR in Southeast Asia. However, because of both economic and military limitations, China was constrained to relatively low-level and low-cost operations in support of national revolutionary movements and anti-imperialist forces there and elsewhere.

During the Geneva Conference on Laos, which extended from May 1961 through July 1962, the Chinese and the Soviet Russians appeared to cooperate in the neutralization of the country and the development of a coalition government under Souvanna Phouma.[38]

The USSR and the People's Republic of China had also been supplying economic and military assistance to Ho Chi Minh's regime in the north, but neither had expressed much concern over South Vietnamese affairs. With increased United States involvement in Laos and South Vietnam, however, Chinese Communist spokesmen began to issue warnings against "United States imperialist aggression" and to assert that the security of Vietnam and China was indivisible.[39] Guerrilla units in increasing numbers began infiltrating south of the seventeenth parallel, and supplies were made available to resistance groups in increasing quantities.

Political unrest in South Vietnam gave rise to a series of military coups. The United States joined with the Saigon regime in planning political and economic reforms, and on January 27, 1964 Secretary of Defense McNamara predicted major withdrawals of United States troops within the following eighteen months. Three days later another coup took place, however, and there were intensifications of the guerrilla war. In March the United States promised assistance and support for the South Vietnamese regime as long as it was needed.

Details of what happened during the Gulf of Tonkin incident are still not firmly established. On August 2, 1964 the North Vietnam government charged that American planes had hit a North Vietnamese village near the Laotian border and that United States ships had bombarded Hon Me Island in the Gulf of Tonkin. During that evening three torpedo boats of the Democratic Republic of Vietnam exchanged fire with the United States destroyer *Maddox*. The next day the United States government reported that this "unprovoked attack" in international water had been repelled, and President Johnson ordered subsequent attackers destroyed.

On August 5, Washington charged that North Vietnamese torpedo boats had attacked two United States ships sixty-five miles from the nearest land. United States aircraft retaliated by bombing a North Vietnamese oil depot and four torpedo boat staging areas. The North Vietnamese government acknowledged the first incident but denied the second. The United States requested discussion of the incidents in the United Nations Security Council. United States reinforcements were dispatched to the area, and President Johnson asked Congress for a resolution authorizing whatever steps might be necessary for assisting any nation of Southeast Asia in defense of its freedom.

The Chinese People's Republic issued a statement on August 6 that referred to the surprise attack of the United States as going over the brink of war. Massive rallies against the United States were held in Peking.

Hanoi protested to the International Control Commission but rejected a United Nations invitation to discuss the crisis. The United States announced that it was suspending patrols over Tonkin Gulf; however, Chinese Communist air patrols were reported off Hanoi, and on August 11 several Chinese MIGs were believed to have landed in Hanoi. There was new unrest in Saigon, and the South Vietnamese government suffered another collapse. Ch'en Yi, foreign minister of the Chinese People's Republic, reiterated that the United States "aggression" must be punished.[40]

The United States government reported a third Tonkin Gulf incident on September 18, asserting that four unidentified vessels had disappeared after drawing fire from an American destroyer. The North Vietnamese and Chinese Communist governments charged that this was a further fabrication. The conflict steadily escalated, and by December the United States troop commitment in South Vietnam had increased from 16,300 to 23,300.

Peking's Relations with the Soviet Union

In the West there had been speculation almost from the start about the reality and durability of the Sino-Soviet partnership. As suggested by Geoffrey Hudson, "It was from the outset reasonable to assume that the Chinese Communists' heritage of national pride, their consciousness of the vast size and population of China, and their sense of achievement in having carried through their revolution with a minimum of Russian aid would render them unwilling blindly to follow the lead of Moscow and inclined to formulate foreign as well as domestic policies of their own."[41] During the first six years, however, there was not much evidence of dissension. On the contrary, there seemed to be "a remarkable degree of harmony."[42] While proclaiming Marxist-Leninist principles, Chinese leaders also underscored their desire to learn from the Soviet experience. Therefore, when the Sino-Soviet conflict first surfaced in the late 1950s, only a relatively few outside observers were prepared to recognize it as genuine.

Chinese and Russian concerns overlapped in Korea, where both leaderships were interested in preventing the overthrow of the communist regime. The Soviet Union not only provided arms, equipment, and valuable training, but also threatened to intervene if the war should encroach upon Chinese territory. It is not entirely clear how successfully the two countries collaborated after Communist China's entry into the Korean conflict, or how much friction there may have been under the surface, but in general we can probably assume that common interests tended to sustain a considerable amount of cooperation during that period.

The first overt and serious evidence of difficulty between Peking and Moscow emerged from the Twentieth Congress of the CPSU over Khrushchev's attack on the memory of Stalin.[43] As suggested by Hudson, "It was noticed at the time by some Western observers that the terms of eulogy in which mention of Stalin was made in Mao Tse-tung's message of greeting to the Congress were so contrary to the tenor of Khrushchev's speech to the secret session a few days later as to require the inference that the Chinese Leader had either not been informed of what was about to be done or had disagreed with it."[44]

Early Sino-Soviet tensions

What brought about the striking change in relations between the two communist states? We know that Mao Tse-tung had carried on guerrilla warfare against Japanese forces and against warlord and Nationalist armies with very little material assistance from Moscow. And after World War II Stalin was apparently dubious about Chinese Communist ability to overthrow Chiang Kai-shek's government. Seemingly, Stalin was ready to settle for a Nationalist government — for the time being, at least — in which the Chinese Communists would hold some posts and exert a certain amount of influence.[45] But the Chinese, as Stalin conceded later, had proceeded to conquer the mainland (with the aid of captured Japanese rifles turned over to them by the Russians but without much direct Soviet assistance).

From early days of the Kiangsi Soviet and during the years of border region governments in Yenan, Mao's policy, for the most part, had been to pay lip service to Stalin as a great communist leader but then to conduct the Chinese revolutionary struggle largely as he himself saw fit. After the Soviet leader's death, on the other hand, Mao and his colleagues probably saw little reason for paying any great deference to Khrushchev and other Russian leaders who, in many respects, could not boast of as much practical revolutionary experience as the Chinese Communist leaders could.

It was also noted by Western observers that the USSR and Communist China were in quite different stages of their revolutions and in quite separate phases of economic and technological development. There were also historical differences between them. However, "The primary cause of the Sino-Soviet rift," according to William E. Griffith, "has been the determination of Mao and his associates that China should become a superpower and the determination of the Soviet leadership to prevent it."[46] It can be asserted in somewhat similar terms, perhaps, that a primary cause of the Sino-Soviet controversy was attempts on the part of the USSR to inhibit — at least in part — certain aspects of Chinese Communist development and increases in national power. The proposition has been advanced, for example, that Stalin drove an unequal bargain with the Chinese during negotiations for the 1950 Treaty of Friendship and Alliance and that subsequent Chinese moves to redress the balance contributed to the Sino-Soviet controversy.[47]

Specifically, it has been argued that Soviet leaders, while negotiating the Treaty of Friendship and Alliance in early 1950, took advantage of China's relative weakness to make heavy demands upon the Chinese Communists for concessions in Sinkiang. The treaty provided for mixed Sino-Soviet companies to provide civil air service for ten years and for the exploitation of oil and nonferrous metals for the next thirty years. To the Chinese these arrangements may have appeared reminiscent of earlier agreements with the imperialist countries for the exploitation of Chinese resources.[48] Admittedly, the treaty further provided compensation to the USSR for expenses incurred in the construction of installations connected with the Changchun Railway, Port Arthur, and Darien — although it might be argued that the Soviet Union had already received compensation from expropriating goods in Manchuria and stripping Manchurian industries following World War II.[49]

Under the 1950 treaty Peking also affirmed the independence of Outer Mongolia, once a part of the Chinese Empire, on the basis of a

1945 referendum carried out by the Nationalist government — despite the fact that all agreements between that government and the USSR were declared null and void.[50] The treaty was probably more generous to China than most that had been concluded by the Nationalist and other governments with foreign powers, but it granted less than one might expect one communist country to receive from another communist country genuinely determined to redress the imperialist balance.

Subsequently, especially after Stalin's death, these stipulations were modified in ways suggesting that, as Chinese bargaining power increased, Peking was able to insist upon more favorable terms than the USSR had been willing to grant when Soviet leaders were in a better position to dominate the negotiations.

If these assertions are legitimate, the causes of Sino-Soviet relations can be explained to a considerable extent in the same general context as other aspects of China's foreign policy: in terms of the long-range aspirations of Mao Tse-tung and his colleagues to reestablish the country in the configuration of world powers by installments, so to speak, and also in terms of Soviet attempts to maintain preeminence and, insofar as possible, to dominate the Chinese or at least keep them under some measure of comradely restraint.

Issues in the Sino-Soviet dispute

In many ways, the death of Stalin opened a Pandora's box for his successors in the USSR to the extent that the Soviets might try to dominate other countries in the Communist bloc as well as China. This became evident almost from the movement of Khrushchev's initial step toward de-Stalinization. "It was the paradox of this extraordinary episode," according to Geoffrey Hudson, "that Khrushchev in demanding that other communist parties simply fall into line with a decision taken in Moscow to degrade Stalin was invoking precisely that supreme authority over the international movement which Stalin had acquired and which largely depended on his prestige as an almost superhuman being. Once the former 'leader of progressive mankind' had been denounced as a tyrant and a fraud, the question was inevitably asked among communists—and not only in Peking—whence Khrushchev could derive the right to issue instructions to the comrades of all lands."[51]

The Chinese Communists may have sought early and immediate advantage from the uncertainties and weaknesses of post-Stalinist collective leadership in Moscow. The feeling of Mao and his colleagues seems to have been that the communist states should be free of Soviet Russian interference in their domestic affairs, but ought to acknowledge Soviet primacy in the making and carrying out of common policy. This predisposition temporarily gained for the Chinese People's Republic a reputation as the champion of liberalism within the Communist bloc and as supporters of the Poles, for example, in their struggle for a "Polish road to socialism."[52] On the other hand, the Chinese soon revealed themselves as rigorous in their condemnation of Tito and his position of neutrality between the two world camps.

The implications of Chinese Communist policy became clearer during the autumn of 1956, in terms of the troubles in Poland and Hungary. As suggested by Geoffrey Hudson and his colleagues, the Polish armed forces remained under strict control. The revolt played itself out within the Communist party itself, and the Soviet-Polish alliance was not threatened. Under these circumstances, the Chinese Communists supported Gomulka and are believed to have tried actively to restrain the USSR from military action. This outcome was in sharp contrast to what happened in Hungary, where the party lost control of the armed forces and dissidents pushed for multiparty democracy and international neutrality. Under these circumstances, the Chinese Communists urged ruthless military intervention at a a time when the Russians were hesitating. "The Chinese attitudes were opposite in the two cases, but each was judged on a consistent principle."[53]

In a sense, however, it was not the Chinese positon on specific issues that was most significant here. More startling and epoch-making was the fact that the People's Republic "claimed the right to have a say in what Russia should do about their affairs and sent Chou En-lai to assist in their settlement."[54] This was a significant change from earlier days when Mao, whatever his innovations, had been careful to pay lip service (sometimes quite extravagant lip service) to Stalin's genius and authority. Between June and December 1957, the Soviet Union and the People's Republic of China appeared to reverse roles; that is, the Chinese seemed to argue for greater centralization within the bloc, at the same time urging a more aggressive response to the West, whereas the Russians, at least relatively, seemed to be in favor of a certain pluralism, a loose confederation of Soviet states, and a somewhat more flexible policy toward the West. To some degree, this switch in positions seems to have come about as an outcome of maneuverings on the part of Russians and Chinese in their competition for influence within the bloc and also as a consequence of changing power relations.

A major underlying factor exacerbating Sino-Soviet relations at the Twentieth Congress was undoubtedly the nuclear weapon issue.[55] During the years when the Chinese Communists were consolidating their power over Mainland China, "nothing less than a revolution in weaponry and strategic doctrine" had taken place elsewhere. For a few years, however, there was not much evidence to suggest that Mao and his colleagues were aware of what was happening.[56]

Alice Hsieh has pointed out two major shifts in Chinese foreign policy that have coincided with major developments in Soviet military thought and weaponry: "China's adoption in 1954 of a policy of peaceful coexistence in relation to her Asian neighbors occurred shortly after the initiation in the Soviet Union of a debate on the implications of nuclear weapons for modern warfare. Similarly, China's apparent loss of interest in peaceful coexistence and her more bellicose political approach to Asia followed within a matter of months the Soviet Union's launching of earth satellites in the second half of 1957."[57]

The Soviet Union tested its first successful ICBM in late August 1957. A few weeks later, at a conference of communist parties and states held in Moscow, the Chinese presented a new assessment of the world situation. Chinese leaders saw the first Russian sputniks as marking a new turning point in world affairs. Mao presented this viewpoint in November 1957 to a group of Chinese students at Moscow University and later to an assemblage of Russian leaders.[58] "I consider that the present world situation has reached a new turning point," Mao asserted. "There are now two winds in the world: the east wind and the west wind. There is a saying in China, 'If the east wind does not prevail over the west wind, then the west wind will prevail over the east wind.' I think the characteristic of the current situation is that the east wind prevails over the west wind; that is, the strength of socialism exceeds the strength of imperialism."[59] From the Maoist point of view there was now much less need to rely upon peaceful coexistence, and much less risk in a more aggressive policy.

The Chinese believed that this crucial shift in world power had already begun well before the successful ICBM tests in the USSR. During World War II, as Peking saw it, the Soviet Union had played the major role in defeating Nazi Germany, not the United States and Great Britain. In the Chinese war of liberation against Japan, the Chinese Communists had turned the tide, not Chaing Kai-shek and the United States. In Korea, the Chinese and North Korean forces had successfully turned United States and United Nations forces back from the Yalu. In Vietnam, Ho Chi Minh had defeated United States-supported troops of France and forced them out of the country. During the Suez crisis, a warning from the USSR had halted the British, French, and Israeli "aggression."

All around the world Western imperialist forces had been withdrawing from colonial and semicolonial areas. "It goes without saying," a Chinese Communist editorial asserted, "that these withdrawals resulted from the double blows to imperialism dealt by the socialist forces, and the nationalist forces which oppose colonialism. The superiority of the anti-imperialist forces over the imperialist forces demonstrated by these events expressed itself in even more concentrated form and reached unprecedented heights with the Soviet Union's launching of the artificial satellites."[60]

According to the Chinese, on October 15, 1957 the USSR offered to support China in achieving nuclear weapons, but two years later, on

June 20, 1959, the promise was formally abrogated, This Russian decision may have been based partly on a general caution resulting from a new awareness of the profound implications of nuclear weapons for all of mankind and partly on a fear of how the Chinese might employ nuclear capability if they achieved it. With nuclear weapons and a delivery system at their disposal, the Russians appear to have become considerably less militant. In retrospect, even the initial Soviet commitment to help Peking construct its own nuclear weaponry began to look more and more like a token gesture.

The Chinese Communists began asserting that the most decisive consideration in warfare was the human element, not weaponry, however advanced and sophisticated. Nuclear devices had been seriously overrated, they said, and China had nothing to fear from a nuclear war. Indeed, the Chinese could lose half their population and still be the largest nation on earth. Although they later issued qualifications, Chinese spokesmen also made initial claims to the effect that imperialist war was beyond human will to avoid. Peking declared that it was the unmistakable duty of the Chinese people to make a timely exposure of those who, through their advocacy of peaceful coexistence, had moved "from fear of war to fear of revolution" and "from not wanting revolution themselves to opposing other people's carrying out revolutions."[61]

Over succeeding years the Russians argued repeatedly that neither side could win a nuclear war and that the outcome was likely to be disaster for all mankind. A major war, moreover, was not fatalistically inevitable. Dialectic materialism did not require it. The Soviet Union had sufficient strength to protect itself from any aggressor, and communism could, and would, triumph by economic, political, psychological, and technological means rather than by military force.

In part, then, the Sino-Soviet conflict emerged from differences in emphasis and in the ways they calculated the probabilities of future developments. The Soviet Russians did not deny the possibility of nuclear war, but they saw it as less probable, or potentially less probable, if world leaders made the correct decisions, than did the Chinese. On their side, the Chinese Communists did not deny the possibility of winning victories in some places through relatively nonviolent struggle, but they saw such efforts as less decisive than did the Russians.

Increasingly, Chinese Communist leaders were forced to conclude that they could no longer rely on Soviet assistance in pursuit of Maoist goals of rapid economic growth and enhanced capabilities in the international arena. The only alternative seemed to involve achieving economic and nuclear goals through what looked to many Westerners like a bootstrapping operation, a "labor-intensive, extremist policy."[62]

In general, the Chinese Communists probably did not envision a large-scale, direct confrontation with the United States. Rather, their predispositions were in the direction of expelling American influence through Sino-Russian military assistance to wars of national liberation in the underdeveloped, nonwhite regions of Asia, Africa, and Latin America.[63] Moscow, of course, was not averse to such a general strategy, but Soviet leaders were disinclined to favor the national liberation struggle at the expense of the world socialist system, its security, and general welfare. The Russians were especially sensitive to the possibility that a war of national liberation, if pushed too far, might invite American intervention and even escalate to a nuclear level.[64]

Development of the controversy

Khrushchev's refusal to support the Chinese People's Republic against the United States and against India, in terms of more extensive economic and nuclear aid, appears to have convinced Mao Tse-tung by 1958 or thereabouts that Soviet policies constituted a serious threat to China's legitimate and fundamental interests.[65] When Khrushchev visited the United States in the early autumn of 1959, and again as the Russians and Americans were making plans for a summit meeting in mid-1960, Chinese Communist charges of revisionism reached a crescendo. It was as if the eventuality that Chinese leaders could least tolerate were a lowering of tensions between the United States and the USSR. As the Sino-Soviet controversy developed, there were repercussions throughout the Communist bloc, with Chinese Communists attacking Yugoslav revisionists when they meant the Russians, and the Soviet Russians using Albania as a whipping boy for the Communist Chinese.[66] The conflict steadily ramified and spread almost literally around the world, often creating divisions in major communist parties both inside and outside the bloc. In some parties, the older, more entrenched members, especially those holding party office, tended to support the CPSU, while younger, dissatisfied, more militant elements looked more and more toward Peking.

The Chinese People's Republic seized upon the occasion of Stalin's birthday anniversary, December 21, 1959, to remind the whole world in general and Khrushchev in particular that the deceased Soviet leader had been an "uncompromising enemy of imperialism"[67] Again on Lenin's birthday anniversary in late April 1960, Chinese Communist spokesmen leveled bitter accusations against revisionists in the socialist camp and charged them with menacing the international communist movement. By implying that the imperialists of the world had changed their nature in some fundamental way, these misguided comrades had betrayed the revolutionary spirit of true Marxism-Leninism and had emasculated its doctrines. In their effect on the revolutionary movement, these revisionists were allying themselves with the imperialists and driving a wedge into the heart of the Communist bloc.[68]

127

By this time the Sino-Soviet controversy was beginning to have an effect within the Chinese Communist leadership itself. Various considerations—the excesses and failures of the Great Leap Forward, the Tibetan crisis, deteriorating relations with India, and the intensification of the Sino-Soviet controversy—may have influenced Defense Minister P'eng Teh-huai to hold private talks with Soviet leaders during a visit to Eastern Europe in the spring of 1959. Presumably encouraged by Soviet agreement with many of his views, P'eng is believed to have tried, on his return, to achieve a reversal of Chinese Communist policy with respect to these and other fundamental issues. Outvoted at the Eighth Plenary Session of the Central Committee of the Chinese Communist party held August 2-16, 1959 at Lushan, Kiangsi, he was dismissed and replaced as defense minister by Marshall Lin Piao—just prior to a visit by Khrushchev to Peking.

At about this juncture the USSR issued a statement of neutrality in the Sino-Indian border dispute, and a week later Khrushchev, without consulting with the Chinese, went to Camp David for talks with United States President Eisenhower. As if this were not sufficient insult, the Soviet leader, according to Chinese Communist reports, even suggested that Mao Tse-tung accept a "two Chinas" solution to the Taiwan issue. And on January 14, 1960 Khrushchev called for limited unilateral disarmament—a proposal that Peking shortly repudiated.

Sino-Soviet relations and the respective influence of the Moscow and Peking leaderships were put to the test at the Bucharest Conference of representatives of the Communist bloc states in late June 1960 when Soviet delegates circulated, somewhat behind the scene, a letter calling attention to Chinese shortcomings and soliciting support for the position of the USSR. Chinese delegates refused to sign a conference communiqué and at the same time circulated a private communication that the Communist party of the Soviet Union had sent to the Communist party of China. Khrushchev retaliated with an angry tirade. Soon after the meetings had come to a close, the USSR announced that Soviet technicians had been withdrawn from China.

It was now evident that the Sino-Soviet dispute was being extended into the international front organizations and the congresses of other Communist parties in various parts of the world. After largely inconclusive preparatory meetings in September and October 1960, a conference of eighty-one Communist parties was convened to discuss and, if possible, resolve the major differences between the Chinese and Soviet parties. There were further exchanges of inflammatory documents, but the 81-Party Conference, which opened November 11 in Moscow, ended in something of a stalemate. Albania clearly sided with Peking, but most of the other delegations took positions closer to that of the CPSU. The principle of polycentrism was acknowledged, including Peking's right to oppose the Soviet line. In one sense, this was a victory for Peking, but it had the paradoxical consequence of undermining the very principle of socialist unity for which the Chinese claimed to be fighting.[69]

Albania, having been excluded from the forthcoming 22nd Party Congress of the Communist party of the Soviet Union, sent a letter to the CPSU Central Committee on October 12, 1961 urging rejection of what was referred to as the "Khrushchev group." In retaliation, Khrushchev denounced Albania in his opening speech at the congress and publicly supported the pro-Soviet wing of the Albanian communist movement. Peking then published a speech on Chinese-Albanian friendship. Chou En-lai criticized Khrushchev for his attack, placed a wreath on Stalin's tomb, and returned to Peking a whole week before the congress ended.[70] The Albanians denounced Khrushchev as a traitor.[71]

In March 1963 the Chinese Communists, angered by Khrushchev's further attacks on China and irked by his reference to the colonial vestiges at Hong Kong and Macao, raised publicly for the first time issues connected with Sino-Soviet boundaries, referring specifically to unequal treaties imposed on China by the Russian tsarist government at the conclusion of the nineteenth century. The documents to which Peking referred were the Treaty of Aigun (1858), the Treaty of Peking, (1860), and the Treaty of Ili or St. Petersburg (1881). The Chinese Communists did not question earlier treaties with Russia, such as the Treaty of Nerchinsk (1689), which located the far eastern boundary of the Chinese and Russian empires along the Stanovoi Mountains, or the Treaty of Kiakhta (1727), which undertook the delimitation of the boundary between Outer Mongolia (then under Chinese suzerainty) and Siberia.[72]

Crucial issues were also raised, or reraised, by Soviet spokesmen.[73] Marxist-Leninist parties throughout the world had the same ultimate aim: "to mobilize all forces in the struggle for the winning of power by the workers and the laboring peasantry, and to build socialism and communism."[74] But a world war was not fatalistically inevitable. "With the balance of forces increasingly tipping in favor of socialism and against imperialism, and with the forces of peace increasingly gaining weight over the forces of war," the possibility of world war could be ruled out even before socialism really triumphed—with capitalism still existing in certain parts of the world.[75]

Charges and counter-charges exchanged

The contradiction between capitalism and socialism remained the chief contradiction of our epoch.[76] The destinies of peace, democracy, and socialism depended to a decisive extent on the outcome of the struggle of the two world systems.[77] But according to Moscow, it was perfectly obvious that the main content and the chief trends of human society's development "were no longer determined by imperialism, but by the world socialist system, by all the progressive forces struggling against imperialism for the reorganization of society along socialist lines."[78]

From a Chinese Communist viewpoint, all this was evidence that the Soviet Union had again failed its responsibilities to the world revolutionary movement, thereby inviting, encouraging, and facilitating further acts of imperialist aggression against the oppressed nations throughout the world.[79] Peking issued new charges. Recently, certain persons had asserted that revolutions were entirely possible without war. But what type of war were they referring to—a war of national liberation, a revolutionary civil war, or a world war? If they were referring to a war of national revolution or a revolutionary civil war, then such a formulation was wholly incorrect. On the other hand, if they were referring to a world war, then, although world wars inevitably led to revolution, no true Marxist-Leninist had ever held or ever would hold that revolution must be made through world war.[80] Also, certain persons had been one-sidedly exaggerating the role of peaceful competition between socialist and imperialist countries. "According to their preaching it would seem that imperialism" would automatically collapse in the course of this peaceful competition and that "the only thing the oppressed peoples and nations" had to do was "wait quietly" for that day. Such a view had nothing to do with Marxism-Leninism.[81]

On the other hand, Soviet theoreticians argued that revolutions were quite possible without war. The people who were fighting for national liberation or who had already won political independence had ceased, or were ceasing, to serve as reserves for imperialism. This meant that the balance of world influence and power was tipping against the imperialists. "We fully stand for the destruction of imperialism and capitalism," Soviet leaders asserted.[82] But this destruction could be accomplished without large-scale war. No one—and this included the big states—had the right to play nuclear games with the destiny of millions of people.

The Chinese responded in terms of "resolute struggle."[83] This was the road to world peace, the only road. The war and peace theory of Soviet leaders, the Chinese charged, was one of forbidding revolution.[84] Chinese spokesmen thought that their own intentions and meaning were amply clear: China wanted peace, not war; it was the imperialists, not the Chinese, who wanted to fight; a world war could be prevented, but even in the eventuality that imperialism should "impose a war on the people of the world and inflict tragic losses on them," it was the imperialist system, and not mankind as a whole, that would perish from the earth, and the future of the world would still be bright.[85]

The Chinese accused the Russians of setting China up as a bogey, of "making such a noise" about the "theory of the Yellow Peril," which, in fact, was a legacy of Kaiser Wilhelm II, "a bigwig in his day" and a "snow man in the sun."[86] Khrushchev, the Chinese charged, was "singing to the tune of the neocolonialists." And with respect to the Cuba crisis of October 1962, Chinese Communist leaders accused the Russians of wantonly attacking the Chinese Communist party, alleging that China "hoped for a head-on clash between the United States and the Soviet Union and tried to provoke a nuclear war." This, according to Peking, was "thoroughly disgusting."[87]

Soviet Russian negotiations for a nuclear test-ban treaty with the United States also irked the Chinese. Even tacit understandings between the USSR and the United States seemed to put the imperialist and socialist camps on a par. Soviet spokesmen took sharp issue. Did the Chinese comrades realize what sort of ruins a nuclear-rocked world war would leave behind?[88] Peking's response was not conciliatory. The Soviet government had been insolent enough, the Chinese charged, to say that "we are able to criticize them only because China enjoys the protection of Soviet nuclear weapons. Well, then, leaders of the Soviet Union, please continue to protect us a while with your nuclear weapons. We shall continue to criticize you, and we hope you will have the courage to argue the matter with us."[89] The main issue was, as Peking saw it, that Soviet leaders held "that China should not, and must not, manufacture nuclear weapons, and that only a few nuclear powers, and particularly U.S. imperialism, the enemy of the people of the whole world," were entitled to the continued production of nuclear weapons.

The Chinese reasserted that a third world war could be prevented, provided the people of the whole world became united, following a correct line—presumably the Peking line—and persevered in the struggle. But imperialism had been, and would continue to be, the source of modern war, and United States imperialism was the main force of aggression and war. Consequently, unless a resolute struggle were waged against United States policies, defense of world peace would be completely out of the question.

Soviet leaders had predicted that nuclear war would burn everything to ashes, and that the three billion people of the world would all die. "We do not agree with this pessimistic and despairing view of theirs. We say that if imperialism should unleash a nuclear war and the worst came to the worst, half of the world's population would be killed. We are optimistic about the future of mankind." In their arguments the Soviet leaders had "simply collected the spittle of the imperialists and the renegades."

As the charges and countercharges were intensified, the controversy began to cut deeper and deeper into relationships among the

131

communist states. The Russians accused their Chinese comrades of "impudently interfering in the internal affairs of fraternal parties, stubbornly thrusting their own views and tactics upon them," and pouring "filth" on the guiding figures of the French, Italian, United States, Indian, and other fraternal parties.[90] The Chinese Communists retaliated by accusing the Russians of revisionism and by denouncing them as the greatest splitters of our times. Never before had the unity of the international communist movement been so gravely threatened.[91]

The Bandung Policy: A détente with certain countries

About the time of the Geneva Conference, on June 28, 1954, Prime Minister Chou En-lai of the People's Republic of China joined Prime Minister Nehru of India in issuing the *Panch Shila,* or Five Principles, that was intended to guide relations between the two states: (1) mutual respect for each other's territorial integrity and sovereignty, (2) nonaggression, (3) noninterference in each other's internal affairs, (4) equality and mutual benefit, (5) peaceful coexistence.[92] Chinese Communist relations with India and also with Burma were further stabilized by visits by Chou En-lai to New Delhi and Rangoon and by Nehru and U Nu to Peking. Through these various discussions and negotiations it was agreed that India and Burma would observe strict neutrality in the cold war and maintain friendly relations with China. The Peking regime agreed, in turn, to refrain from aggression along Indian and Burmese frontiers and to negotiate on the difficult issue of the citizenship of overseas Chinese. These and other discussions paved the way for the Asian-African Conference held at Bandung, Indonesia in April 1955. During the Bandung meetings, Chou En-lai added further elements to the *Panch Shila* affirmations: recognition of racial equality and respect for the rights of the people of all nations to choose their own ways of life and their own political and economic systems.[93] A final public announcement issued by the conference urged participating nations to "practice tolerance and live together in peace with one another as good neighbors and develop friendly cooperation" on the basis of ten principles derived from earlier statements.[94]

The change of Chinese Communist policy suggested in the Bandung Conference initiatives did not by any means signal an end to conflict or armed confrontations and struggle in eastern or southern Asia. The People's Republic of China and the United States-supported Nationalists still faced each other in Taiwan Straits, there were continuing difficulties in Vietnam, and new tensions began to arise in Chinese Communist relations with Burma, Indonesia, and India. The Bandung phase of Chinese Communist foreign policy was characterized, in part, by a campaign for the peaceful liberation of Taiwan through negotiation and agreement, as opposed to armed conflict, with the Nationalists.[95] Tensions were lowered, but they did not disappear. Nationalist and Communist intents and purposes remained largely at an impasse.

During some fifty years of sovereignty over Burma, Great Britain had negotiated certain sections of the country's common border with China, but in general the results had been inconclusive and unsatisfactory. After coming to power, the Chinese Communists had tended to regard Burma as a vestige of Western imperialism. Border disagreements were exacerbated by the presence in northern Burma of Chinese Nationalist army contingents as well as civilians who had taken refuge there after the Chinese Communist takeover. The Chinese Communists also tended to support communist bands in the area, as well as Kachin and other dissident minorities. Finally on November 9, 1955, Burmese authorities announced that the Chinese People's Republic had made a fair and reasonable proposal, and during the next spring U Nu met with Chou En-lai at Kunming to conclude a border agreement.

While the Bandung Conference was in session, Chou En-lai had signed with the Sastroamidjojo government of Indonesia, which was neutralist and somewhat leftist, a treaty providing the opportunity for local Chinese residents to give up dual citizenship and opt for either Indonesian or Chinese citizenship. The terms, written largely in line with Indonesian predispositions, tended somewhat to minimize the number of Chinese who would opt for and acquire Indonesian citizenship. Despite these considerations, however, the treaty became an irritating political issue in Indonesia, and it was not ratified there until late in 1957. Even then, it failed to take effect.

Post-Bandung Quarrels with Asian States

Despite Bandung, Chinese disputes with Asian countries began to develop. For years, even generations, some two and one-half million Chinese had constituted a largely unassimilated minority group in Indonesia. Since 1909 they had enjoyed dual citizenship. During 1957 the Indonesian government began to regulate the financial activities of this community, and Chinese residents in towns and villages began revolting against forced resettlement. In Peking, Chinese

Communist leaders took specific exception to a series of Indonesian ordinances restricting retail—in effect, Chinese—traders in rural areas. Inasmuch as the Indonesian government had not yet agreed to reciprocal ratification of the 1955 treaty with the Chinese People's Republic, it was difficult for local Chinese residents to acquire Indonesian citizenship and thus achieve immunity from discriminatory treatment. In response to this situation the People's Republic, by mounting an intense political and diplomatic campaign, succeeded in bringing about, on January 20, 1960, an exchange of ratifications. The resolution of the crisis, signaled by the signing of the Treaty of Dual Nationality, presented political gains for both sides, although the People's Republic made the greater concessions.

At the 1954 Geneva Conference, which, formally at least, marked an end to hostilities in Indochina, it became evident that the USSR had no intention of increasing its priorities in Southeast Asia at the expense of Soviet commitments and purposes in Europe. This circumstance opened important opportunities for Communist China. With the achievement of at least temporary stability with respect to Korea, Taiwan, and Indochina, the Chinese People's Republic began to focus more and more upon relations with neutral Asian states in directions it had been exploring for the previous two or three years. However, such policies could not be undertaken without challenging Soviet Russian influences to some extent.

Soon there was a trend toward Sino-Soviet rivalry in south and Southeast Asia. Indeed, by the latter part of 1959 and early 1960, Sino-Soviet interests in that region had reached a point of conflict that was increasingly acknowledged by both sides. Thereafter, the USSR sought control over communist movements—and also increased influence over nationalist parties and governments—at what was viewed in Peking as the expense of Chinese Communist interests. Especially, the Soviet Union began strengthening its relations with India at a time when conflicts were becoming more intense between Peking and New Delhi over the Sino-Indian border.[96]

On the surface, Chinese Communist relations with India seemed to be friendly, sometimes even sentimental, during the early 1950s, but potentials for conflict were present between the two nations all along—especially with respect to the Tibetan-Indian border. Beginning in 1951 there were reports of Chinese Communist political infiltration of Nepal from Tibet,[97] of the emergence of an active Nepalese Communist party, and local prediction of a Chinese Communist takeover within the span of a few years.[98] Chinese Communist influence was said to be growing in Afghanistan, Bhutan, and Sikkim as preliminary to penetration of India.[99]

During the autumn and early winter of 1956-1957, Chou En-lai visited Afghanistan, Pakistan, India, Burma, Nepal, Ceylon, Cambodia, and North Vietnam—possibly to offset, in part at least, the effects of the Hungarian crisis and to make some advantage out of the Suez crisis. Of all the capitals, it was only in New Delhi that Chou encountered serious difficulties.

In many respects Tibet offered a source of particularly troublesome conflict. For the most part, the people of that region did not submit willingly to the reestablishment of Chinese Communist authority over the country, and the years 1951-1958 revealed evidences of considerable discontent. On April 29, 1954 the Chinese People's Republic reached an agreement with India that recognized the Chinese claim to Tibet—referred to as "the Tibet region of China"—and incorporated the Five Principles of Peaceful Coexistence, but omitted, by common agreement, any determination or definition of the border between the two countries. At that time, surface relations between India and the People's Republic still seemed cordial. Indeed, as late as February 1958, Chou En-lai, was making favorable public reference to "our great neighbor India."

Two months later, in April, Prime Minister Nehru announced that he planned a Tibetan visit in an effort to support the Dalai Lama's hopes for a more moderate Chinese policy in that country. The announcement came at a time when Peking was showing considerable concern over tendencies toward revolt in eastern Tibet. But in July, at Chinese insistence, Nehru canceled his visit. At about that time the Peking regime published a map that restated the Chinese version of the Sino-Indian border. A recently built Chinese military highway was shown crossing territory that Indian maps designated as part of Ladakh.[100]

In November 1959 Chinese Communist authorities proposed a mutual withdrawal and released Indian prisoners. New Delhi responded with a withdrawal plan of its own. The outcome was a de facto settlement with limited territorial gains for China. The Five Principles of Peaceful Coexistence had clearly suffered damage, however, and Indian leaders, especially Prime Minister Nehru, began to express disillusionment with the People's Republic. Among Chinese authorities there seems to have been a genuine fear that, unless the border were firmly secured, Tibetan dissidents who had escaped to India and Nepal might secure access to arms and ammunition, reenter, and pursue their rebellious activities.

Tibetan unrest continued to grow, and in March 1959 local governments and reactionary, that is, anti-Chinese, cliques undertook armed rebellion against Chinese Communist authorities in Lhasa. The People's Liberation Army was ordered to initiate punitive actions, and troops and reinforcements were rushed to Lhasa. By the month's end, Chinese authorities had suppressed the rebellion, in which an estimated 65,000 Tibetans lost their lives.[101]

As Chinese authorities restored order, the Dalai Lama took refuge in India, where he was warmly received by the Indian government and people. Chinese Communist pressures and penetrations were reported from Sikkim and Bhutan, the north Indian states of Uttar Pradesh, Jammu, and Kashmir, and the Kameng area along the northeastern Indian border. By this time the People's Republic published claims to nearly 40,000 square miles of territory that the Indians considered theirs, and accused India of aggression.[102] Thereafter the Peking regime tended more and more to perceive India, whose sympathy with the Tibetans was unmistakable, as a foreign enemy with whom the rebels were in league.

The precise location of the Indo-Tibetan boundary, never satisfactorily determined, became a sore issue as Tibetan refugees sought sanctuary beyond it. Sino-Indian relations were further aggravated as Tibetan guerrillas received supplies by way of India and Nepal. There were border clashes, and Prime Minister Nehru charged the People's Republic with a clear case of aggression. A Soviet Russian assertion of neutrality in the conflict amounted to a diplomatic jab at Peking.

The conflict did not escalate further, but both nations lost substantial trade, and Chinese Communist prestige among some Asian neutrals was somewhat damaged. Talks between Chou En-lai and Nehru in April 1960 were in most respects a failure, and this unsatisfactory outcome may have strengthened the growing Chinese predisposition to view India as essentially hostile.

After their confrontations in 1958-1959, the Chinese People's Republic and India held a series of conferences, but without conclusive results. There were intermittent border clashes over much of the succeeding two years.[103] As it became clear that diplomatic methods were not succeeding, Prime Minister Nehru announced on October 12, 1962 that the Indian army had undertaken a new offensive to drive Chinese troops out of territory claimed by India. On October 20, coinciding with the Soviet-American confrontation over Cuba, Chinese Communist forces responded to Indian probes with major offensives.

Declaring a state of national emergency, the Indian government called for a return to positions held in early September, but Chinese Communist advances continued. New Delhi requested British and United States assistance. The Soviet Union, deeply involved in the Cuban crisis, initially expressed mild support for China, but later retreated to a more neutral position, admitting continued aid to India. On November 5 Peking charged that Khrushchev was playing "the Munich scheme against the Cuban people." Khrushchev retaliated with the charge that the Chinese People's Republic had tried to incite a world war over Cuba.

Peking proposed to New Delhi a cease-fire and compromise border settlement similar to the Chinese proposal of 1959. In mid-

November 1962, after India had rejected this proposal, Chinese forces renewed military operations, and again they were successful. Then on November 21, the Chinese Communists abruptly halted their forces, and Peking announced a unilateral cease-fire that was to be followed by Chinese withdrawal to a proposed de facto border. A week later Chinese authoritites began withdrawing border patrols from the areas under dispute, but civil police were allowed to remain. By this time, however, indications of a forthcoming American military aid program had strengthened the Indian position somewhat.

While nations of the Colombo Conference worked to arbitrate the dispute, Peking rescinded an earlier demand for the withdrawal of Indian troops from positions they then held, and on January 9, 1963 Prime Minister Nehru expressed satisfaction with Chinese withdrawals. The People's Republic emerged from the crisis with minor territorial gains and uncontested leadership on the Asian mainland. India had clearly suffered a humiliating defeat, and subsequently budgetary allocations for national defense became an added burden to an already strained economy.

Early Chinese Relations with the Middle East and North Africa

The entrance of the People's Republic into Middle Eastern and African affairs may be traced from the Bandung Conference of April 1955 when Premier Chou En-lai met President Nasser. Full diplomatic relations between Cairo and Peking were established a little more than a year later.[104] These events were followed in December 1957 by the Afro-Asian People's Solidarity Conference, which met in Cairo and established a permanent international secretariat there. "Riding the tide of such recent events as the winning of independence by Morocco, Tunisia, and Ghana, the Suez war, and the Algerian rising," this conference, according to Zbigniew Brzezinski, "became the first great continent-wide rally of awakening anti-Western nationalism and Pan-Africanism of various types."[105] The Chinese Communist embassy in Cairo soon became "the first basis for Chinese activity in Africa."[106] At the conclusion of his visit to Cairo in late 1963, Premier Chou En-lai was assured by Nasser of support for Peking's efforts to regain Taiwan.[107] Peking established diplomatic relations with four Middle Eastern countries — Egypt, Syria, Iraq, and Yemen — and maintained cultural and commercial contacts with others, such as Saudi Arabia, Jordan, and Lebanon.

Leaders in Peking saw conflicts in the Middle East as a reflection of wider, global struggles. Hence, a major Chinese Communist objective in Middle Eastern regions was to disrupt Western influence and alliance systems there through political action. The whole Palestinian problem was perceived as a result of an Anglo-United States struggle for control of the Middle East. In essence, according to Peking, the Middle East issue was a question of aggression versus anti-aggression, a question of the Palestinian and other Arab peoples striving for national liberation.[108] The Chinese government and people thus firmly denounced the political fraud concocted jointly by the so-called superpowers for a so-called peaceful settlement of the Middle East question. The first non-Arab government to recognize the Palestine Liberation Organization, the People's Republic began as early as 1964-1965 to train Palestinian guerrilla groups, extend economic and military assistance, and support Palestinian claims and methods of operation.[109]

During the Middle Eastern crisis in the summer of 1958, the People's Republic strongly supported Arab nationalism and called upon the Soviet Union to intervene, at least with volunteers, against the imperialists. In this situation, as in many others, Chinese Communist leaders seem to have felt that the Soviet Russians were too cautious. In any case, Peking's efforts were not unreciprocated.

On January 12, 1958 the People's Republic agreed to send technicians and other skilled workers to Yemen under a ten-year arrangement; a five-year trade agreement was also signed, and Peking affirmed its support of Yemen's claim to territories under British protection.[110] At about that time the New China News Agency announced that Egypt and the People's Republic had signed a trade agreement for the exchange of $72 million worth of goods during 1958.[111] There was considerable interaction between the two countries over the next few years, and in April 1965 a group of Egyptian scientists were reported to be flying to Peking "to acquaint themselves with various aspects of progress in the field of atomic research achieved by Chinese scientists."[112]

The efforts of the Peking regime were extended also into North Africa. The first contact between Peking and the Algerian National Liberation Front (FLN) took place in December 1958 when Mao Tsetung received a small delegation.[113] The People's Republic granted de facto recognition to the FLN and became the only nation promptly to recognize the Algerian provisional government proclaimed by the FLN. During the spring of 1959 an Algerian military mission arrived in the Chinese capital. By the end of that year the People's Republic was reported to have given the Algerian nationalist insurgents the equivalent of some $10 million in credits for the purchase of war materials and for carrying out propaganda and administrative functions.[114]

China and Black Africa

In sub-Saharan Africa the People's Republic in the 1960s began to concentrate on militant anti-imperialist movements. "If a government is identified with such a movement or effectively committed to its support," Zbigniew Brzezinski asserted at the time, "Peking will back it to the hilt. If the government is 'subservient to the imperialists' or suspected of seeking a deal with them, Peking will as resolutely back the opposition."[115]

As more and more African nations began achieving independence, a contest for recognition developed between the Chinese People's Republic and the Republic of China on Taiwan, each country seeking votes in the United Nations General Assembly on the issue of which regime should represent China in the United Nations. During the early 1960s a number of sub-Saharan countries — Brazzaville, Burundi, Congo, Ghana, Guinea, Mali, Somalia, Sudan, Tanzania, Uganda, Kenya, and Dahomey — established relations with Peking. Thirteen others recognized the Republic of China on Taiwan.[116] The Nationalist government also sought recognition with the Republic of the Congo, but Peking scored first. Taipei set up an embassy in Brazzaville after establishing formal relations on September 10, 1962, but severed relations in 1964 after a new government had recognized Peking. Taipei established relations, with the Congolese government in Leopoldville on August 10, 1960. The Camaroons became independent on January 1, 1960, and the Republic of China quickly recognized the new African country. On February 10 the two countries established diplomatic relations. By year's end the Nationalists had set up an embassy in Yaounde, the capital, and had appointed an ambassador.[117] A message was waiting from Peking when the Central African Republic proclaimed its independence — although Taipei also offered recognition and sent its ambassador to the independence ceremony.[118] Three African nations — Mauritania, Nigeria, and Senegal — recognized both Peking and Taipei, but established relations only with the latter. Ethiopia recognized Peking but did not establish relations with it at that time.

In seeking to extend their influence south of the Sahara, Chinese Communist leaders drew important distinctions between conditions there and the situation in North Africa and the Middle East. Countries in the latter regions were viewed as having been essentially semi-colonial, rather than colonial, and thus in a better position to gain independence by armed struggle than was the case in sub-Saharan Africa. It must be assumed, according to Harold Hinton in the mid-1960s, "that the CPC is disgusted at the fact that, because of 'imperialism's' relatively speedy and almost voluntary withdrawal from much of Africa, not a single sub-Saharan country that has gained its independence so far has done so primarily by means of 'armed struggle.' Another significant difference between Africa and the Middle East is that the former is even more immature, although not necessarily more unstable, from the political standpoint and much less homogeneous from the ethnic and cultural standpoints."[119] This latter consideration means that the strong emotions in sub-Saharan Africa often tended to be tribal or ethnic rather than nationalistic.

Peking's objectives in Africa during the early 1960s included gaining access to resources and markets, minimizing and counteracting the influences of the United States, Soviet Russia, Yugoslavia, India, Israel, the United Arab Republic, and other countries active in the region, and competing with the Nationalist government on Taiwan — as noted above — for recognition by African countries with potentially valuable votes in the United Nations General Assembly.[120]

The major goals of the People's Republic were probably associated with longer range considerations, however. The Chinese Mainland press gave the events of the January 1959 riots in the Belgian Congo great publicity. According to Peking, the Congo was "no longer an oasis of stability of the Eastern colonialists."[121] The Congo became formally independent on June 30, 1960, but Peking had already sent congratulatory telegrams to Patrice Lumumba and Joseph Kasavubu and had extended recognition.[122] Sekou Toure of Guinea, the first African president to visit the People's Republic, arrived in Peking on September 10, 1960 to be greeted by Liu Shao-ch'i, Chou En-lai, and a reported crowd of half a million people along the airport road. The week that followed was filled with banquets, speeches, talks with top leaders including Chairman Mao, a visit to Shanghai, and the signing of a Treaty of Friendship and also trade and economic agreements amounting to $23 million.[123] The Chinese People's Republic invited Malonsa Allias, the secretary general of the General Union of the Confederation of Peasants and Workers Trade Unions of the Congo, to Peking; he went in January 1962.[124] In August 1965 President Nkrumah of Ghana visited Peking.[125]

These interchanges, together with various Chinese Communist statements, offer a strong clue to Peking's expectancies at that time. "When the opportunity is ripe," Peking asserted in 1961, "the wave of revolution will roll up the continent of Africa like a mat so that more than 200 million Africans will become world leaders."[126]

Early Chinese Attitudes Toward Armed Struggle in Latin America

The course of early Chinese Communist relations with Latin America is even more difficult to trace than the pattern in Asia and Africa. A number of Latin American leftists visited Peking on the occasion of the World Federation of Trade Unions Conference there in November 1949 and again at a peace conference there in 1952. But relations between the People's Republic and the various regimes and revolutionary movements in Latin America remained limited, although Peking consistently emphasized wars of national liberation there until Latin America's partial rapprochement with the United States in the early 1960s.

In 1943 the USSR gave military support, through some of the East European countries, to a Guatemalan regime that was coming increasingly under local communist control. However, an opposition movement supported by the United States overthrew the government in June of 1943 without Soviet intervention. The failure of the USSR to act decisively in this situation, contrasted with Soviet intervention in Hungary two years later, may have created the impression that Moscow was not willing to take the same order of risk in Latin America it had been willing to take in Eastern Europe. Beyond this, the Cuban crisis of October 1962 seemed to indicate clearly a deep caution on the part of the USSR to make use of its ICBM capability in support of a communist state. For many Latin American communists at that time, the Chinese policy of armed struggle may have appeared somewhat more promising than Soviet Russia's policy of peaceful paths to power.[127]

Chinese Communist leaders were well aware that Latin American countries contain about one-third of all American foreign investments and had been under the influence of the United States for a long time. Moreover, they viewed the whole region as politically restless and unstable. During the late 1950s, and especially after the visit of Vice President Richard Nixon to the area in the spring of 1958, the People's Republic began increasing its political, economic, and cultural activities in Latin America, with particular attention to Mexico. But later, with Fidel Castro's achievement of power in early 1959, Chinese leaders became interested in Cuba, although earlier contacts had been with the Soviet-oriented Popular Socialist (communist) party.

Shortly after Castro's victory, Chou En-lai announced that China was "ready to give support and assistance to the fullest extent of [its] capabilities to all national independence movements" in Latin America, as well as Asia and Africa.[128] The Cuban revolutionary leader Che Guevara visited Peking in December 1960, but it was not until Castro had identified himself as a genuine Marxist-Leninist in early 1962 that Chinese Communist leaders began referring to the new Cuban regime as socialist.[129] During the Cuban missile crisis of October 1962, Peking gave the Cubans vociferous support and criticized Khrushchev for a "Munich policy."

During the early 1960s the Peking regime paid considerable attention to agrarian unrest in Bolivia, Colombia, Peru, and elsewhere, and had not hesitated to side with Panama in its disputes with the United

States. For the most part, however, Peking's interest in Latin America, as in Africa, seemed to be relatively long-range in major focus. In shorter range, the regime appeared to regard Latin America "simply as one more battlefield in its struggle to wrest the international communist movement from Soviet control, or failing that, to wreck it in order to make it ineffective as an instrument of Soviet policy."[130] Chinese Communist leaders also referred to countries south of the Rio Grande as constituting the "backyard" of the United States, which, as viewed from Peking, had remained economically and strategically dependent upon them. Commentators in Peking wrote hopefully of "lighting fires of revolution" there.[131]

On the basis of a proposal concerning the general line of the international communist movement put forward by the Chinese Communist party in 1963,[132] one would have expected a considerable Chinese effort to support revolutionary struggles in Latin America with material and organizational assistance to guerrilla groups operating in various parts of the region. However, as pointed out in the latter 1960s by Ernest Halperin, "Chinese support has so far been largely verbal" and directed more against Soviet influence there than against "United States imperialism."[133] Rebel movements in Bolivia, Brazil, Argentina, Colombia, Ecuador, the Dominican Republic, Guatemala, Peru, Uruguay, and Venezuela received such verbal support, and unrest in these countries was given periodic publicity by the Chinese. But few of these movements became involved in actual fighting along lines called for by the Chinese theory of people's war. According to one observer, at least "the only case of a Chinese-inspired people's war led by an established Communist Party" was the one inconclusively conducted (circa 1968-1970) by the Ejercito Popular de Liberacion (People's Liberation Army), the military wing of the pro-Peking Communist party of Colombia (Marxist-Leninist).[134]

Between 1960 and 1965 the Chinese had expressed respect for Ernesto (Che) Guevara's writings on guerrilla warfare and had tended to gloss over differences between his revolutionary theories and their own. By 1966, however, Sino-Cuban relations had worsened to the point where the Chinese "said nothing even remotely favorable about Guevara's activities in Bolivia from 1966 to late 1967," discouraged pro-Chinese Bolivian Communists from participating in his movement, and, after his death, publicly attacked his movement through those same Communists.[135]

During the 1960s "there was not an armed movement of any consequence in Latin America that did not receive at least implicit support from Peking," but after 1971, with the Sino-United States rapprochement, the Chinese turned to more open, conventional relations with Latin America and largely refrained from overt support to insurgent groups—at least in those countries with which the People's Republic had achieved friendly relations.[136]

Early Chinese Foreign-Aid Programs

Major Chinese Communist purposes in approaching the underdeveloped countries of Asia, Africa, and Latin America appear to have been primarily political, but many of their instruments were economic. In 1956 Peking initiated what was to become an extensive program of economic aid to a considerable number of less developed countries of the noncommunist world. For the next three years Chinese Communist aid extensions averaged somewhat less than $30 million per year. Only seven countries were involved: Cambodia, Ceylon, Indonesia, Nepal, the United Arab Republic, and Yemen. But during the six or seven years after 1960, average extensions of aid rose to about $125 million per year and twenty-one nations were involved:[137] eight in Asia (Afghanistan, Burma, Cambodia, Ceylon, Indonesia, Laos, Nepal, and Pakistan), ten in Africa (Algeria, Central African Republic, Congo (Brazzaville), Ghana, Guinea, Kenya, Mali, Somalia, Tanzania, and Uganda), and three in the Middle East (Syria, United Arab Republic, and Yemen).

These considerations suggest that, in pursuing such relations with underdeveloped countries in Asia, Africa, and Latin America, the Chinese People's Republic has been motivated as much, if not more, by political rather than economic considerations.[138] In part, of course, the Chinese People's Republic proposed to encourage political and economic developments according to the Maoist model. In this connection, Peking's leaders sought to present their country as a rapidly industrializing and expanding society that could supply capital goods as well as "textiles, fountain pens, and bicycles" and compete with the USSR for economic and political influence.[139] No doubt Chinese Communist aid programs in these regions were designed to perform somewhat similar functions. Many countries in Asia, Africa, and Latin America were hoping to achieve rapid industrialization, and the Chinese Communists wanted to see their program used as a model. "The spirit of frugality and sacrifice," according to Alexander Eckstein, "coupled with high rates of saving and investment, the large allocations of investment to heavy industry, and the emphasis on catching up rapidly with the West are all elements of the strategy which have a strong potential appeal in newly emerging nations."[140] In many cases, however, the major underlying Chinese purpose in Asia, Africa, and Latin America was probably to facilitate conditions for armed struggle and to lay the foundations for a trained Maoist leadership and a revolutionarily conscious rank and file.

In part, at least, frequent Chinese Communist references to Peking's respect for the sovereignty of receiver countries, the absence of imposed conditions, interest-free or low-interest loans, concessions on repayments, and so forth appear to have amounted to an "ill-disguised effort to draw invidious comparisons with Soviet foreign aid practice and to undermine the attractiveness of the Soviet program."[141] On the other hand, from its position of greater strength, the Soviet Union could afford to deal more freely with noncommunist governments: "Why ... rely on the uncertain success of communist parties in the relatively distant future when noncommunist leaders already in control of their governments" could be dominated now or in the much nearer future?[142]

During a widely publicized visit to Africa in 1964, Premier Chou En-lai advanced eight principles of foreign aid that emphasized (1) equality and mutual benefit, (2) respect for the sovereignty of other countries, (3) the availability of interest-free or low-interest loans with flexible time limits, (4) encouragement of self-reliance and independent economic development, (5) building projects requiring less investment and yielding quicker results, (6) providing quality equipment and materials of Chinese manufacture, (7) the mastering of techniques by personnel of the recipient country, (8) the expectation that Chinese Communist experts and advisory personnel would restrict themselves to the standards of living to which their counterparts in the recipient countries were accustomed.[143]

The number of Chinese technicians sent to foreign countries under technical assistance programs increased rapidly after 1960. "Although Communist China accounted for less than ten percent of all communist aid in less developed countries, its share in the total number of communist personnel in developing countries nearly doubled in 1965, exceeding the number of technicians from Eastern Europe, and numbering about half the 9500 Soviet technicians in the field."[144] To a considerable extent, this disproportionate number of Chinese technicians was attributable to the labor-intensive nature of many Chinese projects and the consequent numbers of manual laborers.

Chinese Communist aid projects emphasized geological surveys and feasibility studies, delivering machinery and equipment, and training indigenous personnel. A further component of Chinese Communist aid programs was awarding full scholarships for academic study in communist countries for periods of up to five and six years.

Except for military aid to North Korea, North Vietnam, and other countries or revolutionary movements near the Chinese periphery, the Peking regime tended to focus on economic and technical assistance as a channel for political influence. Indeed, whatever ideological differences might be apparent in Soviet and Chinese propaganda attitudes toward "bourgeois nationalist" governments in developing countries, more than a decade of foreign aid revealed China's "willingness to develop economic ties with a remarkable variety of such leaders in the pursuit of its ambitions in the area."[145] But Chinese Communist expectations had been inhibited in Africa and in some other places, no doubt, by the fact that former colonial areas were now being ruled by local elites with growing stakes in their own status quo. However, the overshadowing phenomenon was the Sino-Soviet conflict, which in many regions tended to create schisms in local communist parties, to fracture communist-led revolutionary movements, and to distort the day-to-day policies of both the Chinese and Soviet governments and parties in ways that, to the detached observer, often seemed dysfunctional to overall communist goals.

The Countryside Will Envelope the Cities

In an essay of September 1965 Lin Piao predicted that in time armed struggles in the underdeveloped, essentially agrarian "countrysides" of the world—in Asia, Africa, and Latin America—would envelope the industrial nations—the "cities"—and thus prepare the way for a new communist order, Maoist style. Thus, seemingly weak, newborn forces would eventually triumph over decadent forces that now seem powerful.[146] Meanwhile, the United States had "further weakened itself by occupying so many places in the world, overreaching itself, stretching its fingers out wide and dispersing its strength, with its rear so far away and its supply lines so long." As Mao Tse-tung had said, "Wherever it commits aggression, it puts a new noose around its neck. It is besieged ring upon ring by the people of the whole world." When the United States was hard pressed in one place, it had no alternative but to loosen its grip on others. Therefore the conditions became more favorable for the people elsewhere to wage similar struggles.

In terms of policy, Lin Piao's theses reinforced the idea that history was on the side of Maoist revolution not only in China but around the world. The dynamics for this revolution were seen as generated by objectively existing conditions in the underdeveloped regions that made armed struggles and the eventual triumph of the newborn forces virtually inevitable. These assumptions provided a basis for Chinese Communist foreign policies that were militant and determined, but at the same time somewhat cautious. Armed struggles should be encouraged and facilitated, but, if possible, high risks should be avoided. There was no point in paying excessive costs or even temporarily jeopardizing a revolution that had the force of history on its side in any case. The Lin Piao theses also provided a rationale for Peking's "bargain basement" approach to aiding armed struggles in other countries and a justification for the argument that each people bears the major responsibility for fighting its own revolutions. It could be argued, on the other hand, that under certain circumstances—in a nuclear crisis, for example—the conviction that armed struggles and people's wars were destined to triumph might influence Chinese leaders to take high risks that they would not have taken if they had not been so profoundly confident of the eventual outcome.

In the meantime, Chinese Communist strategists paid most attention to foreign communist parties in those areas where they had hopes of expanding their influence and power at an early date. "If underdeveloped countries are to be brought under Chinese Communist domination," John Kautsky wrote at the time, "then their present governments must eventually be overthrown and replaced by Communist parties looking to Peking for leadership. Hence they want these parties now to oppose the nationalist governments."[147] A major Chinese Communist weapon in these campaigns already operating in former colonial areas through armed struggle was the charge that Soviet Russia's coexistence diplomacy led, for the sake of peace, to betrayal of people's wars and the colonial revolutionary movements.[148]

Despite these sizeable aid commitments to other countries, Chinese Communist leaders extolled the virtues of self-reliance and self-help, attacked Soviet aid to nationalist governments as misplaced because it bolstered such regimes and weakened the position of the revolutionary forces, and gave only nominal support to the idea of economic aid as a significant factor in the national liberation struggle.[149]

Notes

1. John S. Aird, "Population Growth: Evidence and Interpretation," *China Quarterly*, no. 7 (July–September 1961), p. 45.
2. Chiao Kuan-hua, *Peking Review*, no. 47 (November 19, 1971), p. 2.
3. See Herbert Passin, *China's Cultural Diplomacy* (New York: Praeger, 1963).
4. China (People's Republic of China), Political Consultative Conference 1949, *The Common Program*, Article 56.
5. Ibid., Article 55.
6. See David Floyd, *Mao Against Khrushchev* (New York: Praeger, 1963), pp. 10–11.
7. Jan F. Triska, "Pattern and Level of Risk in Chinese Communist Foreign Policy-Making, 1949-1965," report to the Office of Naval Research (Contract N00014-65-A-0112-0005), September 1964. Discussions of these crises in subsequent pages draw to some considerable extent upon the materials of this study.

8.   George Patterson, "China and Tibet: Background to Revolt," *China Quarterly,* no. 1 (January–March 1960), pp. 87–102.

9.   "Discussion of the Report on the Situation in China," *International Press Correspondence* 6, no. 91 (December 30, 1926), pp. 1592-97.

10. A. Doak Barnett, *Communist China and Asia* (New York: Harper and Brothers, 1960), p. 406.

11. *Communist,* Bombay, July 1949, pp. 21–89.

12. The text of Liu Shao-ch'i's speech was transmitted in English Morse to North America, November 23, 1949.

13. Barnett, *Communist China and Asia,* p. 291.

14. Ibid., p. 304.

15. Nobutaka Ike, *Japan's Decision for War* (Stanford, Calif.: Stanford University Press, 1967), p. 66.

16. Ibid., p. 3.

17. Herbert Feis, *The Road to Pearl Harbor* (Princeton, N.J.: Princeton University Press, 1950), n. 16-17, p. 234.

18. Donald Lancaster, *The Emancipation of French Indochina* (Oxford: Oxford University Press, 1961), p. 200.

19. "Liu Shao-ch'i's Inaugural Speech at TUCAA Session," New China News Agency, November 23, 1949.

20. Barnett, *Communist China and Asia,* p. 304.

21. Milton Sacks, "The Strategy of Communism in Southeast Asia," *Pacific Affairs* 23, no. 3 (September 1950), p. 240.

22. Harold C. Hinton, *Communist China in World Politics* (Boston: Houghton Mifflin, 1966), p. 369.

23. George M. Mahin and John W. Lewis, *The United States in Vietnam* (New York: Dial, 1967).

24. Martin Lichterman, "To the Yalu and Back," in Harold Stein (ed.), *American Civil-Military Decisions* (University, Ala.: University of Alabama Press, 1963).

25. *New York Times,* March 2, 1949, p. 22, quoted in Allen S. Whiting, *China Crosses the Yalu* (New York: Macmillan, 1960).

26. Harry S. Truman, "United States Policy Toward Formosa," *Department of State Bulletin,* January 16, 1950, p. 79.

27. Glenn D. Paige, *The Korean Decision* (New York: The Free Press, 1968), pp. 66–68, and Dean C. Acheson, "Crisis in Asia," *Department of State Bulletin,* January 23, 1940, pp. 115–116.

28. Whiting, *China Crosses the Yalu.*

29. Allan B. Cole (ed.), *Conflict in Indo-China and International Repercussions: A Documentary History, 1945-55* (Ithaca, N. Y.: Cornell University Press, 1956), pp. 164–65.

30. Barnett, *Communist China and Asia,* p. 304.

31. Ibid., pp. 304–5.

32. Text in *Documents on International Affairs,* Royal Institute of International Affairs, London, 1954, pp. 140–41.

33. Charles A. McClelland et al., "The Communist Chinese Performance in Crisis and Non-Crisis: Quantitative Studies of the Taiwan Straits Confrontation, 1950-64," Report N60530-11207 to the Naval Ordnance Test Station, China Lake, California, December 1965, pp. 6–9. This type of crisis behavior differs somewhat from behavior in crises that escalate into full-scale war.

34. For the text of the Sino-Soviet joint communiqué, see *New York Times,* October 12, 1954.

35. McClelland et al., "Communist Chinese Performance in Crisis and Non-Crisis," pp. 43–45.

36. *Survey of China Mainland Press,* June 1–July 1, 1962, United States Consulate General, Hong Kong, 1962.
37. See Brian Crozier, "Peking and the Laotian Crisis: A Further Appraisal," *China Quarterly,* no. 11 (July–September 1962).
38. See Arthur Dommen, *Conflict in Laos: The Politics of Neutralization* (New York: Praeger, 1964); and A. M. Halperin and H. B. Ferdinand, *Communist Strategy in Laos* (Santa Monica, Calif.: The RAND Corporation, July 14, 1960), RM-2561.
39. See King Chen, "North Vietnam in the Sino-Soviet Dispute, 1962-64," *Asian Survey* 4, no. 9 (September 1964), pp. 1033–36, and James R. Townsend, "Communist China: The New Protracted War," *Asian Survey* 5, no. 1 (January 1965), pp. 1–11.
40. George M. Mahin and John W. Lewis, *The United States in Vietnam* (New York: Dial, 1967.).
41. G. F. Hudson, Richard Lowenthall, and Roderick MacFarquhar, *The Sino-Soviet Dispute* (New York: Praeger, 1961), p. 1.
42. Ibid.
43. See *The Anti-Stalin Campaign and International Communism: A Selection of Documents* (New York: Columbia University Press, 1956).
44. Hudson et al., *Sino-Soviet Dispute,* p. 1.
45. Vladimir Dedijer, *Tito* (New York: Simon and Schuster, 1953), p. 322.
46. William E. Griffith, *Sino-Soviet Relations, 1964–1965* (Cambridge, Mass.: MIT Press, 1967), p. 4.
47. George Tokmakoff, "The Origins of the Sino-Soviet Split," (Paper prepared for the Far Western Slavic Association Conference, University of British Columbia, Vancouver, B.C., May 4, 1968).
48. Ibid., pp. 7–8.
49. Ibid., p. 6.
50. Ibid.
51. Hudson et al., *Sino-Soviet Dispute,* pp. 2–3.
52. Ibid.
53. Ibid., p. 3.
54. Ibid.
55. *Sino-Soviet Relations and Arms Control, Collected Papers,* vol. 2 (Report to the United States Arms Control and Disarmament Agency, East Asian Research Center, Center for International Affairs, Harvard University, 1966), p. 3.
56. Alice Langley Hsieh, *Communist China's Strategy in the Nuclear Age* (Englewood Cliffs, N.J.: Prentice-Hall, 1962), p. xix.
57. Ibid.
58. "Chairman Mao Meets Chinese Students in Moscow," New China News Agency, in English from Moscow, November 18, 1957.
59. Mao Tse-tung, "Imperialists and All Reactionaries Are Paper Tigers," *Current Background,* no. 537 (November 12, 1958), p. 12.
60. "The Great Revolutionary Declaration," *Survey of China Mainland Press,* no. 1660 (November 27, 1957), pp. 27–28.
61. Lu Ting-i, "Get United Under Lenin's Revolutionary Banner," *New China News Agency,* April 22, 1960. Radio-teletype in English to Europe and Asia.
62. Griffith, *Sino-Soviet Relations,* p. 4.
63. Ibid., p. 5.
64. Ibid.
65. Ibid., p. 4.

66.   For an analysis of Albania in this situation, see Donald S. Zagoria, "Khrushchev's Attack on Albania and Sino-Soviet Relations," *China Quarterly,* no. 8 (October–December 1961), pp. 1–19.

67.   K'ang Sheng, "On the Current International Situation," *Peking Review,* no. 6 (February 9, 1960), p. 6. See also Hudson et al., *Sino-Soviet Dispute,* p. 79.

68.   Lu Ting-i, "Get United Under Lenin's Revolutionary Banner."

69.   William E. Griffith, "The November 1960 Moscow Meeting: A Preliminary Reconstruction," in Walter Laqueur and Leopole Labedz (eds.), *Polycentrism: The New Factor in International Communism* (New York: Praeger, 1962), pp. 105–26.

70.   Stavro Skendi "Albania and the Sino-Soviet Conflict," *Foreign Affairs* 40, no. 3 (April 1962), pp. 471–78.

71.   William E. Griffith, *Albania and the Sino-Soviet Rift* (Cambridge, Mass.: MIT Press, 1963).

72.   W. W. Douglas Jackson, "Borderlands and Boundary Disputes: Issues in Polycentrism," in Edward M. Bennett (ed.), *Polycentrism: Growing Dissidence in the Communist Bloc* (Pullman, Wash.: Washington State University Press, 1967), p. 42.

73.   Letter of the Central Committee of the CPSU to the Central Committee of the Chinese Communist Party (CCP), November 29, 1963, in *Peking Review,* no. 19 (May 8, 1964), pp. 18–21.

74.   Letter from the Central Committee of the CPSU to the Central Committee of the CCP, March 30, 1963, in William E. Griffith, *The Sino-Soviet Rift* (Cambridge, Mass.: MIT Press, 1965), p. 246.

75.   Ibid.

76.   Ibid., p. 244.

77.   Ibid.

78.   Ibid.

79.   "The CCP's Proposal Concerning the General Line of the International Communist Movement, June 14, 1963," in Griffith, *Sino-Soviet Rift,* p. 281.

80.   Ibid., p. 272.

81.   Ibid., p. 268.

82.   The Soviet "Open Letter," July 14, 1963, in Griffith, *Sino-Soviet Rift,* p. 299.

83.   Ibid.

84.   "China Replies to Latest Soviet Attack, September 1, 1963: A Comment on the Soviet Government's Statement, August 21, 1963," in Griffith, *Sino-Soviet Rift,* p. 371.

85.   Ibid., p. 376.

86.   "Apologists of Neo-Colonialism: Comment on the Open Letter of the Central Committee of the CPSU, October 21, 1963," in Griffith, *Sino-Soviet Rift,* pp. 477–78.

87.   "China Replies to Latest Soviet Attack," p. 383.

88.   Ibid., pp. 372–73.

89.   Ibid., p. 371.

90.   "Marxism-Leninism Is the Basis of the Unity of the Communist Movement, *Kommunist,* October 18, 1963," in Griffith, *Sino-Soviet Rift,* p. 471.

91.   Chou Yang, Speech at the Fourth Enlarged Session of the Committee of the Department of Philosophy and Social Science of the Chinese Academy of Sciences, October 26, 1963, *Peking Review* (January 3, 1964), pp. 10–27.

92.   S. L. Poplai, *Asia and Africa in the Modern World* (Bombay: Asia Publishing House, 1958), appendix, vi, p. 206.

93.   George M. Kahin, *The Asian-African Conference* (Ithaca, N.Y.: Cornell University Press, 1956), pp. 60–61.

94.   Final communiqué of the Asian-African Conference, Bandung, April 24, 1955, in Kahin, *Asia and Africa in the Modern World,* appendix, pp. 84–85.

95.   See Chou En-lai's Report to the Chinese People's Consultative Conference, New China News Agency, January 30, 1956.

96.   For an interpretation of these developments by a defector from the Soviet Diplomatic Corps in Burma, see *Experiences of a Russian Diplomat in Burma* (Philadelphia and New York: Lippincott, 1962), especially chapter xi.

97.   *New York Times,* December 13, 1951, p. 1.

98.   Ibid., December 15, 1951, p. 3.

99.   Ibid., August 26, 1952, p. 1.

100. *Concerning the Question in Tibet* (Peking: Foreign Language Press), May 6, 1959, pp. 7–9; "The Revolution in Tibet and Nehru's Philosophy," *Current Background,* no. 570 (May 11, 1959); *New York Times,* September 10, 1959, pp. 1, 4; New China News Agency in English to East Asia, October 26, 1959.

101. Patterson, "China and Tibet", p. 93.

102. P. H. M. Jones, "Passes and Impasses: A Study of the Sino-Indian Border Dispute," *Far East Economic Review* 39, no. 9 (February 28, 1963), pp. 443–58.

103. George W. Patterson, *Peking versus Delhi* (New York: Praeger, 1964).

104. Zbigniew Brzezinski (ed.), *Africa and the Communist World* (Stanford, Calif.: Stanford University Press, 1963) pp. 150–51.

105. Ibid., p. 154.

106. Ibid., p. 152.

107. "Developments of the Quarter: Chronology," *Middle East Journal* (Spring 1964), pp. 236–37.

108. Vice-Premier Li Hsien-nien, New China News Agency, Peking, July 17, 1970, in *Current Background* (November 12 and 17, 1970), p. 54. See also, Vice-Chairman Tung Pi-wu, New China News Agency, Peking, August 2, 1970, ibid., p. 54.

109. Yitzhak Shichor, "The Palestinians and China's Foreign Policy," in Chün-tu Hsüeh, *Dimensions of China's Foreign Relations* (New York: Praeger, 1977), p. 157.

110. "Developments of the Quarter: Comment and Chronology," *Middle East Journal* (Spring 1958), p. 193.

111. "Developments of the Quarter: Comment and Chronology," *Middle East Journal* (Winter 1958), p. 67.

112. "Developments of the Quarter: Comment and Chronology," *Middle East Journal* (Summer 1965), p. 352.

113. "Chairman Mao Greets FLN Delegation," New China News Agency (December 7, 1958).

114. "Developments of the Quarter: Comment and Chronology," *Middle East Journal* (Winter 1960, 1966, and Summer 1958), p. 298.

115. Brzezinski, *Africa and the Communist World,* p. 162.

116. See "Africa and the Two Chinas: A Summary of Known Facts (As of January 1, 1965)," *Africa Report* (January 1965), back cover.

117. Loren Fessler, "Chinese Interests in Africa," *The China Mainland Review* 1, no. 2 (September 1965), p. 15.
118. Ibid., p. 20.
119. Harold C. Hinton, *Communist China in World Politics* (Boston: Houghton Mifflin, 1966), p. 189.
120. Leon M. S. Slawecki, "The Two Chinas in Africa," *Foreign Affairs* 41, no. 2 (January 1963), pp. 398–409, and George T. Yu, "Peking versus Taipei in the World Arena: Chinese Competition in Africa," *Asian Survey* 3, no. 9 (September 1963), pp. 439–53.
121. Fessler, "Chinese Interests in Africa," p. 14.
122. Ibid., p. 19.
123. Ibid., p. 21.
124. Loren Fessler and Min S. Yee, "Chinese Interests in Africa," *The China Mainland Review* 1, no. 3 (December 1965), p. 26.
125. Ibid., p. 25.
126. Quoted by John W. Lewis, *Chinese Communist Party Leadership and the Succession to Mao Tse-tung: An Appraisal of Tensions* (Washington, D.C.: External Research Staff, Policy Research Study, Department of State, 1964), p. 27.
127. Hinton, *Communist China in World Politics.*
128. Robert L. Worden, "China's Foreign Relations with Latin America," in Hsüeh, *Dimensions of China's Foreign Relations,* p. 195.
129. Ernest Halperin, "Peking and the Latin American Communists," *China Quarterly,* no. 29, (January–March 1967), p. 114. See also Peter S. H. Tang and Joan Maloney, *The Chinese Communist Impact on Cuba,* Research Institute on the Sino-Soviet Bloc Studies, monograph series no. 12 (Chestnut Hill, Mass., 1962) for a somewhat different assessment.
130. Halperin, "Peking and Latin American Communists," p. 154.
131. Peter Van Ness, *Revolution and Chinese Foreign Policy* (Berkeley: University of California Press, 1971), p. 147.
132. Reproduced in Griffith, *Sino-Soviet Rift* p. 265.
133. Halperin, "Peking and Latin American Communists," p. 111.
134. Worden, "China's Foreign Relations with Latin America," p. 197.
135. Daniel Tretiak, "China's Relations with Latin America: Revolutionary Theory in a Distant Milieu," in Jerome Alan Cohen (ed.), *The Dynamics of China's Foreign Relations* (Cambridge, Mass.: Harvard University Press, 1970), p. 102.
136. Worden, "China's Foreign Relations with Latin America," p. 197.
137. Kovner, "Communist China's Foreign Aid to Less Developed Countries" in *An Economic Profile of Mainland China,* vol. 2, p. 611.
138. Alexander Eckstein, *Communist China's Economic Growth and Foreign Trade* (New York: McGraw-Hill, 1966), p. 5.
139. Ibid., pp. 5–6.
140. Ibid., p. 6.
141. Kovner, "Communist China's Foreign Aid to Less Developed Countries," pp. 617–18.
142. John H. Kautsky, *Communism and the Politics of Development,* (New York: Wiley and Sons, 1968), p. 119.
143. *Peking Review,* no. 34 (August 21, 1964), p. 16.
144. Kovner, "Communist China's Foreign Aid to Less Developed Countries," pp. 614–15.
145. Ibid., p. 611.

146.   Lin Piao, "Long Live the Victory of People's War!" in Griffith, *Sino-Soviet Relations,* p. 432.
147.   Kautsky, *Communism and the Politics of Development,* p. 119.
148.   Brzezinski, *Africa and the Communist World,* p. 170.
149.   Ibid., p. 611.

Chapter Six

Recent Chinese Communist Relations With the Major Powers

Year by year, Sino-Soviet polemics — along with other contributing factors — affected the Communist bloc, the world configuration of power, and international relations everywhere. In the days when the USSR had been the only communist-governed state and all the other communist parties had lacked control of state power, "it had been natural enough," as suggested by Geoffrey Hudson, "for all non-Russian communists to look to the Kremlin for guidance, which had been in practice words of command, but now that there were several other communist parties with the powers and responsibilities of sovereign governments — and one of them ruled over the most populous nation in the world — it was no longer appropriate for a single party to lay down articles of faith and policies for all."[1] Increasingly, the situation now demanded some new machinery for interparty consultation.

During the early 1950s, the Peking regime had seen a close unity of outlook and policy between liberated China and the Soviet Union, then still a socialist country. But with the 20th Congress of the Communist Party of the Soviet Union, according to a Westerner who has lived and worked in China and has interviewed Chinese leaders, the USSR embarked on a capitalist road. In the later 1950s, differences arose between the parties of the two countries, but "unity was still the main content of the relationship."[2] At first, the struggle over these differences played a secondary role, but as it became evident that they were irreconcilable, the interparty struggle came into public view. "Struggle became primary but unity was still possible on a number of issues." However, in the late 1960s and early 1970s the situation worsened, until between China and the Soviet Union today "there is only all-out struggle. No basis for unity on any major issue exists."[3] Moreover, as ties between the USSR and the People's Republic deteriorated, China's relations with the United States, Japan, and Western Europe improved somewhat.

Sources of the Continuing Controversy

The Sino-Soviet controversy is often assumed to be primarily ideological, and certainly the polemics have seemed to support this view. But environmental differences and differences in historical experience have contributed directly to political conflict and also to differences in ideology. This complexity of issues between the two communist states cuts straight to the heart of the disagreements between those who believe that environment, experience, and interaction come first, followed by ideas and ideology, and those who believe that ideas and ideologies come first and are the prime movers. The viewpoint of this book is that, fundamentally, this is a chicken-and-egg situation; that environment, experience, interaction, ideas, and ideology are highly interdependent, and that any effort to separate them is artificial and arbitrary. People's ideas and ideologies tend to be reflections of the physical universe and of perceptions of themselves as they react and relate to others. But human beings cannot even conceive of the physical universe, of other people, or of themselves except through ideas, and hence their ideas as well as the realities of their environment shape their behavior. To separate environment and ideas as if either had human significance without the other seems a futile exercise. Changes in the environment and changes in ideas go along together, and it cannot be otherwise. That is the human condition.

Undoubtedly, there have been many different factors contributing to the Sino-Soviet conflict — some historical, some ideological, some related to Chinese and Russian nationalism. The course of events suggests, however, that different levels of capability and dissatisfaction, different interests, and different political cultures in Communist China and Soviet Russia have combined to set the stage for and give impetus to the differences in outlook between the two countries. The USSR is generally more powerful than China, although Peking has been bending every effort — including the establishment of nuclear capability — to enhance Chinese influence and strength. But Chinese inferiority is evident on many levels.

Overall, the Soviet Union has a larger territory (22,402,000 square kilometers) than Mainland China (9,561,000 square kilometers), smaller population (249,000,000 as compared with up to 900,000,000 or more Chinese), more resources, and lower population density (11 persons per square kilometer in the USSR as compared with about 83–86 in Mainland China). The Russian and Chinese economies are on wholly different levels of growth. The USSR is a highly industrialized nation, second only to the United States. China is still in an intermediate stage of industrialization. The Soviet Russian GNP has been calculated at $624,000,000 in contrast to a Chinese figure of $180,000,000. The Soviet Russian per capita GNP is $2498 according to 1975 estimates; the Chinese $221.[4]

In terms of capability, Communist China is still low compared with the Soviet Union. But Chinese dissatisfactions, determination, and will appear high relative to those of the USSR (although the latter should not be considered low). Domestically, the Russians have more to protect; the Chinese have more to gain. Traditionally, Chinese leaders have tended to view their country as rightfully a great power and sometimes as the greatest power. After generations of weakness and humiliation at the hands of foreigners, many Chinese understandably compare their country with other countries, including the Soviet Union, and look forward to the reestablishment of China's primacy. From the viewpoint of Chinese Communist leaders in a hurry, the USSR never provided assistance enough. From a Chinese perspective, moreover, the Soviet Union — situated along China's longest border — has become increasingly an expansionist, social imperialist power with a tendency to exploit weaker countries and a desire for world domination.

Social imperialism

In Peking's view "social imperialism" had come about because leadership in the USSR had been usurped by a "revisionist renegade clique," with the result that the Soviet state was "no longer an instrument with which the proletariat suppressed the bourgeoisie," but had become "a tool with which the restored bourgeoisie suppresses the proletariat." Under these conditions, the Soviet revisionist renegades were turning the USSR "into a paradise for a handful of bureaucrat-monopoly-capitalists of a new type, a prison for the millions of working people."[5] The People's Republic attacked the USSR for being soviet only in name and accused Brezhnev for talking "humbug" about Soviet democracy and a Soviet socialist state of the whole people. Judging by what had been done by the Soviet Union in Czechoslovakia, according to Peking, it was not hard to see what the "Soviet leadership supports, what it opposes, and on whose side after all it stands."[6]

The linkage between United States imperialism and social imperialism did not mean that the People's Republic of China had to have a common policy for the two countries, however. To "put down the revolution of the world's oppressed nations and people," United States imperialism and social imperialism were clearly in collusion, but at the same time, in order "to satisfy their own imperialist interests," they were in bitter contention — in Europe, the Middle East, and the Mediterranean Sea. Such contentions were growing sharper and sharper.[7]

The Chinese Communist view of the world was illustrated by the argument put forward by Peking's representatives in the United Nations with respect to disarmament. China had always been in favor of disarmament, but the blame for the arms race could not be place on all countries, nor could disarmament be demanded of all countries alike. Many Asian, African, and Latin American countries were being subjected to threats and aggression. The peoples of Vietnam, Laos, and Cambodia were "engaged in a war against United States aggression and for national salvation." The Palestinian and other Arab peoples were struggling for their right to national existence and for the recovery of their occupied territory. Guinea and several other African countries were engaged in struggles against the colonialists' armed aggression and threats of subversion. The people of Mozambique, Angola, Zimbabwe, Azania, and Namibia were engaged in struggles for national liberation against the white colonialist rule and racial oppression.

Such countries had taken up arms because they were compelled to do so, and for them it was not at all a question of an arms race. The two superpowers, however, had established thousands of military bases abroad. It was these superpowers that had obstinately rejected the prohibition and destruction of nuclear weapons, meanwhile "contending with each other for nuclear superiority" in order to "press forward with their policies of blackmail, expansion, aggression, and war." The threat to world peace originated "precisely from these two superpowers."[8] The problem facing China was to locate the contention and underlying contradiction, identify the principal enemy, and apply a revolutionary combination of alliance and struggle.

During its more crucial phases, the Great Proletarian Cultural Revolution appears to have intensified the conflict between Chinese Communist leaders and the USSR. The Soviet Union, for example, seems to have seized upon some of the excesses of the Cultural Revolution as a rationale for termination of a post-Khrushchev policy of avoiding public polemics with the People's Republic.[9] As suggested by Thomas Robinson, by the latter part of 1966 events in China "were opening that country to ridicule the world over" so that the USSR "had nothing to lose and much to gain from moving into a full-scale denunciation of the Maoist regime."[10]

A series of violent incidents ensued. A Soviet ship, the *Zagorsk*, was detained for twenty days in the Chinese port of Darien because of an alleged refusal of the Soviet captain to obey a Chinese pilot. When the ship was released, its sides had been painted with Chinese slogans. Then a scuffle took place between Chinese students and Soviet citizens in front of Lenin's tomb. Outside their embassy in Moscow, Chinese staff members erected an anti-Soviet showcase that was promptly demolished by Russian chain saws. Worker delegates nailed protests on the Chinese embassy gate.[11] At one point Sinkiang appeared to be in turmoil, and there were also reports of Soviet troop movements close to the Chinese border.[12] Diplomatic relations were on the point of complete rupture.

United States intervention in Vietnam may have had different effects upon Sino-Soviet relations at different times, depending upon certain other factors. Initially, the escalation of United States troops in support of the Saigon government and the bombing of North Vietnam seem to have put heavy additional strains upon the Sino-Soviet relationship. However, the movement of Soviet Russian supplies across Chinese territory in support of North Vietnamese troops required some minimal modus vivendi between Moscow and Peking. If relations became too hostile and this supply route were cut off, the USSR would be forced to depend upon sea access through Haiphong, which, in turn, would greatly enhance the probability of a United States–Soviet confrontation and even the outbreak of World War III almost on China's borders. This was an eventuality that the Peking government could not have courted with equanimity.

Sino-Soviet competition and hostility had not only been evident along their common border, but also in Indochina, where during the late 1950s and early 1960s Moscow and Peking had vied for influence. This competition had been especially apparent in the 1961–1962 Laos crisis.[13] Subsequently, the establishment of the Chinese-sponsored Indochinese United Front against the United States in April 1970 and the residence of Prince Sihanouk of Cambodia in Peking marked the relative decline of Soviet influence in Southeast Asia. But events in Bangla Desh and the strengthening of Soviet naval influence in the Indian Ocean did much to readjust the balance. An examination of any globe would reveal that from the viewpoint of Peking, the People's Republic was all but surrounded by

Soviet territory and influence on three sides, and by the forces of the United States on remaining flanks.

By early 1967, the extreme intensities of Sino-Soviet recriminations and threatening activities, together with realities of the Vietnam War, "brought both the Russians and the Chinese to the realization"—temporarily, it turned out—"that their interrelationship had reached its nadir, from which point it could no longer descend. The result was that, from mid-February 1967 forward, Sino-Soviet relations were carried out by both sides on a plane of reality different from what had been the case previously."[14]

Then, on March 2 and 15, 1969, armed clashes occurred between Chinese and Soviet frontier guards along the Ussuri River, which forms the border between China's Heilungkiang Province and the Soviet Far East. The scene of the fighting, which resulted in considerable loss of life, was a small, uninhabited island known to the Chinese as Chenpao Island and to the Russians as Damansky Island. The boundary in this region is regulated by the Treaty of Aigun (1858) and the Treaty of Peking (1860). Both of these treaties had been imposed on the Chinese Empire by the tsarist government at a time when China had been weakened by war with France and Britain. With the deterioration in Sino-Soviet relations, numerous minor incidents had occurred along this and other sectors of the international boundary since 1960. In February 1964 boundary negotiations had begun in Peking, but had been suspended the following August without any progress having been made.

Further clashes occurred over the next few months of 1969—both along the Ussuri and Amur rivers, and on the border between Chinese Sinkiang and the Soviet Republic of Kazakhstan. In the wake of the most serious confrontation, which took place August 13 on the Sinkiang border, the People's Republic undertook active preparations for a possible Soviet attack. Meanwhile, Chinese irritation had been exacerbated by a Soviet decree replacing the Chinese or Manchu names of a number of towns in the Soviet Far East with Russian names.

China denounced the Soviet invasion of Czechoslovakia as a "monstrous crime" and a manifestation of "imperialist jungle law."[15] The impact of this Soviet act on Chinese foreign policy far exceeded the impact of the Cultural Revolution. Indeed, within a few days a Chinese commentator used the words "social imperialism" borrowing from Lenin, who had referred in this way to social democrats, whom he viewed as socialist in name but imperialist in their actions. Later, this term was changed to "socialist imperialism" for use specifically against a socialist country.[16]

Following the death of Ho Chi Minh, Premier Chou En-lai flew to Hanoi on September 4, 1969, but returned to Peking the following day. His failure to attend the funeral was criticized by the Russians as disrespectful to Ho, and was widely attributed to his desire to avoid meeting Kosygin in Hanoi. After having left Hanoi for Moscow, however, Kosygin turned back from Tajikistan and flew east to Peking, where he and Chou conferred for six hours and issued a joint communiqué. After this conversation, no further frontier clashes were reported, and the number of Soviet propaganda attacks launched against the People's Republic diminished, although China continued its public criticisms of the USSR.[17]

Despite deteriorating relations between the two countries, China and the Soviet Union signed trade and payments agreements on August 5, 1971 and June 13, 1972, and on January 30, 1974, a non-stop air service was inaugurated between Peking and Moscow. Overall, however, Sino-Soviet trade had deteriorated since reaching a peak in 1959. The United States dollar value of Chinese trade with the USSR in 1941 had been $750 million; by 1959 the total had reached $2,055 million; by 1970 it had dropped to only $45 million; by 1974 total trade between the two countries had risen to $280 million—roughly the 1950 level.[18]

Soviet criticisms of China increased with the announcement in July, 1971, of President Nixon's forthcoming visit to Peking, but waned somewhat after the flight and death of Lin Piao in September —perhaps because of an unfounded anticipation on the Russians' part of a political change in the People's Republic favorable to them. However, anti-Chinese diatribes increased again in December when the Soviet Union supported India while China and the United States supported Pakistan in a war that broke out between the two South Asian countries.

Linking the United States and USSR

For several years during the 1960s Chinese Communist spokesmen had tended more and more to link United States imperialism and Soviet social imperialism as if they were a single enemy—much as many Westerners had perceived the USSR and the People's Republic as a threatening monolith in the early 1950s. In the public press Chinese leaders asserted their opposition, in 1971, to the hegemony of one or two superpowers and insisted that the People's Republic would "never seek big power status." The country would "stand forever side by side with all nations subjected to aggressive control, intervention, or subversion by superpowers."[19] But with the continuation of Sino-Soviet diatribes, waning United States enthusiasm for the Vietnam War, the admission of the People's Republic into the United Nations, the emerging of new alignments in South Asia, President Nixon's projected visit to Peking, and the like, it seemed more and more plausible that a significant shift in the world configuration of power might be in the making.

Soviet leaders refused to sign an agreement on maintaining the status quo of the Sino-Soviet border that would have precluded the use of force between the two countries. "They even deny the existence of the disputed areas on the Sino-Soviet borders," Chou En-lai told the 4th National People's Congress.[20] With variations in its intensity, the Sino-Soviet propaganda war continued throughout the period from 1971 through 1975. Peking accused the "Soviet propaganda machine" of "repeatedly spreading the fallacy of 'two-Chinas' " and "openly prettifying the Chiang Kai-shek clique" by suggesting that "the status of Taiwan" remained to be determined.[21] An article published July 1, 1971—the fiftieth anniversary of the founding of the Chinese Communist party—denounced Soviet leaders as "renegades" and "world storm troopers opposing China, opposing Communism and opposing the people." In March 1974 Sino-Soviet relations reached their lowest level since the 1969 border clashes as the People's Republic expelled five Soviet nationals, including three diplomats, for alleged espionage, whereupon a Chinese diplomat was expelled from the USSR on similar charges.

During much of the 1960s and early 1970s, the United States and the Soviet Union were perceived from Peking as more or less equal enemies of China and as threatening the emerging nations of the Third World and the independence of the lesser industrial countries of the Second World. Under these conditions, China had seen the need for a worldwide united front against the two superpowers. The task had been to mobilize the Third World and unite with forces of the Second World willing to oppose the United States and the Soviet Union.

The two superpowers were not only the biggest international oppressors and exploiters; they were also the source for dangerous world conflict. "Their fierce contention is bound to lead to war some day," Chou told the 4th National People's Congress in January 1975. "The people of all countries must be prepared."[22] The contention for hegemony between the two superpowers was becoming more intense, Chou En-lai told the Congress, and had extended to every corner of the world.[23]

The New Main Danger

On his return from a visit to the People's Republic in early 1976, William Hinton, a Western observer who, along with many years' experience in China, has often been extremely critical of the United States' role in eastern Asia, was asked: "Do the Chinese consider the two superpowers to be equal dangers to the people of the world?" His answer revealed the extent to which the configuration of world power was perceived by Peking to have changed:

> *Not any more. There was a period when the super-powers were seen as more or less equal enemies threatening not only the emerging nations of the third world, but also the independence of the lesser industrial nations of the second world. What China called for then was a worldwide United Front against the two superpowers. . . Today there is still a major contradiction between the people of the world and the two superpowers, but as between the two superpowers, one—the Soviet Union—is more dangerous than the other. It is, in fact, the* main danger *confronting the whole world today.*[24]

Among many issues in the Sino-Soviet dispute, the People's Republic was especially concerned about Soviet economic and strategic expansionism beyond its territorial borders. For example, Peking accused the USSR of using technical cooperation and joint stock agreements in order to plunder Mongolia of copper and other mineral resources.[25] Also, from a Chinese perspective, the USSR was reaching for maritime supremacy in order to extend its influence on the various continents and thus establish world domination.[26] On a relatively unobtrusive, nonviolent level, the Soviet Union was "extending its fishing operations to distant waters" not only in order to "plunder the world's fishing resources" but also to "raise their bid for world maritime hegemony against the other superpower."[27] At the same time, the USSR was strengthening its naval forces and changing its strategy from 'offshore defense' to 'attack in the distant seas'." Ostensibly, all this was being done in order to defend the "security and interests of the Soviet Union." But what interests did the Soviet fleets have to safeguard in places several thousand kilometers away from the Soviet coasts, the Chinese wanted to know. And who was threatening Soviet security? [28]

Changing Relations with the United States

Among factors influencing new Chinese views and assessments of the world configuration during the 1960s and early 1970s were the continuing conflict with the USSR, United States difficulties at home, the Vietnam stalemate, waning United States enthusiasm for the war and eventual withdrawal, the rapid technological and economic growth of Japan, and China's own economic development and advancement in nuclear technology.

During the late 1940s and early 1950s world communism had looked to many Americans and other Westerners like a single, monolithic, threatening power bloc. By the middle 1960s the unmistakable trend was toward the fractioning of this bloc into many national communist states with distinct national interests and often at odds with one another. Some critics contended, however, that the United States government often proceeded as though Stalin were still alive and the Communist bloc far more united than perhaps it had ever really been. Defenders of United States policy argued that communists were still communists, despite their polemics, and that the country could not afford to alter its basic policy of containment. But during the 1960s, policymakers in Washington and Peking became aware of a shifting distribution of interests in the world and a gradually changing configuration of power.

According to one of his closest advisers, President Kennedy "felt dissatisfied with his administration's failure to break new ground" with respect to China policy.[29] He concluded, however, that any United States initiative toward negotiations, diplomatic recognition, or admission to the United Nations would be interpreted by the Chinese as rewarding their aggressiveness. He was also concerned about how any such initiative would be received by Congress and by the country as a whole. There was one difference between Kennedy's policy toward China and that of Eisenhower. The previous administration had seemed committed to the idea of a single China — governed, preferably, by Chiang Kai-shek. Like many other United States liberals, however, Kennedy was prepared to think in terms of a two-Chinas solution — a position that may have influenced Mao's conclusion that he, Kennedy, was worse than Eisenhower. From Mao's viewpoint — as well, indeed, as from Chiang's — there was only one China. The issue between Mao and Chiang was who should govern it.[30] In any case, the Kennedy administration decided to defer any major changes in United States China policy until a second term.

Contacts between the Chinese and United States governments were even more infrequent and tenuous under the Kennedy administration than they had been previously. In October 1961 Foreign Minister Ch'en Yi hinted that the People's Republic was still interested in ministerial level discussions with the United States, as they had been during the Eisenhower administration. But in response, Kennedy and Secretary of State Rusk confined themselves to noting that the two countries were already involved in ambassadorial meetings in Warsaw and in a Geneva conference in Laos. From that point on, the frequency of the Warsaw meetings declined further. However, the Kennedy administration did alter the United States position toward China's admission to the United Nations, abstaining on a resolution to postpone discussion and securing a favorable vote to make the representation of the People's Republic an important question requiring a two-thirds majority to be passed. The 'important question' device was to be successful in excluding the PRC from the U.N. for another ten years."[31]

Shortly after President Kennedy's assassination, Assistant Secretary of State for Far Eastern Affairs Roger Hilsman gave a speech on China policy. While criticizing Chinese leaders for their "hatred," "obsessive suspicion," and "paranoid view of the world" and identifying the regime as one "which finds no ground of common interest with those ideals it does not share," Hilsman asserted, nevertheless, that "we pursue today toward Communist China a policy of the open door," and are determined "to keep the door open to any possibility of change, and not to slam it shut."[32]

The Johnson administration made a number of overtures toward the People's Republic, but United States involvement in the Vietnam War on China's southern flank and its continued support of the Nationalist regime on Taiwan were undoubtedly major factors in preventing substantive progress. "The Chinese people are ready to make all necessary sacrifices in the fight against imperialism" Ch'en Yi told a press conference September 29, 1965. "It is up to the U.S. President and the Pentagon to decide whether the United States wants a big war with China today."[33] China had been waiting sixteen years for the United States to attack, he added. "My hair has turned grey in waiting."[34]

In a statement before the Subcommittee on the Far East and the Pacific, of the House Committee on Foreign Affairs (March 16, 1966), Secretary of State Dean Rusk asserted on the one hand that the United States should do nothing that might encourage Peking or anyone else "to believe that it can reap gains from its actions and designs." It was as essential to "contain Communist aggression in Asia" as it was in Europe. On the other hand, the United States must "continue to make it plain" that if Peking were to abandon its belief "that force is the best way to resolve disputes" and to give up "its violent strategy of world revolution," an era of good relations with China would be welcomed in Washington.[35]

Soon after, on April 10, Chou En-lai issued the Four Point Statement on China's policy toward the United States: The People's Republic would not take the initiative to provoke a war with the United States; but if any country in Asia, Africa, or elsewhere met with aggression "by imperialistic actions headed by the United States," China would give support, just as the Chinese would rise in resistance against a United

States attack on the People's Republic. No matter how many United States "aggressor troops" might attack, they would "certainly be annihilated in China;" once such a war broke out, there would be no boundaries.[36]

A month later, Chou revealed an eighteen-month-old Chinese proposal for a Sino-United States agreement on no-first-use of nuclear weapons.[37] Secretary of State Rusk, questioned about it at a press conference, asserted that "mere declarations of words on such matters would not be adequate." But at a subsequent ambassadorial meeting, the United States inquired whether China would be prepared to sign a partial test-ban treaty in return for a United States no-first-use pledge. The answer was "no."[38] Noting various United States statements calling for reconciliation, building a bridge, and entering into peaceful competition with China, Peking charged in September 1966 that the United States government for seventeen years had pursued a policy of hostility and aggression with respect to the People's Republic and had engaged in military provocation and war threats. These activities had proved irrefutably that the United States government did not have "the slightest sincerity about easing Sino-U.S. relations."[39]

Nixon and improved relations

It remained for the Nixon administration to bring about a significant alteration in relations between the two countries. In his inaugural address, President Nixon referred to some of the rethinking he had done in the course of many foreign trips since the days of his vice-presidency. "He believed that an era of negotiation was now succeeding the period of confrontation" and referred to the possibility of improved relations with China.[40] Then he spoke of upcoming negotiations with China in Warsaw. "We will be interested to see what the Chinese Communists may have to say at that meeting, whether any changes of attitude on their part on major substantive issues may have occurred."[41]

The Cultural Revolution was formally brought to an end during the 9th Congress of the Chinese Communist party in April 1969. At that point, the People's Republic resumed its interest in foreign relations and began returning the country's ambassadors to their posts.[42] And at Guam in July 1969 Nixon enunciated what became known as the Nixon Doctrine, which seemed to foreshadow a lessening of the United States commitment to Asia. Specifically, it indicated that in future Vietnam-type situations, the United States would "look to the nation directly threatened to assume the primary responsibility of providing the manpower for its defense."[43]

While reducing United States military strength in Vietnam, Nixon in July 1969 also undertook a series of small steps relaxing travel and trade restrictions with China, "clearly signalling to Peking his hopes of a genuine dialogue." Already in his foreign policy message to Congress on February 25, 1971, the President had emphasized the need to draw the People's Republic into a "constructive relationship with the world community."[44]

Early in April 1971 the United States table tennis team, which had been playing in the World Championships in Japan, accepted — along with other teams and with the blessings of Washington — an invitation from the Peking leadership to tour Mainland China.[45] Chou En-lai, who received the group, noted that "Contacts between the people of China and the United States had been very frequent in the past, but lately they were broken off for a long time. Your visit to China on invitation has opened the door to friendly contacts between the people of the two countries. We believe that such friendly contacts will be favored and supported by the majority of the two peoples."[46]

On April 14—four days after the table tennis team's arrival in China—President Nixon announced a relaxation of the United States embargo on direct trade with the People's Republic, and on June 10 a list was published of goods that could be sold freely to China, including wheat and diverse manufactured goods. And in a television broadcast on July 15, President Nixon announced his acceptance of an invitation to visit the People's Republic.

Sino-American relations are no less complex than Sino-Soviet ties, but for the first time in twenty-two years both Peking's and Washington's policies showed notable improvement. Chinese willingness to develop a new relationship with the United States might have been in considerable part a consequence of a Chinese expectation of prolonged disagreements with the Soviet Union taken together with the Chinese leadership's apparent desire to avoid risking simultaneous Sino-American and Sino-Soviet high-level conflict.

The impediments to the achievement of a full-blown détente were impressive, however. Of primary concern to the Chinese leadership was Washington's military and political support of the Taiwan regime. Chou En-lai, the Chinese premier, on July 19, 1971 once again stated Peking's position: "Taiwan is a province of China and it is an inalienable part of China's territory. And after the second World War Taiwan had already been restored to China. And the liberation of Taiwan by the Chinese people is an internal affair which brooks no foreign intervention."[47] On the surface, then, Sino-United States relations did not appear to be entirely propitious for a new and better turn. "No one imagined that President Nixon would go to China. He had been a hard-liner toward Communism at home and abroad and especially toward China."[48] Moreover, from the time of Nixon's first press conference, Chinese comment on his administration had become increasingly critical.

Nevertheless, at the invitation of Chou En-lai, the President of the United States visited the People's Republic from February 21 to February 28, 1972. In the course of this sojourn, President Nixon and Premier Chou held "extensive, earnest, and frank discussions" of the normalization of relations between the two countries "as well as on other matters of interest to both sides." Talks in the same spirit were held between Foreign Minister Chi Peng-fei and Secretary of State William Rogers.

A basis for improved relations between the United States and the People's Republic was suggested in a banquet toast made by Premier Chou En-lai to President Nixon:

> *The social systems of China and the United States are fundamentally different, and there exist great differences between the Chinese Government and the United States Government. However, these differences should not hinder China and the United States from establishing normal state relations on the basis of the Five Principles of mutual respect for sovereignty and territorial integrity, mutual non-aggression, non-interference in each other's internal affairs, equality and mutual benefit, and peaceful coexistence; still less should they lead to war.*[49]

On February 21 Chairman Mao and President Nixon "had a serious and frank exchange of views on Sino-U.S. relations and world affairs."[50]

The two countries agreed in a joint communiqué that both wished "to reduce the danger of international military conflict"; that "neither should seek hegemony in the Asia-Pacific region" and that each was "opposed to efforts by any other country or group of countries to establish such hegemony"; and that neither was "prepared to negotiate on the behalf of any third party or to enter into agreements or understandings with the other directed at other states."

The People's Republic reaffirmed its position that the Taiwan situation posed the "crucial question obstructing the normalization of relations" with the United States; that the government of the People's Republic was the "sole legal government of China"; that Taiwan was "a province of China"; that the "liberation of Taiwan" was China's "internal affair in which no other country had the right to interfere"; and that all United States forces and military installations must be withdrawn from Taiwan. The Chinese government expressed its firm opposition to such concepts as one China, one Taiwan, one China, two governments, two Chinas, or an independent Taiwan. Peking also opposed the proposition that the status of Taiwan remained to be determined.

The United States acknowledged for its part that "all Chinese on either side of the Taiwan Strait" maintained that "there is but one China and that Taiwan is a part of China." The United States government asserted that it did not challenge that position, but reaffirmed "its interest in a peaceful settlement of the Taiwan question by the Chinese themselves." With this prospect in mind, the United States affirmed "the ultimate objective of the withdrawal of all U.S. forces and military installations in Taiwan." Meanwhile, the United States would "progressively reduce" such forces and installations as tension in the area diminished.[51]

Both countries were in agreement that "it would be against the interests of the peoples of the world for any major country to collude with another against other countries" or for major countries "to divide up the world in spheres of interest."

Encouraging as these interchanges were from many viewpoints, they did not inhibit the Chinese leadership from criticizing United States policies in Southeast Asia and elsewhere. During the early summer of 1972 Chinese sources condemned the escalation by the United States of "its war in Vietnam by mining and blockading" North Vietnamese ports and also the expansion of the war through the dispatching to Thailand of large numbers of additional aircraft and the use of "Thai reactionaries."[52]

Peking also publicized charges from Hanoi that condemned the United States for other "imperialist crimes" against the Vietnam people. "By continually attacking dike systems and other hydraulic works in the midst of the wet monsoon season," a North Vietnamese spokesman was quoted as asserting, "the U.S. imperialists attempted to cause big floods so as to jeopardize the lives and property of millions of people."[53] Also, Peking saw recurrent crises of the dollar — an outcome of "wild expansion abroad" and "wars of aggression" — as an indicator of a decline in United States imperialism,[54] as contrasted with an expanding socialist imperialism on the part of the USSR.

However, with the withdrawal of United States forces from Southeast Asia, Chinese assessments of the world configuration of power began to change, and these changes seemed to require a reassessment of the United States role in the world. From Peking's perspective, relations between the People's Republic and the United States had moved through a development directly opposite to that taken by Sino-Soviet relations. "During the liberation war in China and the Korean War there had been all-out struggle between China and the United States." Later, with the exacerbation of the Sino-Soviet conflict, Peking had perceived both the USSR and the United States as enemies. But now that situation had begun to change, and while the United States and

China were still in conflict on many fronts, unity was possible on specific issues. Specifically, the two countries shared an interest in resisting the spread of Soviet power in Asia, Europe, and elsewhere.[55]

Chinese leaders saw the United States "in its total, all-around ability to command world resources, to produce, and to make war" as still the world's strongest power. But this power was perceived as limited in many ways and difficult to mobilize. The United States was overextended and had suffered two major defeats overseas (Korea and Vietnam). Its imperial ambitions had been exposed "before the world's people and before the people of the U.S." In short, Chinese leaders saw the United States as an empire in decline that would not bring its great strength to bear in crucial world events.[56] Under such circumstances, Chinese criticism of the United States was directed more and more against signs of weakness, policies of détente and any United States tendency to compromise with or yield to the USSR. Peking was thus severely critical of the Sonnenfeldt Doctrine, a statement made by Helmut Sonnenfeldt, counsellor to the United States State Department, at a December 1975 meeting in London of United States ambassadors in Europe. Identifying an urge by Eastern European countries since World War II to break out of the Soviet economic and political straightjacket, Sonnenfeldt at the same time referred to United States policy as striving for an evolution in the relationship between the Eastern European and the USSR as an organic one so that those relations would not sooner or later explode into World War III.[57]

Just previous to the Sonnenfeldt statement, however, President Ford, in a speech at the East-West Center in Honolulu, reiterated the United States commitment to strengthen its presence in Southeast Asia and, with the cooperation of Japan and the People's Republic, to ensure a stable balance in the Asian Pacific. In what he referred to as a Pacific Charter, the United States president — like the PRC—supported the idea of strengthening the Association of South East Asian Countries (ASEAN), a grouping of noncommunist nations.

As will be evident farther along, these new events and emerging relationships required some adjustments in Chinese attitudes toward Hanoi, North Korea, Japan, and the Philippines, together with new policies toward guerrilla movements in various parts of the world.

Chinese leaders saw Japan as dangerously vulnerable to attack. Thus, until Japan could build adequate defense forces, it would have to continue relying on alliance with the United States. On the other hand, it was prudent for the Philippines to demand that the United States vacate its bases one by one. But complete withdrawal would leave the islands vulnerable to Soviet incursion. Thus, the Philippines also required time to develop adequate bases.

However, the Peking regime considered Europe to be the main center of conflict, the necessary base for any plan for world domination, and, for the Russians, the main prize. Soviet social imperialism was thus making "a feint to the east while attacking in the west."[58] No country in Europe could stand alone "against overt and covert pressure from the USSR," and hence, according to Peking, it was necessary for them to maintain their NATO alliance with the United States.[59]

Changing Relations with Europe

During the 1960s and early 1970s, the People's Republic had perceived the well-being of Europe as closely tied to the policies of both the United States and the Soviet Union. Thus, in order to ensure peace and security there, it had been necessary "to oppose firmly the aggression, interference, subversion, and control by the two superpowers, to disband the military blocs, criticize the presence of foreign armed forces and bring about peaceful coexistence of the European countries on the basis of independence and sovereignty, mutual non-aggression, non-interference in each other's internal affairs and equality and mutual benefit."[60]

Once having identified the USSR as the main enemy, however, the People's Republic was forced to alter its view of and attitudes toward Europe. Europe was central, as it always had been, to any plan of world domination, and it was therefore the main center of conflict. However, since the Russians wanted control of it, the principal danger came from the Soviet Union, and it was of utmost importance that any threat from that direction should be blocked.

The danger to Eastern Europe emerged from the economic and political imperialism practiced there by the USSR. Through the Council for Mutual Economic Assistance (CMEA) in the Eastern bloc, the USSR was working on so-called economic integration in Eastern Europe in order to "control, exploit and plunder" other countries belonging to the Council and "to practice neocolonialism in them."[61] Since capitalism had been restored in the Soviet Union in all spheres of endeavor, it was therefore inevitable that "internationally the Soviet revisionists will grab raw materials, seize outlets for investment, scramble for markets and contend for world hegemony."[62]

In this connection, Peking accused the Soviet Union of taking advantage of the need by East European countries for certain important industrial resources by monopolizing the supply of fuel and other raw materials to them "under the pretext of the international division of labor" and "fraternal cooperation." These tactics had enabled the

USSR "to blackmail the East European countries" into providing "loans, equipment and labor to help the Soviet Union tap its own resources and build factories."[63] But the main prize for the USSR, according to Peking, was Western Europe. The danger lay in a serious weakening of NATO forces and the possibility of a Soviet attack. European unity was of utmost importance.

Returning a visit to Peking by Sir Alec Douglas-Horne, United Kingdom foreign and commonwealth secretary, Foreign Minister Chi Peng-fei in July 1973 had carried on a series of talks in London on Korea, Vietnam, the Indian subcontinent, East-West relations, and European security. An agreed statement welcomed increased contact between Britain and China and expressed hopes for the further development of cultural and commercial relations. Then, during a four-day visit to Paris, Chi conferred with President Pompidou, Prime Minister Messmer, and Foreign Minister Jabert and, at a banquet in his honor, asserted that China supported the efforts of West European countries "to unite on the basis of equality and reciprocal advantage in order to make themselves powerful."[64]

At about the same time, *Peking Review* noted the failure of the thirty-five nation Conference on European Security and Cooperation to reach agreement on substantive questions, but underscored European criticisms of Soviet policy, warning against a sense of false security in Europe, and the dangers of "big power hegemonism by one or two superpowers."[65] *Peking Review* also called attention to French reports of "an exceptional reinforcement of Soviet troops stationed in Eastern Europe and the considerable increase in their fire power,"[66] and quoted the West German newspaper *Die Welt* as estimating "the superiority of the conventional armed forces of the Warsaw Pact over that of NATO's" as "more than two to one" and continuing to grow. "Détente is a word," *Die Welt* was quoted as editorializing, "while armament is a fact." Additionally, *Peking Review* called attention to a communiqué reporting upon talks between the United States secretary of defense and the West German defense minister proclaiming their determination to "proceed with important force improvement within the framework of NATO plans" and the need to strengthen further the cooperation of the European allies in "improving the European defense contribution" in the face of Soviet arms expansion.[67]

Later, in May, 1975 then senior Vice-Premier Teng Hsiao-P'ing and Foreign Minister Ch'iao Kuan-hua paid an official visit to France on the invitation of the French government. No formal communiqué was issued, but the two countries reached a number of agreements that amounted to new departures in relations between them. Specifically, regular Sino-French consultation at the foreign ministerial level was agreed upon, a joint economic commission would be established to promote Sino-French bilateral trade, and the French president and prime minister accepted Teng's invitation to visit the People's Republic the following year.[68] At about the same time, an agreement was reached between China and the European community to establish formal relations, and on September 15 the official ambassador from the People's Republic was accredited in Brussels.

During September of the same year, Edward Heath, the former prime minister of Britain, visited China and had meetings with Vice-Premier Teng and with Mao which covered the whole field of international affairs. In part, Heath subsequently attributed the latter meeting to Mao's "intense personal interest in European affairs and the part Britain plays in them." The Chinese, Heath reported, were fearful that the Europeans "might be kidding themselves" about the value of the Helsinki agreement, anxious lest the USSR acquire bases in Vietnam, and afraid that a major war might break out between the two superpowers.[69]

And during a visit to China in late October and early November 1975, West German Chancellor Helmut Schmitt reached agreements with the Chinese on maritime transport and civil aviation. Differences over east-west détente were not narrowed, according to unofficial reports, but there had been unanimity on Chinese support for political efforts toward German reunification and for the unification of Europe.[70]

Identifying Soviet Russia as the main danger, according to the Chinese leadership, required a thorough understanding of the new relationship of forces that had developed in the world. For, in terms of this new relationship, the immediate task was to "strike the main blow at the Soviet Union." This meant that Peking was not interested in détente so much as in maintaining in Europe forces capable of blocking a Soviet invasion. Within such a framework, Chinese leaders tended to prefer hard-liners in high office both in Europe and the United States—Heath rather than Wilson, Strauss rather than Brandt, and Schlesinger rather than Kissinger.[71] According to a West German radio report, the Chinese deputy foreign minister in that country had quite openly demanded that Europe should protect itself from the Soviet threat by intensified cooperation with the United States in political, military, and currency matters.[72]

The People's Republic in the United Nations

By 1970, support among member countries in the United Nations for admission of the People's Republic of China had been growing for several years, and the issue increasingly was not whether but when? A serious obstacle, however, was the fact that Chiang Kai-shek's Republic of China on Taiwan was a permanent member of the Security Council, enjoying veto power, and a charter member of the United Nations.

During early months of 1971 the United States — in line with the general softening of its attitudes toward the People's Republic — moved from its long-standing policy of opposing Peking's admission to what amounted to a fairly explicit two Chinas position. In his annual Report to Congress on American Foreign Policy on April 17, President Nixon expressed the readiness of the United States to establish a dialogue with Peking, but he warned that an honorable relationship could not be achieved at the expense of Asian countries allied with the United States — among which was the government of the Republic of China on Formosa. With respect to the United Nations, this meant, from the United States viewpoint, that a formula should be found for admitting the Peking government without displacing the Nationalist government on Taiwan.

On July 15 Albania, Algeria, and fifteen other countries (Cuba, Guinea, Iraq, Mali, Mauritania, the People's Democratic Republic of Yemen, the People's Republic of the Congo, Rumania, Somalia, Sudan, Syria, the United Republic of Tanzania, Yemen, Yugoslavia, and Zambia) successfully tabled a draft resolution that would have provided for the inclusion in the United Nations of both the Republic of China and the People's Republic. Citing this tabling action with approval, the Ministry of Foreign Affairs in Peking unequivocally denounced the whole two Chinas concept.[73] On the other hand, Secretary of State Rogers announced explicitly on August 2 that the United States, while supporting the admission of the People's Republic to the United Nations, would oppose any action to expel the Republic of China (Taiwan) or otherwise deprive it of representation in the United Nations.[74]

After considerable parliamentary maneuvering and application of pressure by both sides, the United Nations General Assembly on October 25, 1971 defeated a United States resolution to declare the expulsion of Taiwan an "important question," which requires a two-thirds majority, and voted overwhelmingly to admit the People's Republic and to expel the Chinese Nationalist government. The final vote came on a resolution sponsored by Albania and twenty other countries (Algeria, Ceylon, Congo (Brazzaville), Cuba, Equatorial Guinea, Guinea, Iraq, Mali, Mauritania, Nepal, Pakistan, Rumania, Somalia, Southern Yemen, Syria, Sudan, Tanzania, Yemen, Yugoslavia, and Zambia). The resolution was adopted 76 – 35, with 17 abstentions. At the plenary meetings of the 26th Session of the United Nations on November 15, 1971 representatives of 57 countries made speeches to welcome the delegation of the People's Republic of China.[75]

As a United Nations member, the People's Republic has been active in many specialized agencies of the organization and has supported numerous issues concerning countries of the developing world.

In the mid-1970s, the world was still characterized by grossly unequal access among the various countries to vital resources and to the technologies that might help to improve conditions in those societies that were less favored. depending upon one's criteria for national independence and sovereignty, about ten countries of the world had per capita GNPs of $5,000 for the year 1973. The figure for the United States was $6,100 that year, and for the USSR it was $2,030. By contrast, some 82 nations had per capita GNPs of $500 or less in 1973, and the per capita GNPs for about 16 were less than $100 for the year. The 1973 figure for China was $270.[76] Similarly, in 1975 about 17 countries had per capita consumptions of 5000 or more kilograms of coal equivalent (all forms of commercial energy translated into coal equivalents). The figure for the United States was 11,485 and that for the USSR was 5,252. But about 74 nations consumed less than 500 kilograms of coal equivalent per capita that year, and approximately 17 consumed less than 100 kilograms of coal equivalent. The figure for China was 650.[77] Although the figures for individual countries tend to rise somewhat year-by-year, the gap between the poor nations and the rich, industrialized countries seems to widen.

Under such circumstances, the poor nations have found since their emergence from foreign suzerainty, "that political liberation does not necessarily bring economic liberation" — although economic independence tends to be impossible without political independence. Regardless of their respective ideologies and forms of government, these poor nations "have been forced to question the basic premises of an international system which leads to ever-widening disparities between the richest and poorest nations and to a persistent denial of equality of opportunity." Over recent years there has been a growing tendency among these disadvantaged nations, again irrespective of ideology or form of government, to call for a drastic restructuring of the world economic order.[78]

To some of these nations at least, the People's Republic of China represents a poor country that understands their difficulties, that has developed its own relatively successful path to development, and that appears willing as a member of the United Nations to support them in a number of specific ways. For example, in the Committee on Commodities of the United Nations Conference on Trade and Development, meeting in Geneva during February and March 1973, the People's Republic took a strong stand in support of the improvement of trade in primary products for the developing countries.[79] Similarly, in various conferences on the sea bed and the law of the sea, the Peking regime has stood with numbers of Third World countries in denouncing the superpowers, especially the Soviet Union, for trying to protect their maritime hegemony at the expense of weaker nations. China consistently supported Latin American countries in safeguarding the principle of a two hundred nautical-mile offshore limit as opposed to Soviet and United States support for no more than a twelve-mile limitation.[80]

At the month-long 4th Session of the United Nations Conference on Trade and Development held in Nairobi during May 1976, the Chinese delegation supported Third World demands for improving terms of trade for developing countries, confirming their right to fix prices in the world market, resisting usury imposed by the superpowers, alleviating debts, obtaining more control over transfers of technology, and establishing means of regulating multinational corporations.[81] "The repayment of heavy foreign debts has drained the developing countries of a great part of their hard-earned foreign exchanges. Every year these 86 developing countries have to put aside 10, 20, or even 30 percent of their foreign exchange as debt payments."[82]

Notes

1. G.F. Hudson, Richard Lowenthall, and Roderick MacFarquhar, *The Sino-Soviet Dispute* (New York: Praeger, 1961), p. 2.
2. William Hinton, "China's World View," *The Guardian,* May 5, 1976, p. 17.
3. Ibid.
4. Ruth Leger Sivard, *World Military and Social Expenditures 1976* (Leesburg, Virginia: WMSE Publications, 1976), pp. 21, 22, 24, 26. For more recent and slightly different figures, see UNCTAD, *Yearbook of International Trade Statistics,* 1975.
5. "Long Live the Victory of the Dictatorship of the Proletariat," *People's Daily,* March 17, 1971.
6. "What Are Indian Expansionists Trying to Do?" *Peking Review,* no. 16 (April 16, 1971), p. 8.
7. "Statement of the Ministry of Foreign Affairs of the People's Republic of China," *Peking Review,* no. 35 (August 27, 1971), p. 12.
8. Chiao Kuan-hua, Chairman of the Delegation of the People's Republic of China, at the Plenary Meeting of the United Nations General Assembly, November 24, 1971, as cited in *Peking Review,* no. 49 (December 3, 1971), p. 14.
9. Thomas Robinson, "Sino-Soviet Relations During the Cultural Revolution" (paper delivered at the Far Western Slavic Association Conference, University of British Columbia, Vancouver, B.C., May 4-5, 1968), p. 1. See also Thomas W. Robinson, "The Sino-Soviet Border Dispute," *The American Political Science Review* 66, no. 4 (December 1972), 1175–1202.

10. Robinson, "Sino-Soviet Relations During the Cultural Revolution," p. 22.
11. Ibid., p. 33.
12. Ibid., p. 38.
13. Brian Crozier, "Peking and the Laotian Crisis: An Interim Appraisal," *China Quarterly*, no.7 (July–September 1961), pp. 130–132 and 136.
14. Ibid., p. 2.
15. *Peking Review*, no. 34 (August 23, 1968), supplement, pp. vi and viii.
16. Ishwer C. Ojha, *Chinese Foreign Policy in an Age of Transition* (Boston: Beacon Press, 1971), p. 237.
17. Ibid., p. 245.
18. Nai-Ruenn Chen, "China's Foreign Trade, 1950-74," in *China: A Reassessment of the Ecomomy* (Washington, D.C.: U.S. Government Printing Office, 1975), p. 648.
19. Editorial, *People's Daily* (January 23, 1971).
20. Chou En-lai, "Report on the Work of the Government," *Peking Review*, no. 4 (January 24, 1975), p. 24.
21. "Soviet Revisionism: Two China Fallacy," *Peking Review* 16, no. 51 (December 21, 1975), p. 21.
22. Chou, "Report on the Work of the Government," p. 24.
23. Ibid.
24. Hinton, "China's World View," p. 15.
25. "Mongolia: Soviet Revisionists Plunder Mineral Resources," *Peking Review* 17, no. 27 (July 5, 1974), p. 29.
26. Chiang Chien-tung, "Soviet Social Imperialism: Maritime Hegemonic Features Fully Exposed," *Peking Review*, no. 18 (April 30, 1976), p. 25.
27. Chin Ti, "Soviet Fishing Industry: A Case of Expansionism," *Peking Review*, no. 19 (May 7, 1976), p. 23.
28. Chiang, "Soviet Social Imperialism: Maritime Hegemonic Features Fully Exposed," p. 26.
29. Theodore C. Sorensen, *Kennedy* (London: Hadder and Stoughton, 1965), p. 665.
30. Roderick MacFarquhar, *Sino-American Relations 1949-71* (New York: Praeger, 1972), pp. 182-84.
31. Ibid., pp. 184-86.
32. Speech to the Commonwealth Club, San Francisco, December 13, 1963, from extracts quoted in MacFarquhar, *Sino-American Relations*, pp. 201-205.
33. MacFarquhar, *Sino-American Relations*, pp. 221-22. See also *Peking Review*, no. 41 (October 8, 1965), p. 14.
34. MacFarquhar, *Sino-Soviet Relations*, pp. 221- 22.
35. Extracts in MacFarquhar, *Sino-American Relations*, pp. 222-25.
36. "Comrade Teng Hsiao-ping's Speech at the Shanghai Rally," *Peking Review*, no. 20 (May 13, 1966), p. 5.
37. "Premier Chou's Four Point Statement on China's Policy Toward the U.S." *Peking Review*, no. 21 (May 20, 1966), p. 17.
38. MacFarquhar, *Sino-American Relations*, p. 215.
39. Ibid., p. 231.
40. Ibid., p. 241.
41. Nixon at his First Press Conference, January 27, 1969, in MacFarquhar, *Sino-American Relations*, p. 247.

42. Ibid., p. 242.
43. Ibid., pp. 242-43.
44. Ibid., p. 244.
45. "U.S. Table Tennis Delegation Arrives in Peking," New China News Agency, Peking, April 10, 1971, in *Survey of China Mainland Press*, no. 4880 (April 1971), 115-16.
46. "Premier Chou Meets Table Tennis Delegations," *Peking Review*, no. 14 (April 23, 1971), p. 5.
47. "Interview of Premier Chou En-lai with the Committee of Concerned Asian Scholars, July 19, 1971, held in the Hall of the People, Peking," *Peking Review*, no. 30 (July 23, 1971), p. 20.
48. MacFarquhar, *Sino-American Relations*, p. 243.
49. Chou En-lai, "Toast to President Nixon," *Peking Review*, nos. 7-8 (February 25, 1972), p. 8.
50. "Joint Communiqué Agreed by the Chinese and U.S. Sides in Shanghai," February 27, 1972 in *China Quarterly*, no. 50 (April–June 1972), p. 399.
51. Ibid., p. 402.
52. "No War Escalation," *Peking Review*, no. 27 (July 7, 1972), p. 10.
53. Ibid., p. 11.
54. "Dollar Crisis", *Peking Review*, no. 29 (July 21, 1972), p. 13.
55. Hinton, "China's World View," p. 15.
56. Ibid.
57. "Sonnenfeldt Doctrine Evokes Strong Reaction," *Peking Review* (April 30, 1976), p. 27.
58. Chou En-lai, "Report on the Work of the Government," *Peking Review*, no. 4 (January 24, 1975), p. 24.
59. Hinton, "China's World View," p. 15.
60. Chiao Kuan-hua, *Peking Review*, no. 41 (October 13, 1972), p. 7.
61. "CMEA-Soviet Revisionism's Instrument for Neo-Colonialism," *Peking Review* 17, no. 27 (July 5, 1974), p. 24.
62. "Social Imperialism: Rapacious International Exploiter," *Peking Review* 17, no. 45 (November 8, 1974), p. 16.
63. Ibid., p. 25.
64. *Keesing's Contempory Archives: Weekly Diary of Important World Events* (London: Keesing's Publications, July 16-22, 1973), p. 25991A.
65. "CESC: Outstanding Differences," *Peking Review*, no. 29 (July 20, 1973), p. 19.
66. "Détente and Arms Expansion: Relaxing Vigilance is Dangerous," *Peking Review*, no. 30 (July 27, 1973), p. 17.
67. "FRG–USA: Cooperation within NATO Stressed," *Peking Review*, no. 31 (August 3, 1973), p. 21.
68. "Quarterly Chronicle and Documentation," *The China Quarterly*, no. 63 (September 1975), pp. 590-91.
69. "Quarterly Chronicle and Documentation," *The China Quarterly* no. 64 (December 1975), pp. 812-13.
70. "Quarterly Chronicle and Documentation," *The China Quarterly* no. 65 (March 1976), p. 208.
71. Hinton, "China's World View," p. 15.
72. "Quarterly Chronicle and Documentation," *The China Quarterly* no. 63 (September 1975), p. 590.
73. "Statement of the Ministry of Foreign Affairs of the People's Republic of China," *Peking Review*, no. 35 (August 27, 1971), p. 5. See also "Resolutely Oppose U.S. Scheme of Creating 'Two Chinas'," *Peking Review*, no. 40 (September 30, 1971), p. 5.

74. *Keesing's Contemporary Archives* (August 14–21, 1971), p. 24765.
75. *Peking Review*, no. 49 (December 3, 1971), pp. 28-47.
76. United Nations, UNCTAD, *Yearbook of International Trade Statistics,* 1975.
77. United Nations, *World Energy Supplies, 1950-1974.*
78. Jan Tinbergen, Antony J. Dolman, and Jan van Ettinger, *RIO: Reshaping the International Order, A Report to the Club of Rome* (New York: E. P. Dutton, 1976), p. 15.
79. "China Supports Developing Countries' Demand for Improvement of Trade in Primary Products," *Peking Review*, no. 11 (March 16, 1973), p. 11.
80. Yang Ying, "Maritime Overlord's Alibi," *Peking Review,* no. 48 (November 30, 1973), pp. 21-22.
81. "Third World Wins New Victories in Joint Struggle Against Hegemony: 4th UNCTAD Session," *Peking Review*, no. 24 (June 11, 1976) p. 19.
82. "Third World's Debt Burden and Superpower Usury," p. 21.

Chapter Seven

Asia, Africa, Latin America, and the World Revolution

If capability, dissatisfaction, history, and traditions account for a large part of a country's external behavior, its ideology and world view or belief system frequently shape its expectations of other countries and its own style of behavior. This tends to be particularly true of communist states, in view of the specificity of their ideologies. Marxist-Leninist-Maoist theory defines major issues of conflict, identifies revolutionary and reactionary forces, predicts imperialistic behavior on the part of the United States and other powerful capitalist countries, and specifies modes for bringing dissatisfactions and capabilities to bear upon the worldwide struggle. But although relations between the Russian and Chinese Communist parties have involved considerable conflict since the mid-1920s, few, if any of us would have found much in Marxist-Leninist ideology, per se, to prepare us for the Sino-Soviet controversy.

However, as the Sino-Soviet conflict developed, Peking drew upon Marxist-Leninist writings to define the USSR as a socialist state turned capitalist, to analyze its behaviors as socialist-imperialism, and to define Soviet leaders as antagonists in the world revolutionary struggle. This change in prognosis and the alterations in the configuration of power that underlay it led Chinese leaders to feel that any extension of Soviet power and influence in the Third World amounted to a social imperialist threat in the area, rather than a victory for national liberation, and in the long run a threat to the security of the People's Republic as well. This meant that, along with the threats of western imperialism and United States military presence in

Vietnam, the world with which Chinese leaders had to deal was an extremely complex one indeed. As if all this complexity were not enough, China's foreign policy problems were further compounded by the domestic confusions of the Great Proletarian Revolution.

According to early guidelines for the Cultural Revolution, the revolutionary activities of the Red Guards were to be confined to the party itself and were not to penetrate political, economic, and other governmental organs of the state — although it was recognized that, since most top party leaders were also ranking governmental officials, there was certain to be some spillover. By the autumn of 1966 it became evident, however, that party members under attack as "capitalist roaders" were taking refuge in their state functions and that the field of pursuit must be widened. In November of that year the Red Guard opened a direct attack upon Foreign Minister Ch'en Yi as an ideological backslider. The consequences of this and subsequent attacks were too numerous and complex for treatment here. The essential outcomes were that Chinese diplomats in foreign countries soon found themselves compelled to defend their own ideological positions by any means available while conducting diplomacy on an every embassy on its own basis. Under such circumstances, most Chinese diplomats found themselves in positions where safety, if there were any, seemed to depend upon appearing as revolutionary as possible.

A Policy of Incitement

During the late 1950s and early 1960s, as described in Chapter Six, the People's Republic had gained considerable political attention, if not influence, in many parts of Asia, Africa, and Latin America. Beginning about 1965, however, and seemingly in line with Lin Piao's essay, Peking identified a long list of revolutionary targets, including Burma, India, Indonesia, Israel, Cameroon, Rhodesia, Southwest Africa, Spanish Guinea, and Ecuador.[1] Thus, well before the Cultural Revolution, China had begun openly inciting revolutionaries in countries throughout the world, especially Southeast Asia, to follow the path of armed struggle outlined by Mao, to overthrow their governments by force, and thus to achieve national liberation. Such policies aroused opposition in many quarters that had previously been well-disposed toward Peking and gave rise to considerable conflict. Chinese diplomatic and other official personnel "were expelled from Kenya, India, Indonesia and Mongolia; a Chinese official was stabbed to death in the embassy in

Rangoon." There were anti-Chinese riots in India, Indonesia, Burma, and Nepal and demonstrations nearly every week in Peking outside some foreign embassy.[2] Beginning in January 1967, enormous demonstrations took place in Peking outside the Soviet, British, Indian, Outer-Mongolian, Nepalese, Indonesian, and Burmese embassies.[3]

By September 1967 China had become involved in quarrels of one magnitude or another with thirty-two countries, including Algeria, Iraq, Kenya, Tanzania, Morocco, Tunisia, the United Arab Republic, Zambia, Cuba, Afghanistan, Burma, Cambodia, Ceylon, Japan, Mongolia, Nepal, North Korea, and Singapore.[4] The People's Republic might have appeared to an outside observer as at odds with the world. An incident or confrontation of one kind or another had damaged Peking's relations with almost every government "except ever-loyal Albania, and with many of the noncommunist countries with which Peking had established diplomatic relations as well."[5]

Peking appeared to be particularly disturbed over the revolt under military and militant Muslim auspices in Indonesia, which Chinese Communists interpreted as imperialist intervention against growing communist influence within the Sukarno government. On October 4, 1965, the Chinese People's Republic and an Indonesian delegation issued a joint statement on the "further development of friendship" and "opposition to imperialism, colonialism, and neocolonialism." Just two weeks later, however, the Peking government was protesting Indonesian armed forces attacking and searching the Office of the Chinese Commercial Counsellor, located in the Chinese embassy in Indonesia, and threatening and insulting Chinese diplomatic personnel.[6]

This was only the first of a series of Chinese protests concerning Indonesian raids on Chinese consulates, insults to the Chinese Communist flag, insults to Mao Tse-tung, persecution of Chinese nationals, attacks of right-wing hooligans, wrecking and looting of Chinese shops and schools in Djakarta and elsewhere, illegal seizures of Chinese nationals' properties, attacks by Indonesian armed forces, and the like.[7] Peking accused the Djarkarta regime of "fascist outrages" and "brutal crimes."[8] In East Java, local Chinese held antigovernment demonstrations in response to anti-Chinese measures introduced by the provincial military commander. Numbers of Chinese were killed by police and Chinese shops and homes were ransacked by thousands of young Indonesians in reprisal raids. The Chinese government protested against the bloody persecution of Chinese nationals, "whereupon the Indonesian government accused the Chinese embassy of directing antigovernment demonstrations."[9]

Meanwhile, in August 1965, Pakistani guerrillas had begun infiltrating the Indian sector of Kashmir as a further move in what had become a conflict of nearly two decades' standing. The Kashmiri Revolutionary Council was formed on August 9 to oppose Indian imperialism. Reinforcements were sent to Kashmir from India, and on August 13 Prime Minister Shastri began mobilizing troops to repel what Indians perceived as armed aggression. Three days later Indian troops crossed the truce line. In early September the United Nations called for a cease-fire; Pakistan demanded that a cease-fire should be tied to a plebiscite arrangement. At about the same time the People's Republic of China issued statements in support of Pakistan, announcing a buildup of Chinese troops on the Indian border and offering material as well as moral support for Pakistan in case the situation were aggravated. The USSR, meanwhile, had withdrawn somewhat from an earlier position supporting Indian claims and also called for a cease-fire, offering mediation. Efforts at mediation by United Nations Secretary U Thant were inconclusive.

The USSR on September 13 denounced those forces, meaning China, that were hoping to gain advantage for themselves from a worsening of relations between India and Pakistan. United States Secretary of State Dean Rusk declared that the People's Republic would be well advised to stay out of the conflict. The next day, September 16, Peking issued an ultimatum to India charging border violations and making the demand that certain Indian fortifications in the Sikkim region should be dismantled immediately. The United Nations then called for an immediate cease-fire to take effect before expiration of the Chinese ultimatum. There were clashes between Chinese and Indian troops prior to the acceptance of the cease-fire by the belligerents. Thereafter, Chinese troops withdrew.[10] Indian-Pakistani talks held at Tashkent gave rise to a status quo ante.

The People's Republic also began having difficulties with Cuba. By the end of 1965 China had become a major customer for Cuban sugar and an important supplier to Cuba of Chinese rice. To many outside observers, it appeared that Cuba was serving as a crucial beachhead for Chinese Communist revolutionary influence in Latin America. But in November 1965 Cuban trade delegates in Peking were informed that China would not be able to supply rice during 1966 at the previous year's level. The official reason for the cut involved increased Chinese commitments in North Vietnam, but many outside observers — and probably Castro — saw it as a reprisal for Cuba's failure to turn aside from what Peking viewed as a pro-Moscow course.[11] The quantity of rice was apparently increased somewhat through a trade protocol the following May, but this change may have been a tribute to Castro's tactical skill in maneuvering between Peking and Moscow rather than a reconsideration of Chinese Communist policy. In any case, this and other issues gave rise to further exchanges of bitter charges and recriminations.

To some extent Chinese foreign policy during the years of the Cultural Revolution may have resulted from an overriding preoccupation with domestic crises, efforts at self-preservation on the part of Chinese diplomats, and an inclination toward allowing foreign affairs to drift and, in a sense, seek their own solutions. Retrospectively, however, this period of decline in China's diplomatic activities and influence has been viewed by Party leaders as an ultraleft episode and has been severely criticized by the Chinese themselves as "making revolution by breaking relations."[12]

Within China, the peak of violent activities was reached in August 1969. "After that, the militance of the Great Proletarian Cultural Revolution in terms of its influence on Chinese foreign relations began to subside.[13] Through to the end of the year, however, it was still unclear what new directions foreign policy might take. But during 1970 and 1971 a new pattern increasingly emerged wherein the People's Republic rapidly expanded and improved its relationships with numbers of other countries.

China Reasserts Itself in Foreign Affairs

Following disruptions of the Cultural Revolution, the People's Republic began in about 1970 to reassert itself as a world power. During the single month of June, delegations and important visitors came to Peking from Albania, Czechoslovakia, Rumania, North Korea, North Vietnam, Somalia, Sudan, and Pakistan. Chinese ambassadors were sent (or returned) to Burma, Chile, Denmark, Norway, and Morocco. Diplomatic relations were established with Nigeria, and Austria declared itself willing to open negotiations for recognition.[14] And the list of countries establishing relations continued to grow thereafter—including Austria, Cameroon, Canada, Iran, Kuwait, San Marino, Sierra Leone, Turkey, and others. In July — for the first time since 1964 — Chou En-lai attended a French embassy reception marking France's national day.

"We have never been in favour of adventurist activities of terrorism carried out by individuals or a few divorced from the masses," Chen Chu assured the United Nations in October 1972, "because they are harmful to the cause of national liberation and people's revolution. However, it must be stressed that in referring to the question of violence, one should first distinguish the military aggression and violent repression by the aggressors and oppressors from the struggle of resistance by the victims of aggression and oppression."[15]

However, while improving its relations with many countries in various parts of the world, the People's Republic became increasingly apprehensive as a result of the rapid growth of Japanese commercial and industrial capabilities in the late 1960s and early 1970s — and of the dangers inherent in a potentially powerful and aggressive Japan. Indeed, Sino-Japanese relations were characterized more and more by tough Chinese accusations about the revival of Japanese militarism — although these charges were paralleled with high levels of trade and personal visits to China by large numbers of Japanese.

According to Peking, a revived Japanese militarism "with the fostering of U.S. imperialism" was making "wild attempts to stage a comeback and realize its old dream of a 'Greater East Asia Co-prosperity Sphere,' brazenly stretching its aggressive claws" into South Korea and "our territory Taiwan" and serving as "shock troops for U.S. imperialism in pushing its criminal scheme of 'using Asians to fight Asians'."[16] United States and Japanese reactionaries, "colluding with each other," were directing "the spearhead of their aggression" squarely against the peoples of China, Korea, the three countries of Indochina, and other Asian countries.[17]

In late August 1971 the *Peking Review* published an English translation of a study on policy, by the Writing Group of the Hupeh Provincial Committee of the Communist party of China, drawing some suggestive analogies between the current world situation and the situation in China "when China's War of Resistance against Japan entered the stage of a strategic stalemate and there was a high tide of anti-Communist attacks by the Kuomintang reactionaries."[18] "On Policy" was the title of an essay written by Mao in December 1940;[19] the title which the Hupeh writers gave to their study was "Unite the People, Defeat the Enemy." In 1940, Mao had argued that in making friends with the Kuomintang — in order to defeat the Japanese — the Communists should adopt the policy: "we will never attack [the Kuomintang] unless attacked."[20]

Referring specifically to Mao Tse-tung's policies during the anti-Japanese united front of the late 1930s and early 1940s, the Hupeh writers concluded:

> *If it is only all struggle and no alliance, we will not be able to unite all the forces that can be united and consolidate and develop the revolutionary united front.* We will also not be able to push the principal enemy into a narrow and isolated position *and therefore will not be able to*

*win victory in the struggle against the enemy. If it
is only all alliance and no struggle, we will lose
our revolutionary, principled stand, relinquish the
Party's revolutionary leadership in the united front,
the Party will disintegrate ideologically, politically,
and organizationally, and the revolution will fail.*[21]

A successful united front policy meant "neither all alliance and
no struggle nor all struggle and no alliance," but combined "alliance
and struggle."[22]

Peking was also sharply antagonistic to what was referred to as
Japanese, South Korean, and Nationalist Chinese attempts to exploit
resources of the seabed and subsoil of the waters around the Tiaoyu,
Huangwei, Chihwei, Nanhsiao, and Peihsiao Islands, which are adja-
cent to Taiwan. Japanese reactionaries, Peking charged, were attempting to incorporate into Japan's territory the Tiaoyu and other islands
"and seas which belong to China."[23]

Despite this tough talk, Chinese Communist tendencies toward
aggressiveness beyond the country's borders appear to have been relatively controlled — much less reckless than Western observers had
often expected. During the summer of 1972 Chinese spokesmen saw a
good beginning in early high-level talks by North and South Korean
representatives on critical issues concerning the possible reunification
of the two countries into one.[24] And by the middle 1970s new and
favorable relations with Japan seemed to be developing. This trend was
strengthened on September 29, 1972 when the government of Japan
formally recognized the government of the People's Republic "as the
sole legal Government of China." In a joint communiqué, the Peking
government affirmed that Taiwan is "an inalienable part of the territory of the People's Republic of China," and the Japanese government
declared its full understanding of and respect for this position. The
People's Republic renounced its earlier demands for war indemnities
from Japan, and the two countries agreed to hold negotiations aimed at
the conclusion of agreements on trade, navigation, aviation, fishery,
and so forth.[25]

Relations with South Asia after the Cultural Revolution

Even if Europe is the center of world conflict,
as Peking asserts, it is not there but in the developing nations that

Chinese leaders see early possibilities for significant change in the world at large. But with the identification of the USSR as the main enemy, a somewhat new approach is required in such regions, as well as in Europe. While identifying their own country as "a developing socialist country belonging to the Third World," Chinese leaders perceive Third World countries as the main force in combating colonialism, imperialism, and Soviet hegemonism.[26]

After the admission of the People's Republic into the United Nations in late 1971, the Chinese began to take new initiatives among Third World countries in diplomacy directed toward improving the international position of the so-called developing societies on issues such as trade with industrialized powers and the export of oil and other primary resources.

The Conference of the Foreign Ministers of Non-Aligned Countries, held in Georgetown, Guiana, during early August 1972, was hailed in Peking for taking "a clear-cut position with regard to struggles against imperialism, colonialism and neo-colonialism, racial oppression, the big powers' monopoly over the handling of international affairs."[27]

The People's Republic also gave tacit — and in some instances, open — support to the government of Ceylon in its efforts to crush domestic insurgents.[28] According to a May 27, 1971 agreement, Peking contracted to extend to Ceylon an interest-free loan of 150 million rupees in convertible currency that would be repayable over twelve years with a grace period of three years. Accompanying this agreement was a letter from Chou En-lai to the prime minister of Ceylon, Mrs. Banderanaike, in which he asserted that the People's Republic was "glad to see that the chaotic situation created by a handful of persons who style themselves Guevarists" had been "brought under control."[29]

In early August of the same year Premier Ne Win of Burma visited Peking with his wife for a friendly and informal visit at the invitation of the government of the People's Republic. At a banquet that evening, Premier Chou En-lai extolled the development of good neighborly relations between the two countries and the successful settlement of boundary questions left over by history. The Chinese government had consistently pursued a friendly policy, he said, and had respected and supported the policy of peace and neutrality of the Burmese government. "We are happy to see that over the past two years the relations between our two countries have returned to normal," he continued.[30]

The relations of the People's Republic with Pakistan, India, and Bangla Desh provide some of the more spectacular evidence for the proposition that strategic considerations and the safeguarding of national interests tend to override ideological considerations when the two are at odds. During the early 1950s, the Peking regime had been outspoken in its protestations of friendship with nonaligned India while condemning Pakistan as a feudalistic tool of Western imperialism. But, as recorded earlier, this had turned out to be a short-lived set of relationships. During the 1960s, India had moved closer to the USSR, whereas Pakistan had looked increasingly toward Peking.

The situation was further exacerbated after the termination of the Cultural Revolution — to the point where Peking supported Pakistan proper against the aspirations of East Pakistan for national independence.

In late November 1970, General Yahya Khan, president of Pakistan, paid a state visit to Peking. A joint communiqué reiterated China's support for the Pakistan position on Kashmir. In reporting on the visit and communiqué, the *China Quarterly* noted that interestingly no adverse reference had been made to either the United States or the Soviet Union. The People's Republic promised further assistance to Pakistan, and Chou En-lai promised to pay a visit at the earliest opportunity. According to Karachi Radio, Peking had granted a loan of 500 million yuan for Pakistan's fourth Five Year Plan, to be repaid interest free and in kind over a twenty-year span with a grace period of ten years.[31] According to Peking, Sino-Pakistani friendship had developed on the basis of the five principles of peaceful coexistence — deriving, ironically, from the 1954 statements of Nehru and Chou En-lai — and in the common struggle against imperialism and expansionism.[32]

Early in 1971 the Awami League, in pursuit of far-reaching autonomy for East Pakistan, which encompassed more than half of Pakistan's total population, won practically every seat in East Pakistan at the general election. On March 1, President Yahya Khan announced in a national broadcast that he was postponing indefinitely the opening of the National Assembly, which was due to convene in Dacca on March 3. A basic complaint raised by the Awami League had referred to the colonial status of East Pakistan, the exploitation of the 70 million East Pakistanis, and the transfer of its resources for the benefit of a handful of industrialists and other vested interests in West Pakistan.[33] The Awami League was outlawed by the Karachi government, and martial law was put widely into effect. On March 23 the Pakistani flag was hauled down by East Pakistan dissidents in Dacca and elsewhere and replaced by the flag of a new government, Bangla Desh.

In subsequent weeks India became increasingly involved as millions of East Pakistanis, fleeing civil war in their homeland, sought refuge across the Indian border. This outcome brought the Delhi and Karachi governments into more and more conflict. On April 12 Prime Minister Chou En-lai sent a message to President Yahya Khan pledging China's full support for Pakistan in the situation arising from the civil war in East Pakistan and declaring that if Indian expansionists launched aggression against Pakistan, the Chinese government and people would "firmly support the Pakistan government and people in their just struggle." Then, on August 9, the Soviet Union and India signed the Treaty of Peace, Friendship, and Cooperation concluded in the first instance for twenty years and automatically renewable thereafter for five-year periods unless either of the parties gave prior notice.

Efforts of the Pakistan government to contain the Bangla Desh independence movement in East Pakistan during mid-1971 led to the flight of millions of Hindu refugees across the border into India. In response, toward the end of the year, India — equipped with Soviet Russian tanks and weapons — undertook a full-scale military invasion of East Pakistan. The People's Republic continued to support Pakistan in this crisis and issued a warning against any Indian intervention.

On November 24, 1971 Premier Chou En-lai and Vice-Foreign Minister Han Nien-lung had a cordial and friendly conversation with Pakistan Ambassador to China K. M. Kaiser. Five days later Vice-Premier Li Hsien-nien charged that the Indian government "supported and encouraged by social imperialism" had carried out "subversive activities and military provocations against East Pakistan," thus aggravating tension on the Indian subcontinent. "The Chinese government and people resolutely support the Pakistan government and people in their just struggle against foreign aggression," Li declared, "and in defense of their state sovereignty and national independence."[34]

Before the United Nations, Representative Fu Hao of the delegation of the People's Republic charged "a certain country" with intervention in the internal affairs of Pakistan. "These tactics of interference in the internal affairs of other countries are well known to the Chinese government and people," he asserted, recalling Sino-Indian border conflicts of the past. "In our experience, a certain neighboring country plotted a rebellion in the Tibetan region of our country and carried out subversive activities. When the rebellion it plotted was smashed by the Chinese people, it coerced tens of thousands of Chinese inhabitants into going into its country, creating a question of so-called 'Tibetan refugees' in wild opposition to China." In order to obtain a reasonable settlement of the East Pakistan refugee problem, all interference in Pakistan's internal affairs must first of all be stopped, he said.[35]

The United States, while seeking — and failing — to get India and Pakistan to make concessions, found its own position being interpreted variously as ambivalent, ineffective, and, by some, as inappropriately pro-Pakistani. From an Indian viewpoint, the Pakistani military regime would not have remained in power without arms aid from the United States. Many Indians were also angered by what they considered "phony United States claims to neutrality in the United Nations," where, they believed, President Nixon had "failed to distinguish between the just cause of Bangla Desh and oppression by Pakistan."[36]

Having given all-out support to India, the USSR was seen as emerging with great strategic and diplomatic gains from the first major confrontation with its two rivals, United States and China.[37] From a Chinese Communist standpoint — particularly in view of the Soviet-Indian treaty and of Soviet military aid to India — the growth of Indian influence into East Pakistan and the emergence of Bangla Desh could also be interpreted as a further extension of Soviet influence along China's southern flank — a partial encirclement extending from Vladivostok through Mongolia, along the western borders of Sinkiang and Tibet, and on, with only minor gaps, to the Bay of Bengal. Huang Hua, Chinese delegate to the Security Council, accused the Soviet Union of a monstrous plan to encircle China.[38]

On December 13 the USSR vetoed in the Security Council a United States resolution for an immediate cease-fire and the withdrawal of Indian and Pakistani forces to their own sides of the borders. This was the third Soviet veto of a cease-fire and withdrawal call in the Council in ten days.[39]

The People's Republic was widely perceived as having suffered a major setback — although its losses were judged to be somewhat less severe than those of the United States. Russian observers were quick to link the Chinese position with that of the United States. Soviet commentary underscored that the United States and the People's Republic of China had voted together on the various resolutions pertaining to the India-Pakistan war.[40] "This is the first time in history that the United States and China have been defeated together," a Soviet official at the United Nations was quoted as observing.[41]

During the summer of 1972 the People's Republic vetoed the admission of Bangla Desh into the United Nations. "As is known to all . . .," Peking spokesmen declared, "the Indian government, with the active encouragement and energetic support of the Soviet social-imperialists, brazenly launched a large-scale war against Pakistan and seriously undermined the peace on the south Asian subcontinent."[42] Now the Indian government and its behind the scenes support, the Soviet social-imperialists, aimed at encouraging the aggressor through the instrumentality of the United Nations. On October 20, 1975, the most serious incident on the Sino-Indian border in several years occurred when four Indian soldiers were killed in a clash with Chinese troops about thirty-five miles east of Bhutan. Each side accused the other of transgressing the Sino-Indian boundary.

Two other countries where considerations of power and political or military strategy seemed to override ideological considerations were Nepal and Afghanistan. So-called feudal economic and political systems operated in both these countries, and yet the People's Republic has maintained friendly relations with them for the better part of a decade.[43]

Unexpectedly, from the viewpoint of many Western observers, China appears to have gained little — in terms of communist politics — from developments in Indochina. According to the Institute of Strategic Studies in London, the communist victory there was at best "a mixed blessing to Peking, for whatever ideological solace it might have drawn from Hanoi's triumph was diminished by the thought that it was Moscow, not Peking, that preserved the more significant leverage over North Vietnam." There was also the disturbing possibility that the United States might abandon the western Pacific and leave China to deal alone with the Soviet Union. On this point, at least, the People's Republic and the United States had a common interest.[44]

The People's Republic did little to improve its relations with the Vietnamese when it annexed the nearby Paracel Islands in 1974.

China's Policies in the Middle East and Africa

China's interest in Middle Eastern affairs dates back to the early 1950s. Because of its rich oil resources and its strategic location, the region was perceived by Peking as a vital link in United States and other Western attempts to encircle China, the USSR, and the other communist countries. The Arab-Israeli conflict and the Palestine problem were seen by the Chinese as having been created by an Anglo-American rivalry over control of the Middle East and as providing a major pretext for imperialist interference in affairs of the region.[45] Within this context, China's initial inclination was to improve relations with all Middle Eastern countries, including Israel. It was not until the latter part of 1956 that Peking began to identify Israel as a tool of Western imperialism used for exerting pressure on Arab states and thereby generating tension in the Middle East.

The People's Republic undertook its first major campaign in the Middle East in late 1963. Chinese leaders began making frequent trips to the area, aid was made available, and trade increased considerably. It was at this point that Peking adopted the Arab position on the Palestinian problem (almost in its entirety) and established relations with the Palestine Liberation Organization (PLO). When a PLO delegation visited China in 1965, Mao identified Israel and Formosa for them as the two great bases of imperialism in Asia.[46] From that time on, China recognized the Palestine problem as the crux of the whole Middle Eastern question.

Since the early 1970s, Chinese policies in the Middle East have been increasingly influenced by fear of the Soviet Union. Thus, the whole region is now perceived in terms of a Soviet, rather than a United States attempt to outflank China from the south. And although Peking still refuses to have contact with either the people or the government of Israel, efforts are now made to distinguish between the two. There are some indications that, as perceived by Peking, the restoration of the national rights of the Palestinians may not necessarily require the destruction of the state of Israel.

While Chinese arms shipments and other aids to the PLO have been drastically cut in recent years, China has been developing economic relations with numbers of Middle Eastern countries. Early in 1970 a five-man Chinese delegation visited South Yemen to conduct an economic survey.[47] They followed an earlier group of agricultural experts sent to aid the development of agricultural projects. A South Yemen official asserted that the People's Republic had "expressed its enthusiastic readiness to provide all possible facilities for promotion of trade."[48] Later in the year the name of the People's Republic of South Yemen was changed to the People's Democratic Republic of Yemen.[49]

There were other Chinese efforts that opened doors, but produced much more limited results. Between December 25 and January 3, 1971-1972, a government delegation from the Republic of Iraq, led by a member of the Arab Baath Socialist Party, visited the People's Republic — an event that was hailed in Peking as "of great significance to the strengthening of the friendship between the people of China and Iraq."[50]

The Iranian government announced on April 4, 1971 that thirteen members of a Chinese-backed ring who attempted a coup were being executed. On the other hand, a member of the Iranian royal family visited China and was reported to be optimistic about establishing diplomatic relations with the People's Republic.[51]

The People's Republic has made considerable efforts to strengthen its commercial relations with Middle Eastern and African countries. Egypt has accounted for the greater part of China's Middle Eastern trade. Three countries have accounted for the greater proportion of China's trade with Africa proper — Nigeria, Sudan, and Tanzania.

On January 17, 1971 the People's Republic and Equatorial Guinea concluded agreements on trade and economic and technical assistance.[52] Some months later, the Peking regime agreed to build a road in Sudan from Medaric to Gedaref and to provide a $14.5 million loan for other projects.[53] In December of that year a Sudanese high-status official delegation arrived in Peking, and later the two countries signed an agreement on economic and technical cooperation.[54] In a banquet honoring the delegation, Premier Chou En-lai extolled the "profound militant friendship in the struggle against imperialism and colonialism" that had been forged between the Chinese and Sudanese people.[55]

While accusing Israel of aggression against the Palestinians and various Arab states, the People's Republic condemned Portuguese imperialism in Angola and other colonial possessions and launched attacks against South African and Rhodesian exploitation and racism. Specifically, China published condemnations of Portuguese authorities for their "aggression against the Republic of Senegal and brutal suppression of the peoples of Guinea (Bissau)" and other areas fighting for national independence.[56]

With respect to Rhodesia, Peking identified the white racist regime there as a direct outcome of British colonialist policy.[57] The African people, accounting for more than 98 percent of the population in that country, still suffered racist oppression. China also condemned the South African regime and its policies as producers of racial discrimination.[58] Peking charged United States imperialists with secretly supplying arms to the South African white racist regime and linked this activity with United States racist policies at home.[59]

The Angolan struggle against Portuguese colonialism produced a graphic illustration of the kind of dilemma that can be produced by the Soviet-Union-as-the-Main-Enemy thesis.

During the early phases of the Angolan revolution, the People's Republic had supported, in principle at least, all three of the major dissident groups — the Popular Movement for the Liberation of Angola (MPLA), the Front for the National Liberation of Angola (FNLA), and The National Union for the Total Independence of Angola (UNITA), which were tied into a loose coalition under the Alvor Agreement of January 10, 1975. "When this coalition was disrupted," according to William Hinton, identifying himself as a long-time supporter of the People's Republic, "China stopped all aid and urged that the coalition be reformed. Instead, the MPLA, with Russian arms and Cuban troops, won control of most of Angola."[60] On the other hand, according to Wilfred Burchett, who also identified himself as a long-term friend of China, "The ink, quite literally, was not even dry on the Alvor Agreement before the CIA began to make secret shipment of arms and money to the FNLA–UNITA" . . . which were "getting massive support from the U.S., Zaire and South Africa" against the MPLA.[61] In FNLA hands, Chinese arms were not used against the Portuguese but against the MPLA.

The USSR accused China of subversive activity against the Angolan people and support of pro-imperialist groups. The Chinese, in turn, charged the USSR with "contending for hegemony with the other superpower" and stooping "to anything to frenziedly penetrate and expand in Africa in a vain attempt to replace the old colonialism." In their scramble for African hegemony, the Soviet revisionists were putting "strategically important Angola, which is rich in natural resources, into their neo-colonial spheres of influence."[62]

The question raised by Hinton, reasoning from the main enemy assumption, was "How will the Angolans now deal with the Russians and Cubans, who gave them little help while they were fighting the Portuguese, but poured in arms and men once the Portuguese had been driven out?"

Burchett's perspective was almost the polar opposite: "The FNLA and UNITA, supported to the hilt by the U.S., behaved exactly like the Thieu regime in South Vietnam and used the Alvor Agreement to step up their attempts to wipe out the MPLA and set themselves up as neo-colonialist puppets."

Recent Chinese Policies Toward Latin America

The main trend of Chinese relations with Latin American countries during the 1970s has been away from the support of armed insurgency and in the direction of support for economic independence in Latin America, for just rights, for the establishment of a nuclear-free zone in the region, for increasing levels of Sino-American trade, and the like.

China made its first aid overtures to Latin America in 1971. Since then Chile, Guyana, and Peru have signed aid agreements totalling almost $135 million. In fact, however, the Chilean program has been in suspension as a result of political changes there, and at this writing the Peru and Guyana programs are yet to be implemented. The Sino-Peruvian agreement does provide a clue to China's potential appeal in parts of Latin America. In a document signed in late April 1971 the two countries agreed to expand trade flows and establish mutual trading facilities. Later, in June, the People's Republic agreed to purchase fish powder, fish oil, copper, lead, and zinc from Peru. Considerable emphasis was placed upon China's acceptance of two hundred nautical miles as the legal limit of Peru's territorial waters.[63]

The Chinese Communists expressed approval of measures taken by Mexico in "Mexicanizing" a United States–owned copper company by gaining control of 50.98 percent of its shares. Peking also praised Mexico for supporting Peru, Ecuador, and other Latin American countries "in defending their sovereignty over the 200 nautical miles and opposing the 12 nautical mile territorial water limit imposed by the two superpowers" — the United States and the Soviet Union.[64]

In late December 1971 *Peking Review* quoted Fidel Castro's denunciation of the *Johnny Express* and the *Laval Express*, both seized by the

Cuban government, as "pirate ships" carrying out "criminal acts of aggression" as part of the United States Central Intelligence Agency's aggressive activities against Cuba. The *Peking Review* described the Cuban action as entirely justified and predicted that the "Nixon Government's intimidations and threats" would neither "save U.S. hegemony from its doom nor frighten the heroic Cuban people."[65]

In recent years, Chinese policies in Latin America have been complicated by the Sino-Soviet conflict, with a number of countries and revolutionary movements inclining toward the USSR, rather than the People's Republic. It was a shock to many leftist groups in Latin America when, with the overturn of the Allende regime in Chile, the People's Republic almost immediately recognized the extreme anticommunist group that had overthrown and replaced it.

After a visit to Cuba by Leonid Brezhnev, general secretary of the Communist party of the Soviet Union, and a team of political and economic specialists, a joint communiqué was issued from Havana on February 4, 1974 making veiled attacks on China. This document decried hegemonistic and chauvinistic tendencies contradicting communist internationalism and backed a Soviet proposal for a collective security system in Asia opposed to China. In a presumed reference to the People's Republic, Castro condemned pseudo-leftists and renegades of the revolutionary movement who, from allegedly Marxist positions, had reviled the Soviet Union, "wretchedly betraying proletarian internationalism" and "serving the interests of imperialism." Meanwhile, the Chinese official news agency Hsinhua denounced alleged Soviet economic and military infiltration and expansionism in Latin America.

Chinese Economic Aid Programs

Chinese economic assistance programs deserve special attention for at least two major reasons. First, the aid is being made available by a country that will itself continue to be a developing country for years to come; and secondly, Chinese economic assistance has been offered to recipient countries in ways that make the overall program something of a model.

As assessed by a West German observer, these programs have set new standards in the international community.[66] Earlier inefficiencies and frictions in Chinese aid efforts seem to have been eliminated in recent years, and recipient countries, by and large, appear to have been satisfied with the arrangements. Thus, as compared with other foreign-aid programs during the early and middle 1970s, the Chinese have a good performance record.[67] There is a further consideration, however. What has distinguished China from other donor countries, according to the Bureau of Intelligence and Research, has been "her guiding principle that economic aid must not bring economic profit to the donor."[68]

A central aspect of the overall Chinese program is the consideration that the People's Republic makes economic loans available without interest and subject to more favorable repayment terms "than those granted by any other country, capitalist or socialist."[69] Especially with respect to larger loans, the Peking regime has commonly offered the recipient a grace period of ten years beginning at the time when an economic aid program has been completed. Once repayments have begun, the installments are usually distributed over a twenty-year span.[70]

Chinese economic aid agreements stipulate that technicians and workers sent abroad from China are to be paid in accordance with the standards of the receiving country. Since living standards in most developing countries are low, the cost of aid is thus reduced considerably. According to Bureau of Intelligence and Research estimates, the cost of China's projects may be estimated at about a quarter of that of comparable projects undertaken by capitalist countries.[71]

In 1972 the People's Republic surpassed the USSR as a grantor of economic aid. [72] During the years 1970-1974, China's aid to developing countries averaged about $480 million a year — although there was considerable variability in aid levels from one year to another. About 20 percent of China's overall foreign aid has gone to South Asia — with Pakistan the major recipient. This is all the more remarkable, according to United States State Department analysts, since "Chinese aid to this country did not begin until 1965 when Pakistan and India went to war over the Ram of Kutch." In Pakistan, as nowhere else, Chinese aid since that time has been in direct competition with Soviet economic assistance programs.[73] Ranking third in terms of its overall receipt of Chinese economic aid has been Indonesia.[74]

Prior to 1972, Asian countries had received the greater share of Chinese economic aid loans. After the United States secretary of state's 1971 visit to Peking, the reluctance of many nonaligned countries to accept Chinese economic assistance disappeared, especially in Africa. Thus, whereas only thirteen African countries had been recipients of Chinese aid previously, the number increased to twenty-nine in the course of about thirty months. Thereafter, Africa ranked first in terms of recipients of Chinese loans, and Asia dropped into second place.[75]

Never an important area in terms of Chinese aid, Middle Eastern countries have received less than 10 percent of Peking's more recent undertakings in developing countries. In 1971 Iraq received a $45 million extension of aid. This assistance, along with additional pledges to old clients — the Yemens, Syria, and Egypt — accounted for all of the $185 million of new and old aid to the Middle East during the 1970-1974 period.[76]

Approximately two-thirds of the aid in the early 1970s went to Africa. Tanzania and Zambia were the largest recipients, accounting for over one-third of the total Chinese aid extended to that continent.[77]

Tanzania has occupied second place among recipients of Chinese economic aid.[78] In large part these loans are accounted for by China's extension of almost $100 million annually for construction of the Tan-Zam Railroad, the single most important Chinese aid project.[79] In some part, China's determination to make this project a success stemmed from the fact that the World Bank had declared the undertaking unprofitable, while a mixed French and Canadian consortium, having reached the opposite conclusion, was unable to raise the necessary funds.[80] The railroad links the Zambian copper belt to the Tanzanian port of Dar es Salaam.[81]

China made its first economic aid overtures to Latin America in 1971. Since then, Peking has signed aid agreements amounting to almost $135 million. In Chile, however, that program is currently dormant, and little has been done so far toward implementing aid to Guyana and Peru.[82]

The People's Republic has also made donations or nonrepayable loans to a number of countries including Cambodia, Nepal, Sri Lanka, and Pakistan.

Mobile medical units, a unique feature of China's foreign-aid programs, have had a powerful propagandistic effect in a number of recipient countries. Whereas other Chinese aid personnel are supposed to avoid association with the local population except in circumstances where their work requires otherwise, the mobile medical groups come into direct contact with large numbers of people from all walks of life.[83] Consisting of between twenty and thirty persons, including physicians and medical workers, each group treats about 50,000 outpatients and performs an average of 3,000 surgical operations.

The first Chinese medical group was sent to Algeria in 1963. Since then, comparable groups have gone to North and South Yemen and numbers of African countries.[84]

Overall, in terms of the rivalry with respect to economic aid, the People's Republic predominates in Africa, where Chinese aid surpasses that of the USSR in twenty-two countries, as compared with eight where the Soviet Union predominates. In Asia, by contrast, the USSR has extended more than twice as much assistance as the People's Republic. As compared with Chinese aid programs, those of the USSR also predominate in the Middle East and Latin America.

Notes

1. Peter Van Ness, *Revolution and Chinese Foreign Policy* (Berkeley: University of California Press, 1971), pp. 214–18. See also Robert L. Worden, "China's Foreign Relations with Latin America," in Hsüeh, *Dimensions of China's Foreign Relations*, pp. 195–99.

2. "Quarterly Chronicle and Documentation," *China Quarterly*, no. 31 (July–September 1967), p. 212.

3. Ishwer C. Ojha, *Chinese Foreign Policy in an Age of Transition* (Boston: Beacon Press, 1971), p. 231.

4. "Quarterly Chronicle and Documentation," *China Quarterly*, no. 32 (October–December 1967), p. 221.

5. "Persistently Follow the Road of Seizing Political Power by Armed Force," *Peking Review*, no. 27 (July 2, 1971), pp. 6-11. See also Van Ness, *Revolution and Chinese Foreign Policy*, p. 205.

6. *The China Mainland Review* 1, no. 3 (December 1965), p. 64.

7. Ibid., pp. 62–65; 2, no. 1 (June 1966), pp. 36–40.

8. Ibid. 2, no. 1 (June 1966), p. 41.

9. "Quarterly Chronicle and Documentation," *China Quarterly*, no. 31 (July–September 1967), pp. 218-19.

10. Klaus Pringsheim, "China's Role in the Indo-Pakistani Conflict," *China Quarterly*, no. 24 (October–December 1965), pp. 170-75.

11. Ernest Halperin, "Peking and the Latin American Communists," *China Quarterly*, no. 29, p. 150.

12. Wilfred Burchett, "China's Foreign Policy: A Friend of China Raises Some Questions," *The Guardian*, May 5, 1976, p. 14.

13. Van Ness, *Revolution and Chinese Foreign Policy*, pp. 205-206. See also Sheldon W. Simon, "Some Aspects of China's Asian Policy in the Cultural Revolution and its Aftermath," *Pacific Affairs* 64, no. 1 (Spring 1971), pp. 18–38.

14. "Quarterly Chronicle and Documentation," *China Quarterly*, no. 46 (April–June 1971), p. 392.

15. Statement by Chinese United Nations Representative Chen Chu, *Peking Review*, no. 40 (October 6, 1972), p. 30.

16. Vice-Premier Li Hsien-min, *Peking Review*, no. 37 (September 11, 1970), p. 11.

17. "Premier Chou En-lai's Speech at Welcoming Ceremony at Pyongyang Airport," New China News Agency, Pyongyang, April 5, 1970, in *Current Background*, nos. 912–914 (August 27–28, 1970), p. 65.

18. "Unite the People, Defeat the Enemy," *Peking Review*, no. 35 (August 27, 1971), pp. 10-13.

19. Mao Tse-tung, *Selected Works*, Vol. 3 (New York: International, 1954), pp. 215-24.

20. Ibid., p. 223.

21. Ibid., p. 13. Emphasis added.

22. "Unity of Revolutionary Cadres — A Guarantee of Victory," *Peking Review*, no. 27 (July 7, 1971), p. 9.

23. "Countries Ranged Against U.S. Imperialism to Defend Their Territorial Seas," *Peking Review* , no. 48 (November 27, 1970), pp. 7 – 9.

24. "A Good Beginning," *Peking Review*, no. 38 (July 14, 1972), p. 7.

25. Text in *New York Times* (September 30, 1972), p. 12.

26. Chou En-lai, "Report on the Work of the Government," *Peking Review*, no. 4 (January 24, 1975), p. 24.

27. "Conference of Foreign Ministers of Non-Aligned Countries," *Peking Review*, no. 33 (August 18, 1972), p. 10.

Review, no. 33 (August 18, 1972), p. 10.

28. "Quarterly Chronicle and Documentation," *China Quarterly*, no. 47 (July–September 1971), p. 600.

29. Colombo Radio, as reported by BBC, *Summary of World Broadcasts*, Far East No. 3695, May 26, 1971.

30. "Chairman and Madame Ne Win in Peking," *Peking Review*, no. 33 (August 13, 1971), p. 4.

31. "Quarterly Chronicle and Documentation," *China Quarterly*, no. 45 (January–March 1971), p. 213.

32. Hsio Ching-kuang, Commander of the PLA Navy at a banquet to welcome Pakistani Naval Commander-in-Chief Vice Admiral Muzaffar Hason, New China News Agency, Peking, September 19, 1970, in *Current Background* (November 12 and 17, 1970), p. 103.

33. Sheikh Mujibuo Rahman, at a press conference in Decca, February 24, 1971, *Kessing's Contemporary Archives*, May 1–8, 1971, p. 24565.

34. "Firm Support for Pakistan," *Peking Review*, no. 49 (December 3, 1971), p. 5.

35. "China's Stand on Question of Refugees from East Pakistan," *Peking Review*, no. 48 (November 26, 1971), p. 20.

36. "Indian MP Calls for Attack on USS Enterprise," *New York Times* (December 16, 1971), pp. 1, 20.

37. "India-Pakistan War Damages Influence of Big Powers," *New York Times* (December 20, 1971), p. 1.

38. Ibid., p. 14.

39. "USSR Vetoes U.S. Resolution in Security Council," *New York Times* (December 14, 1971), p. 1.

40. Ibid., p. 17.

41. "India-Pakistan War Damages Influence Big Powers," *New York Times* (December 20, 1971), p. 14.

42. "Consideration of 'Bangla Desh's' Application for U.N. Membership Opposed," *Peking Review*, no. 33 (August 18, 1972), p. 12. See also Mahbubul Hok, "Bangla Desh and China," *China Report* 7, no. 6 (November–December 1971), pp. 3–7.

43. Van Ness, *Revolution and Chinese Foreign Policy*, p. 159.

44. *Strategic Survey* (London: The International Institute for Strategic Studies, 1975), p. 97.

45. Yitzhak Shichor, "The Palestinians and China's Foreign Policy," in Hsüeh, *Dimensions of China's Foreign Relations*, p. 159.

46. Ibid., pp. 167-68.

47. "Developments of the Quarter: Comment and Chronology," *Middle East Journal* (Spring 1970), p. 198.

48. "Developments of the Quarter: Comment and Chronology," *Middle East Journal* (Spring 1971), p. 240.

49. Ibid., p. 240.

50. "Iranian Visit," *Peking Review*, no. 1 (January 7, 1972), p. 5.

51. "Developments of the Quarter: Comment and Chronology," *Middle East Journal* (Summer 1971), p. 376.

52. "Quarterly Chronicle and Documentation," *China Quarterly*, no. 46 (April–June 1971), p. 394.

53. "Quarterly Chronicle and Documentation," *China Quarterly*, no. 47 (July–September 1971), p. 605.

54. "Sudanese High Status Official Delegation Visits Peking," *Peking Review*, no. 52 (December 24, 1971), p. 4.

55. Ibid., p. 9.
56. Huang Hua, *Peking Review*, no. 49 (December 3, 1971), p. 22.
57. Foreign Minister Chi Peng-fei's letter to U.N. Secretary-General, *Peking Review*, no. 5 (February 4, 1972), p. 14.
58. Ibid.
59. "U.S. Imperialism: Arch Criminal in Pushing Racism," *Peking Review*, no. 1 (January 7, 1972), p. 23.
60. William Hinton, "China's World View," *Guardian*, May 5, 1974, p.15.
61. Burchett, "China's Foreign Policy: A Friend Raises Some Questions," pp. 14 and 17. See also C. Clark Kissinger, John S. Paul and "The Editors," "Angola, China and Southern Africa," *The Monthly Review* 28, no. 1 (May 1976), pp. 1-17.
62. Colin Legum, "The Soviet Union, China and the West in Southern Africa," *Foreign Affairs* 54, no. 4 (July 1976), p. 752.
63. "Quarterly Chronicle and Documentation," *China Quarterly*, no. 47 (July–September 1971), p. 602.
64. "Opposing U.S. Hegemony," *Peking Review*, no. 52 (December 24, 1971), p. 23.
65. "Exposing U.S. Imperialist Crimes of Aggression," *Peking Review*, no. 53 (December 31, 1971), pp. 21–22.
66. Wolfgang Bartke, *China's Economic Aid* (London: C. Hurst and Company, 1975), p. 1.
67. Carol H. Fogarty, "China's Economic Relations with the Third World," in *China: A Reassessment*, p. 733.
68. Bartke, *China's Economic Aid*, p. 9.
69. Ibid.
70. Ibid., p. 12.
71. Ibid., p. 26.
72. Ibid., p. 20.
73. Ibid., p. 14.
74. Ibid., p. 16.
75. Ibid., p. 15.
76. Fogarty, "China's Economic Relations with the Third World," p. 733.
77. Ibid.
78. Bartke, *China's Economic Aid*, p. 16.
79. Fogarty, "China's Economic Relations with the Third World," p. 730.
80. Bartke, *China's Economic Aid*, p. 16.
81. Fogarty, "China's Economic Relations with the Third World," p. 733.
82. Ibid.
83. Bartke, *China's Economic Aid*, p. 25.
84. Ibid.

Chapter Eight

Current Chinese Foreign Policies, the Death of Mao, and Future Possibilities

For the People's Republic of China it has appeared that political culture, tradition, changes in capabilities, and conscious choice arising from deep reservoirs of dissatisfaction have all been powerful factors in Chinese behavior. Of these four, capability, tradition, and conscious choice arising from dissatisfaction are still so strong that certain aspects of Chinese policy and behavior would be very likely to continue even if the leadership should change substantially and if specific aspects of the political culture — the Marxist-Leninist-Maoist ideology and style — were to be replaced by something else.

However, the Cultural Revolution cannot be viewed solely as a throwback to an earlier era or solely as a power play. Quite the contrary, certain segments of the Chinese leadership realized that if China were to play an active role in the international system and safeguard her interests in the future, then China's basic capabilities would have to be expanded. In Mao's eyes expanding these basic capabilities required a complete restructuring of Chinese society. Mao felt that only when the cultural impediments to nationalization of agriculture and other productive enterprises were removed would China realize her true potentiality. The Cultural Revolution, then, while frenetic in its impact, represented a calculated attempt to create the social preconditions for the rapid expansion of basic Chinese capabilities.

The Great Leap Forward and the Cultural Revolution were often viewed by outsiders as evidence of self-destructive tendencies within the People's Republic. And, undoubtedly, both these developments involved seriously disruptive tendencies. As explained by Mao and other Chinese Communist writers, however, the seeming chaos was the outcome of social, economic, and political contradictions that could be solved only by a certain amount of struggle that in the longer run would render the regime stronger rather than weaker.

Whether or not one is prepared to accept the explanations of Mao and his colleagues, the fact remains that so far, at least, the People's Republic has not only survived the disruptions of the Great Leap Forward and the Cultural Revolution, but has succeeded in maintaining considerable bureaucratic stability and pursued a remarkably effective course over the more than quarter century of its existence. Against this background, it is possible that during the years immediately ahead Chinese performance will continue to improve even though further economic, political, or other disruptions may contribute to temporary setbacks.

With the deaths of Chou En-lai and Mao Tse-tung, the year 1976 undoubtedly marked a sharp turning point in terms of Chinese leadership, if not in other respects. Suddenly, all kinds of past speculations took on new and immediate importance. What effect would major changes in the top leadership of the People's Republic have over the years to come? Virtually from the establishment of the regime in 1949 down to the present, Western observers have questioned whether the character of the Chinese revolution could be preserved and the momentum sustained on the basis of Maoist traditions and prescriptions for the future.[1] And, more recently, the question has been asked whether the Maoist social and economic patterns that began to prevail even prior to the Cultural Revolution would transform the political system or whether the political system would reassert itself and try to fashion the society in its own image.[2]

The successive leadership changes that took place during 1975 and 1976 confused many outside observers. At the National People's Conference of January 1975, Teng Hsiao-ping had been elevated to the Standing Committee of the Politburo, named a Party vice-chairman, made chief of staff of the People's Liberation Army, and appointed highest ranking vice-premier in the government. But when Chou En-lai died in mid-January 1976, Teng abruptly and unexpectedly dropped from view.[3] In April 1976 the Central Committee of the People's Republic passed two resolutions, one appointing Hua Kuo-feng first Vice-Chairman of the CPC Central Committee and premier of the State Council,[4] the other dismissing Teng Hsiao-ping from all posts both inside and outside the Party.[5] Up to this point, Hua had been considered a relatively junior member of the Chinese hierarchy.

Teng Hsiao-ping was charged specifically with "putting profits and material incentives in command" and attempting to "deny class struggle on the industrial and transport fronts" as a cover-up for his struggle against the proletariat on behalf of the bourgeoisie both inside and outside the Party." In "pushing his revisionist line," he put technique and production ahead of the requirements of social, economic, and political revolution.[6]

The charges leveled against Teng had a theoretical base that was familiarly Maoist. In the period of democratic revolution against the Nationalist leadership, the principal contradiction in the society had been that between the proletariat and the masses of people on the one hand and imperialism, feudalism, and bureaucratic capitalism on the other. Subsequently, after the rule of imperialism, feudalism, and bureaucratic capitalism had been overthrown and the proletariat had led the people of the whole country in seizing the political power of the state, China had then entered a historical period of socialist revolution; the contradiction between the proletariat and the bourgeoisie had become the principal contradiction in the society. From that time on "our struggle against the bourgeoisie both inside and outside the Party ... gradually developed in depth in all spheres, centering on the question of whether or not to carry out the socialist revolution."[7]

When the socialist transformation of the means of production had been basically completed, Teng had "followed Liu Shao-ch'i in trumpeting the theory of the dying out of class struggle, alleging that 'class contradictions have now been solved in the main,' that 'since classes have been limited basically, we should not stress class struggle'."[8] During this later, socialist revolution, according to Mao, the workers and the poor and lower-middle peasants stood still, although they actually wanted revolution. But a number of Party members did not want to go forward. Some moved backward and opposed the revolution. Why? Because they had become high officials and wanted to protect the interests of high officials.[9]

According to Chinese press analyses, once the leadership in certain units or departments had come under the control of "capitalist-roaders" like Liu Shao-ch'i, Lin Piao, and Teng Hsiao-ping, they used the power in their hands

> to energetically push the revisionist line and turn the socialist mutual relations among people into capitalist relations between employers and employees ... to expand bourgeois rights with respect to distribution and to appropriate the fruits of other people's labor without compensation; and ... take advantage of their position and power to dispose of

> *state- or collectively-owned means of production and consumption, with the result that socialist ownership exists only in name but is actually turned into capitalist ownership under the control of the capitalist-roaders.*[10]

The policies of the capitalist-roaders had affected enterprises in many sectors of Chinese society according to Maoist theoreticians. Right deviationists, for example, had "one-sidedly emphasized that Marxism could not replace natural science. Their aim was to oppose using Marxism to guide natural science." They had pushed technology and industrial technique at the expense of class struggle, thus distorting the purpose of Chinese development.[11] In fact, the whole aim of production was "solely to ensure supplies; to meet the needs of socialist revolution and socialist construction and the needs of the people in their work and life; to be prepared against war; be prepared against natural disasters; and do everything for the people."[12] In order to pursue these aims, the People's Republic had to maintain self-reliance — avoiding economic or political dependency on any other nation — and recognize the central revolutionary role of the class struggle.

The End of an Era

On September 9, 1976 Mao Tse-tung died in Peking at the age of eighty-two. People in all parts of the world mourned his passing — including many of those who had criticized him, worked against him, condemned him as long as he was living, and hoped for his early demise.

Although it has been characteristic of Marxist-Leninist regimes that the death of a major leader has triggered struggles for domestic power, there being few institutionalized mechanisms for smooth succession, Chinese affairs proceeded uneventfully, for a time, and many observers began to conclude that the transition might be accomplished virtually without incident. Such was not the case.

On October 12 it was announced that Hua Kuo-feng had succeeded Mao as chairman of the Chinese Communist party and chairman of the Military Affairs Commission. For the time being, at least, he would maintain his post as premier. That same day, however, Hsinhua, the official Chinese news agency, announced that the Party Central Committee under Hua Kuo-feng's leadership, had apprehended a coup attempted by Mao's widow Chiang Ching and her Gang of Four. It was asserted that as a result of "resolute and decisive measures," the Central Committee has successfully crushed "the counterrevolutionary conspiratorial clique and liquidated a bane inside the party." Chiang Ching was accused of plotting to kill Mao on his deathbed. On November 8, it was further charged that two days after the arrest of the Gang of Four, their supporters in Shanghai had mobilized and armed 30,000 militiamen in preparation for an abortive armed attack against the Peking regime.

An extended statement on Mao's death, which was published in the *New York Times* on September 10, had reidentified Teng Hsiao-ping, along with Liu Shao-ch'i and Lin Piao, as having advanced a counterrevolutionary, revisionist line over which Mao himself had successfully triumphed. But during the October disruptions, Teng, who had been ousted as deputy premier in the power struggle of the previous April, was rehabilitated — with Hua Kuo-feng retaining the post of prime minister. The Gang of Four were charged with having attempted to murder Teng.

The foreign minister of China, Chiao Kuan-hua, was dismissed in early December and replaced by Huang Hua, China's ambassador to the United Nations. Chiao reportedly had been linked to the purged Gang of Four. Two weeks later Party Chairman Hua Kuo-feng asserted that a nationwide purge of party and governmental officials who had gained office through the influence of the Gang of Four would be undertaken during the ensuing year.

From an early 1977 perspective, the overall trends in China's foreign affairs do not appear to have undergone any major changes since the death of Mao. As a basic principle, the Chinese leadership has continued to emphasize self-reliance with at least three major objectives in view: (1) to keep the country's financial and strategic dependence on foreign nations at a minimum; (2) to develop in China a self-confident "new Maoist man" and to safeguard him from contamination by alien influences; and (3) to mobilize domestic savings down to the local level in order to economize on scarce foreign exchange and outlays of state investment. But the People's Republic cannot live in isolation from the rest of the world and continue to grow.[13]

Indicators of the Chinese revolution's future direction remain mixed. While one of the major objectives of the Great Proletarian Cultural Revolution was to reduce bureaucracy at all levels and place power in the hands of local revolutionary committees, it is not clear how viable such an uninstitutionalized system may turn out to be.[14] It seems safe to presume, however, that in the short-to-medium run (the next five to ten years) Peking's basic capabilities will still constitute the decisive limitation on the quantity and quality of Chinese participation in the international community; for, as we have seen in the previous chapter, Chinese attempts to build military capabilities through defense expenditures have had an adverse effect on the rate of industrial-technological growth.

China has lacked the resources that would allow it to build capabilities on a level competitive with United States and Soviet capability-building. Consequently, the People's Republic will have to devise a foreign policy strategy that minimizes expenditures abroad so that the resources available for domestic development can be maximized. This also means that Peking will have to channel some of those resources that might be devoted to the larger international system to those areas closer at hand and that are most vital to China's security. In short, China will be most concerned about Japan, Taiwan, Korea, South and Southeast Asia, the Indian Ocean, and the USSR.[15] With world energy shortages, the Peking regime, like many other governments, is likely to be increasingly concerned with events in the Middle East. Since the seating of the People's Republic on the Security Council of the United Nations, these relationships have tended to move closer to the center of the international stage, although the critical center, as perceived by Peking, will continue to be Europe.

Some Problems Facing China

The controversy over priorities as between industrial development and social revolution, along with what Mao Tse-tung and other top leaders have identified as the Red-Expert contradiction emerge as a serious dilemma for the regime as it is now constituted. Partly because the country has lacked the educational and social resources to build a tremendous corps of highly trained technicians and partly because the Chinese leadership fears a technological elite that is politically backward, China has relied on minimal formal education and focused on the creation of worker-peasant technicians who acquire most of their skills through on-the-job training.

While these technicians' feats have been considerable, the pressures for a more regularized training process will become greater as Chinese society becomes even more complex and interdependent. In addition, there has been the continuing problem of the relationship between the more expert Western-style technicians and the more ideologically pure (Red) worker-peasant technicians. Since the mid-1950s China has experienced a steady growth of professionalism leading to greater differences on issues among military leaders, between members of the party apparatus and officers supervised by them, and inside the military establishment between generations of officers.[16] This trend is likely to continue — although the relationships themselves may well grow increasingly complex.

It has been estimated that some 4500 Western and Japanese-trained scientists and engineers "constitute the backbone of China's professional, scientific, and technical manpower."[17] The scientists in charge of recent Chinese development of nuclear weaponry "were all trained in the United States and Western Europe."[18] The full participation of these specialists will probably be required if China is to close its population-productivity gap — at least until larger numbers of specialists can be trained within China itself.

There is the further issue of product distribution within China. To date, the question of for whom increased production is being developed has been settled in favor of the state as a whole and against the individual members of that state. "Increases in [individual] consumption are made, if at all, only grudgingly."[19] However, it remains to be seen if the Chinese people can be socialized to accept nonmaterial incentives for an extended period of time.[20] If experience is any guide to the future, as it may well not be, in the middle and long run Peking will be able to maintain a viable society only to the extent that it makes a growing part of production available to the populace. (On the other hand, the United States, Japan, and other industrialized countries are providing more and more evidence of the relationship between high levels of consumerism and pollution and a whole range of societal imbalances and overloads. In these terms it is at least conceivable that the more China succeeds, the greater the range of new and vexatious problems it will have to confront.) More specifically, future trends in China's economic growth, capabilities, and basic policies are likely to be affected in major ways by problems of Chinese population, technology, and access to resources.

Population, Technology, and the Future

It can be argued that a country's population and technology combine multiplicatively to encourage that country's expansion of interests, activities, and influence, but that such tendencies are often alleviated or modified by domestic area and resources.[21] The reasoning would be somewhat as follows: increases in the number of people produce more and more demand for land and other basic resources and thus give rise to dissatisfactions and perhaps a will for expansion. Such tendencies are likely to be constrained, however, by distance and geographical barriers, by domestic problems, and by resistance of adjoining nations and their allies.

A basic question for oncoming decades is how China's leaders address themselves to the population-technology problem.[22] Anyone seeking to predict future Chinese behavior must keep his eyes fixed upon the rate of investment and the pace of development in agriculture, as well as upon population growth and broad technological advancement.[23] Herein lies the foundation of Chinese capability.

Technological developments may contribute to expansionist tendencies in two ways. Advances in technology often enhance the ability (capabilities) of a growing population to expand and conquer or otherwise acquire new territory. In addition, technological advances frequently create new demands for resources (dissatisfactions) that may be met domestically, but that frequently are not, and that add thus to lateral pressure — a tendency to reach out for resources and markets and to expand activities and national interests in a variety of modes. Technological advances often create military and political power, and very powerful nations are inclined to extend their military activities, as well as their commercial and diplomatic activities, and to become involved in international conflicts and violence.[24]

An increase in territory and resources may tend — at least temporarily — to constrain lateral pressures by meeting many of the needs (reducing the dissatisfactions) of a growing population. This function can also be served by an increase in equal or favorable trade with other people. By extending the resource base of a group of people, trading relations afford a substitute for size of political jurisdiction.[25] Successful trade is almost like a gigantic hand reaching across distance to acquire and move resources and add them to the inadequate supply (or the inadequate diversity) at home. It may reduce dissatisfactions. But if access to resources is blocked by any means — or if the availability of resources is outstripped by the needs of a growing population and its advancing technology — there is likely to be an increase in that country's dissatisfactions and its will toward lateral pressure — expressed in one mode or another — especially if technology continues to develop rapidly. (A major difficulty in studying these factors in a systematic fashion arises from the fact that, over time, area [resources], population, technology [organization and application of knowledge and skills], and trade tend to be deeply interdependent, a change in one often tending to contribute to sometimes quite complex changes in one or more of the others. It is also difficult to develop satisfactory indicators of lateral pressure.) In a world where populations are growing and technologies are advancing, competition for vital resources is likely to increase — unless arrangements for the allocation for such resources can be agreed upon.

Continuing Modernization
Problems in China

Over the long run, China — whatever the nature of its government — cannot hope to maintain domestic stability and external influence, status, and power unless the imbalance between population and technology is corrected. On the other hand, spectacular advances in technology and production are likely to encourage and facilitate the expansion of Chinese activities and interests beyond the borders of the People's Republic.

During the latter part of the nineteenth century and the first decade or two of the twentieth, the Chinese Empire had a large territory, a very large and growing population, and — for a major country of the time — a very low level of technology. There was thus a high ratio of population to employed resources. Under these circumstances, China was not able to exert strong pressures (economic, political, or military) beyond its borders. Indeed, the leaderships had great difficulty maintaining even minimal domestic cohesion. The country was vulnerable to political, economic, and military penetration and exploitation from the outside. Especially after the fall of the ancient imperial government in 1911 and 1912, the country was characterized by domestic disintegration, the loss of political control at the center, division into regional warlord regimes, banditry and other internal disorders, and parceling into treaty ports, concessions, and foreign spheres of influence. China was dissatisfied but incapable.[26]

A part of the technology — the knowledge and skills — introduced from the West were the revolutionary and organizational methods of Marxism-Leninism. As adapted by Mao, these methods were used to establish centralized political and economic controls over the mainland and to mobilize and train the populace in new techniques of communication, transportation, sanitation, medicine, agriculture, and industrial production. Dissatisfactions were harnessed for revolution and building new capabilities. But what can be expected of China in the future — especially now that Mao Tse-tung is dead and as more and more new leaders emerge at the top?

Initially, reliance upon Soviet economic assistance for development of Chinese industry was a central aspect of Chinese policy. The People's Republic was able to keep its defense expenditures low and maintain satisfactory progress toward industrial technological development through commercial and technical cooperation with the Soviet Union. With time, however, the rapid worsening of the Sino-Soviet dispute, the withdrawal of Soviet technicians, and armed clashes on the Sino-Soviet frontier led to an unfriendly nation relationship between China and the USSR.[27] The Soviet Union has effectively imposed restraints on the actions of the People's Republic both domestically and in external spheres. China's trade volume with the Soviet Union declined sharply in the early 1960s, and deliveries of industrial plants were drastically cut back. China was forced to assume the burden of developing and producing its own technological advances in the industrial spheres.[28] The Chinese Communist leaders, on the other hand, have embarrassed and angered Moscow.

China cannot continue to modernize without accumulating capital in one way or another, and — after agriculture — one of the principal means by which China accumulates investment capital is via foreign trade; the exporting of agricultural products has served as a major means through which China has acquired foreign exchange which, in turn, has been used to purchase needed producer goods. Generally, investment has been accorded priority once minimum consumption and defense needs have been met,[29] and on the whole, China has made greater effort toward investment than have other so-called underdeveloped countries.[30] But, in spite of a relatively successful birth control program, population growth has limited the effects of successful investment. China's ability to convert agricultural production into industrial progress (via trade and other means) has been limited by the fact that popular consumption of these agricultural products cannot be pushed below a basic level without severe consequences — both for the general welfare of the population and for the leadership's ability to govern.

In order to move along lines projected by its intricate plans for growth, the People's Republic relies upon the carefully regulated exploitation of newly located resources of oil, natural gas, and other resources that will be used to fuel much of the country's domestic transportation and in industry, to manufacture fertilizers, fibers and plastics, to boost agriculture, and to generate foreign exchange for the importation of critical technology and the development of its own technological, economic, political, and defense capabilities. However, there are serious constraints upon these interlocking activities, some domestic and some external.

China's fuel problem offers an example of important constraints and linkages. Currently, the People's Republic is relying primarily on exploiting oil fields in the eastern and northeastern parts of the country. However, many of its richest fuel reserves are in Sinkiang (close to Soviet borders), Szechuan, which is rich in natural gas, and other relatively peripheral regions. Domestic transportation capabilities are a major constraint there. In addition, the oil now being exploited in China has a considerable paraffin content and is therefore relatively difficult and expensive to refine.

To date the People's Republic has met this problem in large part by exporting unrefined oil to Japan and elsewhere, relying upon the purchasing country to do the processing with its own specialized capabilities. But from the Chinese perspective this strategy creates a certain dependency in capabilities beyond its direct control and thus infringes upon the goal of self-reliance. On the other hand, to reverse this dependency would require the expenditures of limited foreign exchange for the development of appropriate specializations at the expense of competing domestic demands for fuel, fertilizer, fabrics, and plastics.

Meanwhile, the current Chinese strategy appears to have attracted a portion of Japanese attention away from Siberian oil potentials and to some extent may thus have altered other aspects of Russo-Japanese relations. In various ways, such developments may be expected also to influence — directly or indirectly — the course of these three countries' relationships with the United States and other nations.

China's population continues to grow, although the rate of increase has undoubtedly been decreased. Even a growth rate of one percent or less may amount to an annual increase of up to nine million more people each year. Thus, in spite of birth control progress and spectacular advances in the economy, "the Malthusian specter still looms in China's future."[31] At the same time, the Peking regime is committed to the policy of raising the basic living standard of these still increasing numbers of people. We may therefore conclude that access to resources — both domestic and foreign — and their effective use will remain critical considerations for China for a long time to come.

Over ensuing years, if the Chinese population should grow too fast relative to technological development, the country might conceivably lose much cohesion and centralization achieved since 1950 and perhaps suffer fragmentation and even regression to some type of warlordism or other regionalism. Such an outcome might create a political vacuum and bring about penetration and competition for influence within the country on the part of the United States, the Soviet Union, and possibly other powers. In general, this possible outcome seems less likely now than it did a few years back.

In this connection, the suggestion has been made that if organized administration began to disintegrate in north and northeast China, with loss of control by Peking and the threat of chaos along the Soviet or Mongolian frontiers, then it is possible that the Soviet government might consider the use of troops in a preventive occupation of Manchuria, initially in the name of preserving Chinese communism, as well as the protection of the Soviet frontier. The Soviet planners would probably assume that in such a situation the United States would not wish to extend a threat of war to the Soviet Union in order to prevent a Soviet occupation of northeast China.[32] Again, this outcome seems less probable than it did a few years back.

These considerations place a heavy burden on Chinese agriculture as well as upon the country's continuing ability to concentrate and apply capital, develop or otherwise acquire technology, and regulate consumption wisely. For although Chinese agricultural production is likely to increase, there will be many further difficulties to overcome without any high probability of major breakthroughs.[33] "Imports of grain and transfer of agricultural technology from the West, though marginally significant in the short run, do not shift the heavy long-term subsistence burden on Chinese agriculture."[34] In one way or another, China will have to solve the problem, as it has solved so many problems in the past, through domestic organization and ingenuity.

At the same time, if the People's Republic is to continue its development toward a modern industrialized state, an expanded acquisition of foreign goods and technologies will almost certainly be required. Future leadership may be expected to pursue the policy, now well-established, of maintaining full domestic control over imported goods and technologies. But purchases of needed imports nevertheless imply greater contact with the United States and other Western countries, the risk that Maoist revolutionary values may be weakened in the process, and the possibility that foreign involvements may lead to increased entanglements in international competitions and conflicts.[35]

Global Expansion of Chinese Activities and Influence

On the other hand, if Peking begins substantially to close the gap between population and productivity, China's lateral pressure is likely to increase and to be expressed in more aggressive modes — unless the country's requirements for basic resources are adequately met, whether from domestic reserves or from trade or from both. In general, a powerful China is likely to be a militant China, unless needs are met — including demands for territory, such as Taiwan, which the Chinese perceive to be rightly theirs —- and unless the people and leaders become relatively satisfied. (With respect to societies in general, what are defined as needs tend to increase spectacularly with advances in technology. This consideration exacerbates the difficulties inherent in efforts to stabilize the international system over time.) On the other hand, if population further outstrips productivity to the point where the country loses, relatively, what was gained during 1950–1977, again we may expect domestic instability, regionalism, and possibly some new type of warlordism.

These considerations — to the extent that they are valid — present a disturbing paradox: If large-scale war is avoided and production succeeds in overtaking population growth, we might expect China to achieve new levels of domestic cohesion and stability. With respect to foreign policy and actions, however, *the directions in which China develops its technology will probably make a critical difference*. To the extent that technology is used to locate, release, and process resources within China, we might expect Chinese energies to be invested domestically and lateral pressures to be inhibited — or expressed in diplomatic, cultural, or commercial rather than military or political expansionist modes. Something similar could be postulated about successful Chinese trade: the higher the level of favorable trade, combined with availability of domestic resources, the less likely is China of the future to be inclined to extend its territory or seek domination over other, weaker countries. But, conversely, the more China is deprived of resources relative to population and the requirements of a growing technology, the more we might expect a Chinese disposition toward expansionism of one kind or another. (These are general propositions that seem to be widely applicable. Their use here is purely speculative and illustrative and should not be construed as in any sense peculiarly applicable to China.) And the expansion of China's external activities may increase the possibilities for competition and conflict.

While China has enduring domestic problems against which she will have to wage a protracted tit-for-tat struggle, she also has concerns about her relations abroad, most notably her ties with the Soviet Union, Japan, and the United States. Since the establishment of the People's Republic in 1949, Chinese leaders have proclaimed again and again their determination to overtake the major powers in terms of production, power, and influence. Only the time-table has remained controversial and uncertain.

The leaders of the People's Republic "would probably like to sit at the bargaining table as equals with the United States and the Soviet Union" as soon as possible "but they appear to be patient and realistic about attaining this Asian and global power status."[36] In the meantime, however, China's territorial and demographic dimensions, its position as a developing nation with a large army and nuclear capability, its availability as a model for technological and economic development, and its rivalry with the USSR all contribute to the international image of the People's Republic as a country approaching superpower status.

In terms of China's foreign policy, the Sino-Soviet conflict continues to bring about changes that few, if any, observers could have foreseen even a decade ago. Relations between the People's Republic and countries with revolutionary movements in many parts of the world are already being affected. On the one hand, China offers an alternative revolutionary model that suggests to developing countries that they need not follow in Soviet footsteps. On the other, China's conflict with the USSR introduces a certain amount of confusion, uncertainty, and conflict into Marxist-Leninist ideology as well as revolutionary movements throughout the world.

China as Supporter of and
Model for Developing Nations

During recent years the underdeveloped nations of the world have initiated a number of efforts — both within the United Nations and on their own — to improve their conditions. Such undertakings have included the 85-member Movement of Non-Aligned Nations, which at their Fifth Conference in Colomo, Sri Lanka in August, 1976, demanded of the rich countries that they yield more of their wealth in a rearranged world economic order; and the Group of 77 of the United Nations Conference on Trade and Disarmament (UNCTAD), which has called for a restructuring of international trade and finance, diversification of commodity trade, new mechanisms for transfers of technology, price adjustments in raw materials, and new procedures for supply and pricing — all calculated to improve the positions of the poorer nations and to establish a more equitable economic order in the world. Similar efforts have been made by the International Monetary Fund's Group of 25, representing about 100 of the world's poorest nations.

It is still too early to ascertain precisely what role the People's Republic will play in these efforts, but it may be expected to continue aligning itself with many of the poorer nations' interests. It must be noted, however, that China has gone a significant step further than most of the poor nations, which have tended to pursue greater equity in the world at large while leaving many of the gross political, social, and economic inequities within their own domestic societies largely unchallenged. By contrast, China at the very least has substantially reduced economic differentials within the home society, reducing discrepancies between the least advantaged and the most advantaged. The People's Republic does not purport to be fully egalitarian, but the differences separating the rank and file, the cadres, the scientists, and the regional and national leaderships are vastly less than in most other countries today.

Dilemmas Confronting the
Chinese Leadership

While strengthening its own position among developing countries, the People's Republic may be expected to do what it can to reduce Soviet and Western influence in the Third World.[37] But China's identification of the USSR as the main enemy has set in motion a logic that has new and critical implications for Chinese policy everywhere. This logic may tempt leaders in Peking with the oversimplified proposition that a friend of one's main enemy must be an enemy, whereas an enemy of one's main enemy must be one's ally. Perhaps, nowhere have these implications been more explicit than in Angola during the mid-1970s. "What happened in Angola," according to one Western observer, "suggests that in the Third World the Sino-Soviet rivalry with each other has become more important to them than either's rivalry with the West."[38]

It was precisely with respect to the Angolan issue that, as indicated in Chapter Seven, two long-term supporters of the People's Republic found themselves in sharp disagreement over the country's role in the civil war there.[39]

"What China is saying," according to William Hinton, "is that the people of the Third World should conduct their liberation struggles in such a way as to free themselves from all imperialism, not put themselves under the heels of the Russians in their effort to break loose from the Americans."

Wilfred Burchett took strong issue: "China's error in Angola stems from the nature of its struggle with the Soviet Union," which it views as "a fascist, capitalist imperialist power bent on world domination, at least equal to if not far worse than the U.S." An analysis of this kind "can lead one into a policy-making cul-de-sac unless both regional as well as global considerations are kept in mind and unless all the varying and often contradictory concrete conditions are objectively understood. Indeed, the policy of aid to national liberation movements or friendship to certain governments condition on denunciation of 'Soviet social-imperialism' is to run the risk of recruiting the opportunist riff-raff of the world."

The Chinese may well agree that their adversaries have done the same for years, according to Burchett, but a policy of "only those who denounce our enemies are our friends" is a very poor basis for foreign policy. The fact remains that "Fear of possible Soviet hegemony in southern Africa . . . led China into the impossible position of objectively compromising its support of a liberation struggle and of jeopardizing its considerable prestige among progressive African nations."

As long as the People's Republic derives a large part of its foreign policies from the Soviet main enemy principle, we may expect to find similar debates emerging over Chinese positions and activities in Asia, other parts of Africa, and Latin America, as well as in Europe. One might even imagine a crisis or other confrontation somewhere in the world with combinations of capitalist and communist states aligned on both sides.

The People's Republic charged both the United States and the USSR with exploiting Third World countries through moneylending. But although the United States was the biggest creditor country, according to Peking, the Soviet Union was "far more greedy and ruthless than the old-line imperialists." Between 1954 and 1974 "Moscow provided the developing countries with 17,850 million U.S. dollars in economic aid of which 95 percent were furnished in the form of loans which must be repaid." But the strings attached could be described as usury. "For instance, the Soviet Union lent Bangla Desh 12 million pounds in 1974 and charged an annual rate of 4 percent. Usually western capitalist countries would ask 2.5 percent for such a loan." The USSR had been especially "ruthless and unscrupulous in pressing India for debt repayment."[40]

An article in *Peking Review* charged Soviet leaders with identifying proletarian internationalism with the defense, strengthening and support of the USSR and its interests at the expense of people everywhere. "Obviously, as the people's struggle against hegemonism is spreading on a world-wide scale," according to this article, "the true features of the Soviet revisionists as social imperialism have become clearer than ever." As a result of Moscow's "colonial activities in Eastern Europe" the USSR had become involved in quarrels with allies in the Council for Mutual Economic Assistance (CMEA). And in Western Europe the fraternal parties in Italy, France, and elsewhere, "no longer were as docile as formerly in taking Moscow's cue," and were openly refusing to let their countries follow the Soviet example.[41]

Peking accused the USSR of trying to sow discord among non-aligned countries, to gain control of the nonalignment movement, which in the Chinese view constituted "a massive contingent against imperialism, social imperialism, colonialism and hegemonism."[42] More and more nonaligned countries of the world were coming to realize, according to Peking, that "the ever fiercer contention for world hegemony between the two superpowers, which is the root cause of instability in the world, seriously encroaches on or threatens the independence and sovereignty of the non-aligned countries."[43]

Events in Latin America have not entirely substantiated this claim, however. In June 1975 a large meeting of the Communist parties of Latin America and the Caribbean region convened in Cuba. This gathering, which brought together representatives of twenty-four pro-Soviet parties, identified Yankee imperialism as the main enemy and energetically condemned the treasonous foreign policy of the People's Republic. The meeting also criticized China for recognizing Chile's military junta and supporting "groups of pseudo-revolutionaries who divide the left, attack the Communist parties, block the progressive process and often behave as agents of the enemy at the core of the revolutionary movement." The occasion marked the full adherence of the Communist party of Cuba to the company of pro-Soviet Communist parties of Latin America and the Caribbean.[44]

From their record of the 1960s and early 1970s we may conclude that in general the Peking regime had been more successful as a grantor of economic assistance to Third World countries than as advisor or active participant in revolutionary movements in such regions.

Maintaining Chinese Security

The maintenance of adequate security against external attack may be expected to remain a primary objective of Chinese policy. Peking may also reassert control over areas that are viewed as integal parts of China provided the task can be accomplished without undue risk or threat to other aspects of national policy. And the regime will undoubtedly pursue low-cost possibilities for expanding its power and influence in various parts of the world.

During the foreseeable future, however, China's policies and activities in the sphere of national security will be constrained by the technological and resource requirements of other aspects of Chinese society. Thus, the tight resource situation which confronts virtually every sector of the overall economy will "continue to provide incentive for holding military spending down as the tasks of providing for a growing population and modernizing industry continue to mount."[45] For a time, at least, Chinese leaders may well conclude that a strong economy will do more to strengthen the country than a bigger military build-up.[46]

In view of these persisting constraints on military spending Chinese leaders — while pursuing the development of nuclear weaponry — may be expected to maintain relatively heavy reliance upon manpower, as opposed to technology, for military purposes. On the other hand, It is important to keep in mind that China's power is not trivial.[47] As pointed out by an Asian observer: "The great dimension of her land, the mammoth size of her population, her enormous resources and the febrile and dynamic activity of her diligent and disciplined people should enable her to a position of great power, and if to this is added the missionary fervour of her ideology, she seems destined to the status of a superpower."[48] Moreover, in 1974 the People's Republic was one of six countries (United States, USSR, West Germany, United Kingdom, and France) accounting for about 75 percent of the world's military expenditures,[49] and this status may well be enhanced with further developments in Chinese nuclear weaponry and delivery systems.

Both the strengths and the weaknesses of China's military establishment will affect the country's foreign policies in important ways.

Chinese leaders must be fully aware that the Soviet Union and the United States both possess overwhelming superiority in tactical and strategic capabilities. Moreover, even an all-out effort by China would not be sufficient to redress the military balance for some time to come. On the other hand, the Peking regime may well have concluded that its combined nuclear and conventional forces are now sufficient to deter the USSR or any other country from a major attack — a level of sufficiency that Chinese leaders may be satisfied with for some time to come.[50]

Future Policy Alternatives

To the extent that they are viewed in a highly oversimplified way as elements of a single three-power system, Sino-Soviet-United States relations present a problem that defies easy solution. The potential instabilities of a three-power system are illustrated by a simple game wherein three players are to divide a dollar by majority vote. The rules of the game allow for bargaining, coalitions, and side payments. Suppose that A and B agree tentatively to take fifty cents each — freezing C out. But then C offers one of them — B perhaps — a better deal; by deserting A, B may take sixty cents. As compared with the previous arrangement, such a 60–40 split is clearly advantageous to both B and C. If B accepts C's offer, however, he risks losing everything since it will be advantageous both to A and C to freeze B out and split 50–50, thus returning to the starting place. "No matter what arrangement is proposed, it is always possible for *two* of the players to think of a better arrangement (for them); and being a majority, they can defeat the previous proposal. There is *no stable* solution."[51] Fortunately, or unfortunately depending on one's perspective, the actual situation is more complicated than the oversimplified example.

In many respects, a Chinese-United States-Soviet three-way stand-off is certainly difficult to live with, but for the immediate future it may be preferable to any other likely alternative. In fact, of course, the People's Republic, the USSR, and the United States comprise a single, three-power system only to the extent that we choose to view them in that perspective. Britain, France, Italy, Japan, India, and a host of other countries complicate the picture. Thus, it would be closer to the truth to recognize that all three countries are interacting with large numbers of other nations as well as with each other, and are thus able to alter and trim the balance in complicated ways. But this consideration should not obscure the very real difficulties inherent in the three-cornered aspects of Sino-Soviet-United States relationships.

In combination with the Sino-Soviet controversy, the continuing domestic power struggle has left the prospects for Chinese foreign policy in considerable doubt. At one extreme, there is the possibility that at some point factions more favorable to the Soviet Union might be elevated to leadership. At the other, a more moderate leadership group might pave the way for closer alignment with the United States. However, whatever the characteristics of the Chinese leadership at any particular time, the current structure of the international system is such that any Peking regime is likely to do whatever it can to counterpose the USSR and the United States against each other.

In its policies toward China, the Soviet Union has remained essentially hostile, but has also kept the door open for possible rapprochement, asserting that only Mao stood in the way of improved relations. If even a partial rapprochement were to take place, we might expect a number of policy changes including concerted negotiations, improved trade relations between the two countries, a greater flow of Soviet technology into the People's Republic, a troop withdrawal on either side of the border, a demarcation of the border, and possibly a treaty of non-aggression. Such a realignment would tend to isolate the United States and its allies and probably raise specters of a new bi-polar world.

Even in the eventuality of a marked improvement in Sino-Soviet relations, however, the United States would possess considerable leverage, if the United States leadership chose to use it, for maintaining a measure of stability within the Sino-Soviet-American triangle, just as the Chinese might be expected to use Sino-United States relations as leverage applied to the Soviet Union. On the other hand, a prolonged stagnation in Sino-United States relations might contribute to an increase in the power of pro-Soviet elements in the Chinese military or of radical factions in the leadership hierarchy. A coalition of the two groups might be encouraged.[52]

To date, the foreign policy of the People's Republic has continued to emphasize Chinese fear of the USSR, but it has also reflected a cooling of the country's rapprochement with the United States. While continuing to accept improved relations with the United States, China was clearly dissatisfied with what was viewed in Peking as a post-Nixon policy of appeasement of the Soviet Union. Frequent articles in the Chinese press reflected a continuing hope on the part of the leadership that the United States would undertake stronger opposition to the USSR, greater support for NATO, and more vigorous opposition to the expansion of the Soviet influence in South and Southeast Asia, the Middle East, Africa, and Latin America. A further cooling of Sino-United States relations would almost certainly strengthen the position of the USSR, which would then be able to pursue tougher policies in Europe, Asia, the Middle East, and Africa.

According to an Indian observer, a quite different clue to China's future policies can be derived from the often repeated assertion by the

Peking regime that — Soviet-United States proclamations of détente to the contrary notwithstanding — the two superpowers are, in fact, headed for a world war. In terms of this assessment of world trends, the People's Republic may be expected to dismiss any Soviet-United States efforts to improve their relations and limit armaments as "a fraud to cheat the world and lull it into complacency" — and to prepare itself for all that might be required by such an eventuality. To the extent that Chinese leaders are seriously convinced of the inevitability of a world war triggered by a Sino-Soviet struggle for supremacy, they might pursue a policy that would sharpen the conflict and thus contribute a self-fulfilling element to their prophecy.[53] It has been generally characteristic of Mao and his colleagues in the past, however, that they have taken a long view of history and exercised considerable restraint in many — though by no means all — aspects of foreign policy. The possibility therefore exists that, by following a moderate course of action within the Sino-Soviet-United States triangle, Mao's successors may exert a stabilizing influence in world affairs.

Closer relations between the United States and the People's Republic would encourage trade between the two countries, stimulate the flow of United States technology, food, and manufactured goods into China, and reduce many international tensions — not only between the two countries directly, but also in parts of the Third World where Chinese and American economic assistance and security arrangements might develop parallel, rather than in opposition, to each other. On the other hand, such a course of events could seriously threaten the Soviet-United States détente, sharpen many conflicts in Europe, and increase Third World tensions wherever Soviet activities and interests came into confrontation with either United States or Chinese activities and interests. Too close a Sino-United States alignment might thus substitute a new bipolarity for the one that appears to have been left behind.

Notes

1. A. Doak Barnett, *China After Mao* (Princeton, N.J.: Princeton University Press, 1967), p. 34.
2. H. Franz Schurmann, "China's 'New Economic Policy,' Transition or Beginning," in Choh-ming Li, *Industrial Development in Communist China* (New York: Praeger, 1964), p. 91.
3. Roger Glenn Brown, "Chinese Politics and American Policy: A New Look at the Triangle," *Foreign Policy*, no. 23 (Summer 1976), p. 16.
4. "A Great Victory," *Peking Review*, no. 16 (April 16, 1976), pp. 3–4.

5. "Resolution of the CPC Central Committee on Appointing Comrade Hua Kuo-feng Vice Chairman of the CPC Central Committee and Premier of Council;" and "Resolution of the CPC Central Committee on Dismissing Teng Hsiao-ping from all Posts Both Inside and Outside the Party," *Peking Review*, no. 15 (April 9, 1976), p. 3. See also "Counter-Revolutionary Political Incident at Tien An Men Square," *Peking Review*, no. 15 (April 19, 1976), p. 4; and Chih Heng, "A Great Victory for the Dictatorship of the Proletariat," *Peking Review* no. 19 (May 7, 1976), pp. 16–17.

6. Chang Shih, "Criticize Teng Hsiao-ping's Revisionist Fallacies on the Industrial and Transport Front," *Peking Review*, no. 24 (June 11, 1976), p. 8.

7. Fang Kung, "Capitalist-Roaders are the Bourgeoisie Inside the Party," *Peking Review*, no. 25 (June 18, 1976), p. 7.

8. Li Chang, "Teng Hsiao-ping's Total Betrayal of Marxism," *Peking Review*, no. 23 (June 4, 1976), p. 14.

9. Fang, "Capitalist-Roaders," p. 9.

10. Ibid.

11. "Repulsing the Right Deviationists' Wind in the Scientific and Technological Circles," *Peking Review*, no. 18 (April 30, 1976) pp. 6 – 9.

12. Chang, "Criticize Teng Hsiao-ping's Revisionist Fallacies," p. 9.

13. Hans Heymann, Jr., "Acquisition and Diffusion of Technology in China," in *China: A Reassessment*, pp. 678, 679.

14. For more on institutionalization and its role in maintaining political stability, see Samuel P. Huntington, *Political Order in Changing Societies* (New Haven: Yale University Press, 1968), Chapter 1.

15. Robert C. North and Nazli Choucri, "Trend Analysis Study of China in its Relations with the Major Powers and Selected Medium Powers from 1922 until 1968," final report, Contract NONR 225 (82) Modification 10, October 1970, Office of Naval Research. There is strong quantitative evidence to indicate that China tends to be very much aware of relative Soviet and Chinese capabilities.

16. John Gittings, *The Role of the Chinese Army* (New York: Oxford Press, 1967). See Chapters 7 and 8 for a detailed discussion of these questions.

17. Chu-Yuan Cheng, "Scientific and Engineering Manpower in Communist China," in *An Economic Profile of Mainland China*, Vol. 2, p. 542.

18. Ibid.

19. Arthur G. Ashbrook, Jr., "Main Lines of Chinese Communist Economic Policy," in *An Economic Profile of Mainland China*, Vol. 1, p. 43.

20. See E. L. Wheelwright and Bruce McFarland, *The Chinese Road to Socialism* (New York: Monthly Review Press, 1970), pp. 143-53, for an excellent discussion of moral incentives.

21. Nazli Choucri and Robert C. North, "Dynamics of International Conflict: Some Policy Implications of Population, Resources, and Technology," *World Politics* 24, supplement (September 1972), pp. 80 – 122.

22. For additional information on population control efforts being made in China, see Leo A. Orleans, "Evidence from Chinese Medical Journals on Current Population Policy," *China Quarterly*, no. 40 (October – December 1969), pp. 137-146.

23. Dwight H. Perkins, "Economic Growth in China and the Cultural Revolution (1960 – April 1977)," *China Quarterly*, no. 30 (April – June 1967), p. 48.

24. Robert C. North and Nazli Choucri, "Population, Technology, and Resources in the Future International System," *Journal of International Affairs* 25, no. 2 (1971), pp. 224-37.

25. Edward A. Ackerman, "Population and Natural Resources," in Philip M. Hauser and Otis Dudley Duncan (eds.) *The Study of Population* (Chicago: University of Chicago Press, 1959), p. 626.

26. Ibid., p. 626.

27. Malcolm Mackintosh, "Sino-Soviet Relations in a U.S.-China Crisis: The Soviet Attitude," in *Sino-Soviet Relations and Arms Control, Collected Papers*, Vol. 2 (Report to the U.S. Arms Control and Disarmament Agency, East Asian Research Center, Center for International Affairs, Harvard University, Cambridge, Mass., 1966), p. 37.

28. The Soviet "Open Letter," July 14, 1962 in William E. Griffith, *The Sino-Soviet Rift* (Cambridge: MIT Press, 1964), p. 295.

29. Ashbrook, "Main Lines of Chinese Communist Economic Policy," p. 21.

30. Ta-chung Liu, "The Tempo of Economic Development of the Chinese Mainland, 1949-65," in *An Economic Profile of Mainland China*, Vol. 1, p. 64.

31. John P. Hardt, "Summary," in *China: A Reassessment*, p. 16.

32. Mackintosh, "Sino-Soviet Relations," p. 36.

33. Perkins, "Economic Growth in China," p. 365.

34. Hardt, "Summary," p. 16.

35. Eugene A. Theroux, "Legal and Practical Problems in the China Trade," in *China: A Reassessment*, pp. 595 – 96.

36. Angus M. Fraser, "The Utility of Alternate Strategic Postures to the People's Republic of China," in *China: A Reassessment,* p. 439.

37. Carol H. Fogarty, "China's Economic Relations with the Third World," in *China: A Reassessment*, p. 730.

38. Colin Legum, "The Soviet Union, China and the West in Southern Africa," *Foreign Affairs* 54, no. 4 (July 1976), pp. 751 – 52.

39. *Guardian*, May 5, 1976, pp. 14, 15, and 17.

40. "Third World's Debt Burden and Superpower Usury," *Peking Review*, no. 24 (June 11, 1976), pp. 21-22.

41. "Crude Interference in the Non-Alignment Movement," *Peking Review*, no. 25 (June 18, 1976), p. 16.

42. "Crude Interference in the Non-Alignment Movement," p. 16.

43. Ibid.

44. "Cuba," *Latin American Report,* World Affairs Council of Northern California, 3, no. 11 (July 1, 1975), p. 4.

45. Sydney H. Jammes, "The Chinese Defense Burden, 1965-74," in *China: A Reassessment*, p. 464 – 65.

46. Ibid.

47. Robert F. Dernberger, "The Economic Consequences of Defense Expenditure Choices in China," in *China: A Reassessment*, pp. 467–568.

48. K. S. Tripathi, "China's Military Strategy in the Eighties," *China Report* 11, nos. 5–6 (October – November – December 1975), p. 110.

49. Ruth Leger Sivard, *World Military and Social Expenditures 1976* (Leesburg, Virginia: WMSE Publications, 1976), p. 7.

50. Jammes, "The Chinese Defense Burden," p. 464.

51. Anatol Rapoport, "Critique of Strategic Thinking" in Naomi Rosenbaum (ed.), *Readings on the International Political System*, (Englewood Cliffs, N.J.: Prentice-Hall, 1970), p. 213. Emphasis added.

52. Roger Glenn Brown, "Chinese Politics and American Policy: A New Look at the Triangle," *Foreign Policy*, no. 23 (Summer 1976), pp. 20 – 21.

53. Tripathi, "China's Military Strength," p. 110.

Index